Cassell's Rural Scier

Rural Science 2

Bernard Salt

Head of Rural Studies,
King Edward VI School, Lichfield
Chief Examiner, West Midlands Examination Board

Cassell

CASSELL LTD
1 St Anne's Road,
Eastbourne, East Sussex BN21 3UN

First published 1980
Second impression 1981
Third impression 1982
Fourth impression 1984

ISBN 0 304 30425 5

Typeset by Oxprint Ltd., Oxford

Printed and bound in Hungary

Contents

Preface

This book continues in the same style as *Rural Science 1*, with the inclusion of some more difficult language, to suit the older pupil. Each chapter is a complete study, giving teachers the freedom to select their own order of work. Pupils should have studied the first three chapters, before undertaking practical work in the vegetable garden.

Answers to questions raised in the text appear at the end of the book. It is hoped that pupils will be encouraged to make use of both the index and the glossary.

Almost all of the photographs were taken on working farms, and I wish to thank S. J. & W. G. J. Archer, W. J. & A. J. Ryman, and A. W. & E. J. Tipper, who allowed me access to their farms for this purpose.

Special acknowledgement is made to the following examining boards, who have kindly given permission to reproduce questions from their examination papers:
Associated Lancashire Schools Examining Board;
North West Regional Examination Board;
South East Regional Examination Board;
Southern Regional Examination Board;
West Midlands Examination Board;
Welsh Joint Education Committee; and
West Yorkshire and Lindsey Regional Examining Board.

Bernard Salt
Lichfield, 1980

1 Soil science

Life as we know it depends upon the soil. By 'soil' the rural scientist means the layer of material on the surface of the earth in which plants root to obtain support, water and nutrients – the *topsoil* – and the lighter coloured layer underneath – the *subsoil*. Soil is a mixture of: *small rock particles, water, bacteria, humus, mineral salts,* and *air*.

A good method of learning about soil is to carry out the sequence of investigations and experiments which follow.

Investigation 1.1
To prepare and examine a soil profile

Note: in some town schools it may not be possible to dig a soil profile, however all the other experiments in this chapter may be carried out with a sample of topsoil collected from a town garden or park (after obtaining permission).

1. Select a site where the soil has not been disturbed by earth-moving machines involved in construction work (part of the school site may be so affected).
2. Dig a hole 1 m wide and 2 m long, putting the soil in neat piles and keeping the different layers separate in order to return them in the correct order after the investigation is completed.
3. When the hole is about one and a half metres deep carefully clean a vertical face with a trowel and examine it. This face is called a *soil profile* and the different layers are termed *horizons*.

Digging a soil profile

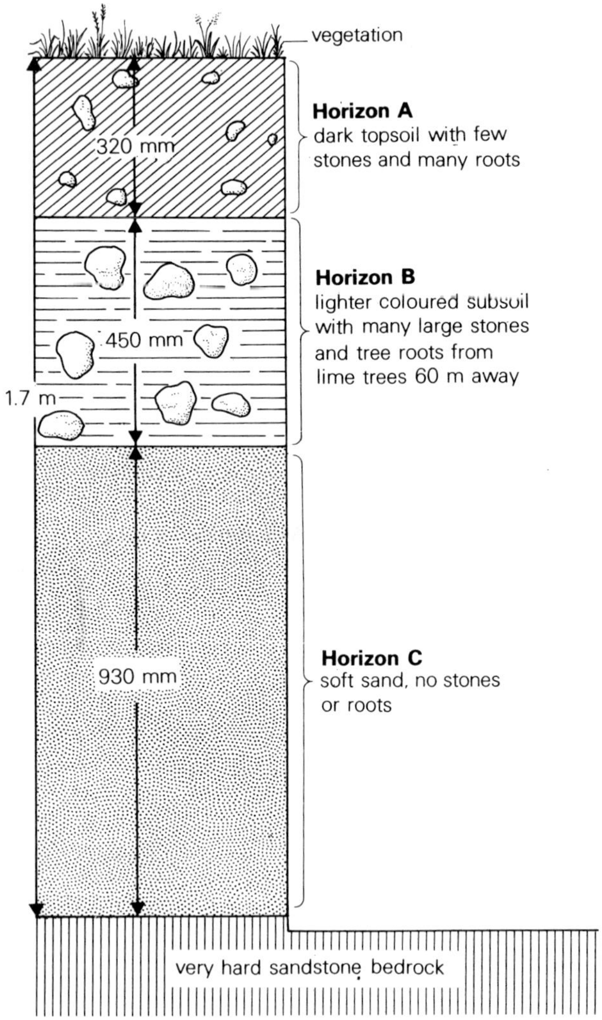

vegetation

Horizon A
dark topsoil with few stones and many roots

320 mm

Horizon B
lighter coloured subsoil with many large stones and tree roots from lime trees 60 m away

450 mm

1.7 m

Horizon C
soft sand, no stones or roots

930 mm

very hard sandstone bedrock

The resulting profile (measurements are approximate)

4. Examine and measure each horizon in turn and make notes about it in a table similar to the one below:

Horizon	Depth, mm	Colour	*Texture	Stones	Roots

5. Collect a sample of about 2 kg from horizon A, put it in a polythene bag and label the bag; also collect about 0.5 kg from each of the other horizons, and bag and label as before. These samples will be needed for further investigations and experiments.
6. Fill in the hole making sure that the topsoil is replaced as the final layer.

*Texture

The soil in the profile will be either sand, clay or a mixture of the two – a *loam*. A guide to the texture of the soil may be made by picking up a handful of moist soil, moulding it in the hand and rubbing a little between the finger and thumb:
A *sandy soil* feels gritty and crumbles easily.
A *clay soil* feels smooth, forms into a ball, the surface of which can be polished by rubbing with the thumb.
A *loam* feels less gritty, it rolls into a ball, but cannot be polished.

Task 1.1
To make a model of a soil profile

1. Take about 40 g from each soil sample, and leave to dry for a few days. Make sure that each sample is labelled.
2. On the left-hand side of a piece of plain A4 paper, draw a vertical column 50 mm wide to represent the soil profile.
3. Using a suitable scale, mark off each horizon on the column, using the measurements for each horizon on the profile you exposed.
4. Paint the column with a quick-setting, clear glue. Crumble the dried soil from each horizon onto the wet glue in the appropriate position.
5. Apply more glue and soil until a good depth of colour is obtained.
6. Write a description alongside each horizon, using the information that you recorded in the field.

The diagram on page 6 shows the soil profile exposed by the two boys in the photograph on page 5. The material in the C horizon was deposited by water thousands of years ago.

In other areas the profile will be different from this—there may be only two horizons, or there may be more than three. If the underlying layers are impervious, the hole may partly fill with water. The various horizons may have formed from any of the different types of rock which solidified as the earth's crust cooled, or from rocks which formed as a result of volcanic activity. Some of the layers may have been transported by glaciers, and others by wind. In some areas the material may be limestone, marl or chalk—formed from the hard part of dead marine animals which accumulated over great periods of time at the bottom of ancient seas.

In all profiles, however, horizon A will contain most humus and will therefore be darker in colour than horizon B.

Experiment 1.1
Soil composition

1. Stopper the end of a wide bore (50 mm) glass tube and put in soil from horizon A to a depth of 250 mm.
2. Dissolve 5 g of sodium carbonate in a litre of water and pour it into the tube.
3. Stopper the open end and shake until the water and soil are thoroughly mixed.
4. Clamp vertically in a stand and leave the contents to settle.
5. Examine the tube. The soil will have separated into different layers, showing that soil is a mixture of various sized particles.

Which particles form the lowest layer, the large or the small? . . . Q.1

The particles are very small pieces of rock, which form the *skeleton* of the soil. Soils which are based on rock particles are called *mineral soils*. A small proportion of soils are formed from partly rotted vegetation, e.g., the peat soils in the Fens, and these are called *organic soils*.

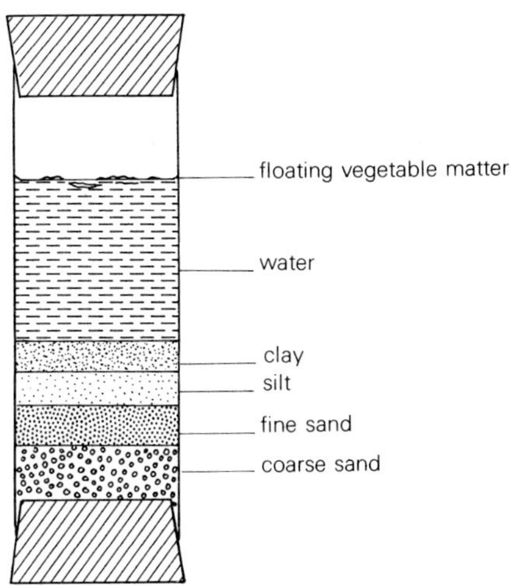

Examine the diagram. Which has the largest particles, sand or clay? . . . Q.2
What size are silt particles? . . . Q.3

Soil particles are given names according to their size:

Name	*Size of particle, mm*
Coarse sand	2.0–0.2
Fine sand	0.2–0.02
Silt	0.02–0.002
Clay	less than 0.002

Sets of *soil sieves* are designed to separate soil particles into the above internationally agreed fractions.

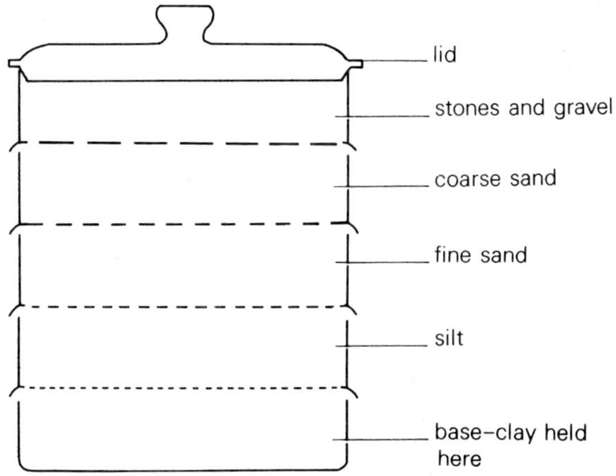

Experiment 1.2
Use of soil sieves to determine the proportions of sand, silt and clay in a soil sample

1. Dry about 250 g of soil from horizon A, in an oven set at 90°C.
2. Using a pestle and mortar, lightly crush any soil crumbs in the dry sample.
3. Place the soil in the top compartment of a set of soil sieves, and, keeping the sieves vertical, shake vigorously for several minutes.
4. Weigh the soil left in each compartment.
5. Using the formula below calculate the percentage of each fraction in the soil sample:

percentage of clay

$$= \frac{\text{weight of particles in the base}}{\text{total weight of soil sample}} \times \frac{100}{1}$$

Particle size

Soils are named according to the proportions of sand, silt and clay that they contain. Soils with fairly even mixtures are called *loams*. The actual soil type for any mixture of particles can be obtained from the triangle below:

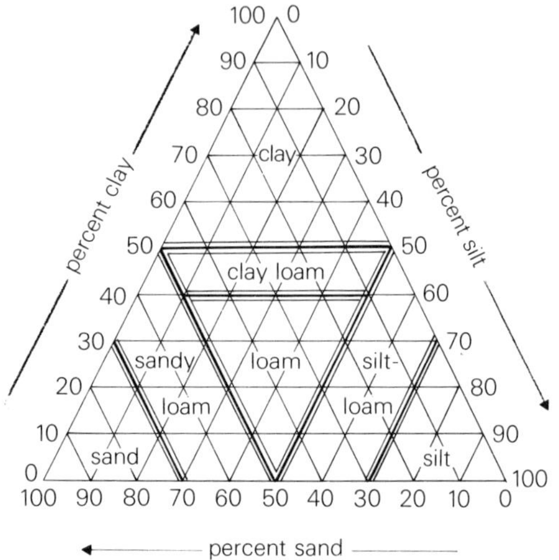

Refer to the triangle above and name a soil that contains 40% sand, 40% silt and 20% clay.

. . . Q.4

Experiment 1.3
To find the percentage of water in a soil sample

The amount of water in a well-drained soil can vary from a maximum (known as the *field capacity*) down to almost none at all. In order to make this experiment meaningful the soil used should be at field capacity, which can be achieved by filling a plant pot with soil, holding it under water until it no longer bubbles and then allowing it to drain overnight.

1. Weigh a clean, dry crucible.
2. Two-thirds fill the crucible with soil from horizon A (which has been brought to field capacity).
3. Weigh the crucible again and calculate the weight of the soil.
4. Heat the crucible over a water bath to dry the soil.
5. Dry the base of the crucible on a piece of filter paper and re-weigh.
6. Return the crucible to the water bath and continue to heat.
7. Dry the base of the crucible and re-weigh. Repeat the heating and weighing until there is no further loss in weight (i.e., the soil is completely dry).

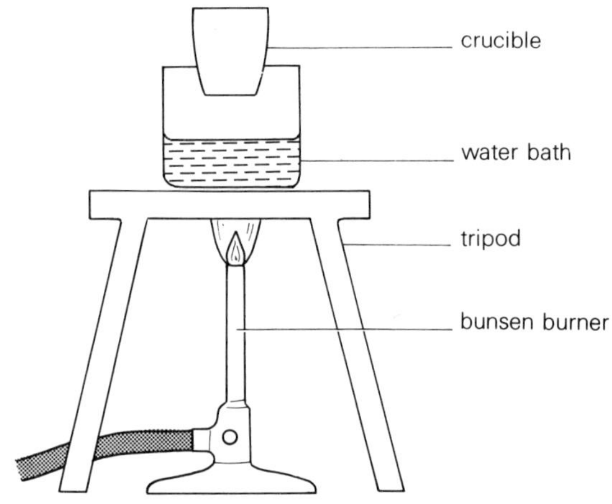

8. Calculate the percentage of water in the soil sample by substituting your results into the following equation:

$$\frac{\text{weight of water}}{\text{weight of soil}} \times \frac{100}{1}$$

= percentage of water in the soil

Retain the dry soil for the next experiment.

Specimen results
(the results of all your experiments should be set out like this)

Weight of crucible	= 12.0 g
Weight of crucible and soil	= 20.0 g
Weight of soil (by subtraction)	= 8.0 g
Weight after first heating	= 18.5 g
Weight after second heating	= 18.0 g
Weight after third heating	= 18.0 g
Weight of water in soil (by subtraction)	= 2.0 g
Percentage of water in the sample	

$$= \frac{2}{8} \times \frac{100}{1} = 25\%$$

The sample of soil under investigation contained 25% water.

Why was the soil not heated for a fourth time? . . . Q.5

In a soil each individual particle is wet, having a layer of water over its surface. As a soil dries the layers of water on the particles get thinner; if water is added, the layers become thicker until a maximum is reached – once this is reached any additional water will drain away.

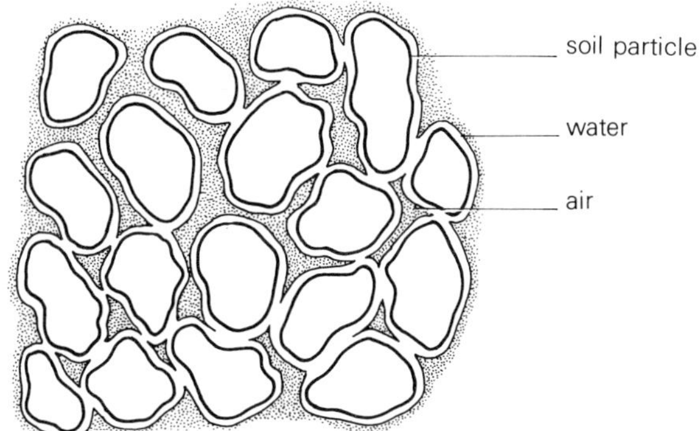

(the water around a soil particle is continuous with the water around surrounding particles; if some water is lost from around one particle water will flow around neighbouring particles to replace it, leaving all of the layers a little thinner)

Soil particles (magnified)

The effect of particle size on the water capacity of a soil

If a soil particle is broken in half two new surfaces are exposed:

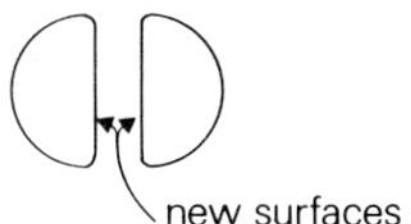

These two new surfaces will hold additional water:

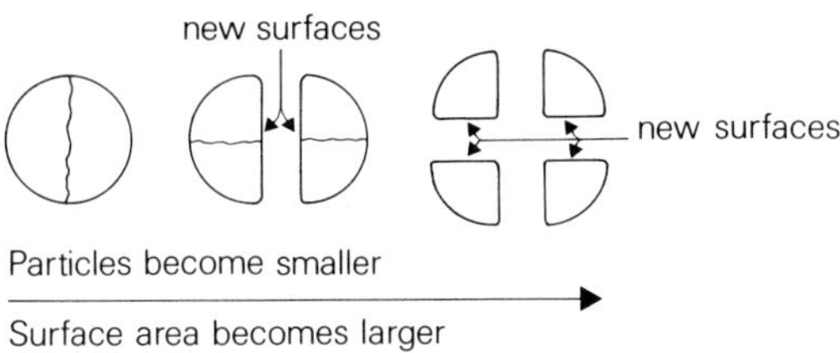

Which will hold most water, a sandy soil or an equal amount of clay soil? . . . Q.6

The dry soil from experiment 1.3 consists of rock particles and a certain amount of organic material called *humus*. Humus consists of dead plant and animal material in its final stages of decay. Millions of bacteria, fungi and other microscopic organisms live in humus. These organisms continue the process of decay, releasing into the soil water inorganic salts, which are taken up by plant roots and used as materials for plant growth. Humus gives the soil its characteristic dark appearance; good soils have a high proportion of humus and poor soils have little humus. The humus in a soil is bound up with the soil particles and cannot be extracted. Humus has the following effect upon soils:

1. It makes the soil dark in colour.
2. It increases the water-holding capacity of the soil.
3. It provides nutrients which make a soil fertile.
4. It holds particles together in a sandy soil.
5. It prevents soil particles from binding together into solid 'bricks' in a clay soil.

Experiment 1.4
To find the percentage of humus in a sample of soil

1. Weigh a clean, fire-proof crucible.
2. Put the dry soil from experiment 1.3 into the crucible, and re-weigh.
3. Place the crucible on a pipe clay triangle and support it with a tripod.
4. Cover the crucible with a lid, to prevent spitting, and heat strongly with a bunsen burner. This heating will burn off the humus (note the smell – like that of a garden fire).
5. Cool the crucible in a desiccator, and weigh when cool.
6. Repeat 4 and 5 until there is no further weight loss (*loss of weight* = *weight of humus*).
7. Substitute your results in the following equation:

$$\frac{\text{weight of humus}}{{}^{*}\text{weight of soil}} \times \frac{100}{1}$$

= percentage of humus in the soil.

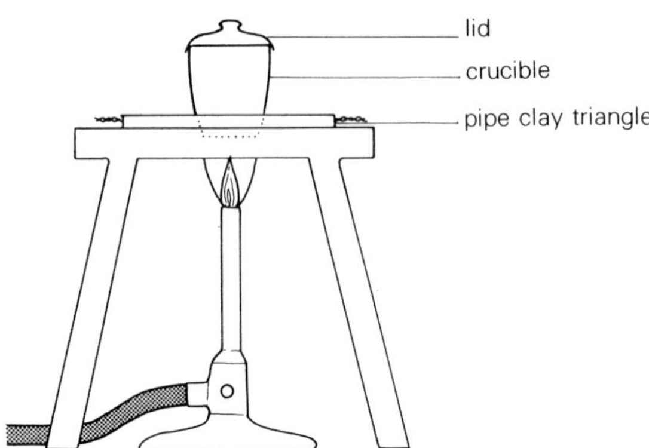

* This weight is the weight of soil *before* it was dried.

Experiment 1.5
To show that soil contains micro-organisms

1. Sort through about 500 ml of top soil and remove any macro-organisms.
2. Divide the soil into two equal parts. Bake one part in an oven at 110°C for 30 minutes to kill any micro-organisms.
3. Put each sample in a muslin bag and moisten by immersing in distilled water. Hang the bags on a thread to drain.
4. Pour 75 mm of clear lime water into each of two gas jars.
5. Suspend one bag of soil in each jar, tying the thread around the jar.
6. Smear vaseline around the top of each jar to form a seal, and cover with a glass disc.
7. Leave the jars in a warm room.

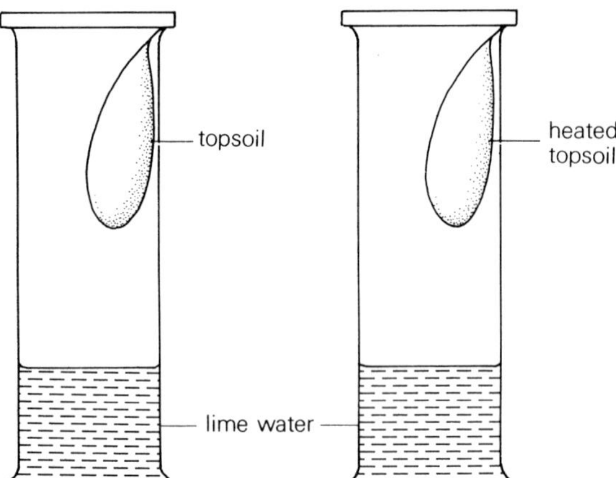

Examine the jars one week later. If there are micro-organisms in the unheated soil the carbon dioxide produced by their respiration will have turned the lime water milky.

The air in soil

If a container of soil is plunged into water, air bubbles can be seen escaping as the air in the soil is replaced by water. When the bubbles stop, the soil in the container is 'waterlogged', i.e., all air spaces are full of water. Plant roots and soil fauna are unable to breath in a waterlogged soil – air is an *essential part of the soil.* The proportion of air in soil is difficult to measure, as the collecting of samples either loosens or compresses the soil, which increases or decreases the amount of air.

Experiment 1.6
To determine the amount of air in a soil (pore space)

1. Measure the volume of an empty tin (e.g., pet food or small baked bean tin) by filling it with water and emptying it into a measuring cylinder.
2. Pierce a small hole in the bottom of the tin.
3. Dig a hole with a vertical side, taking care not to disturb the soil.
4. Fill the tin by pressing it into the soil; take it to the laboratory.

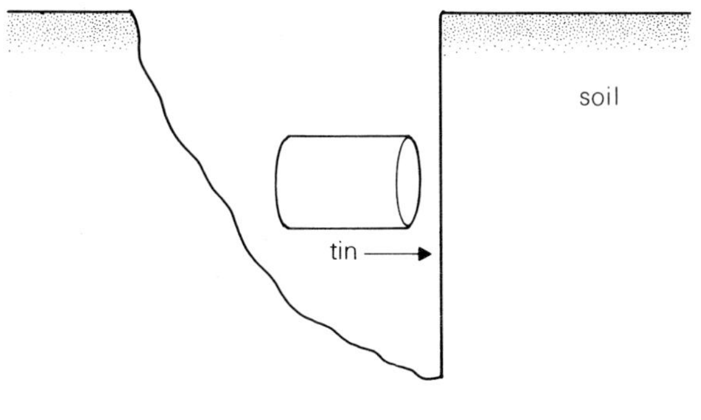

5. Level off the soil by drawing a ruler across the top of the tin.

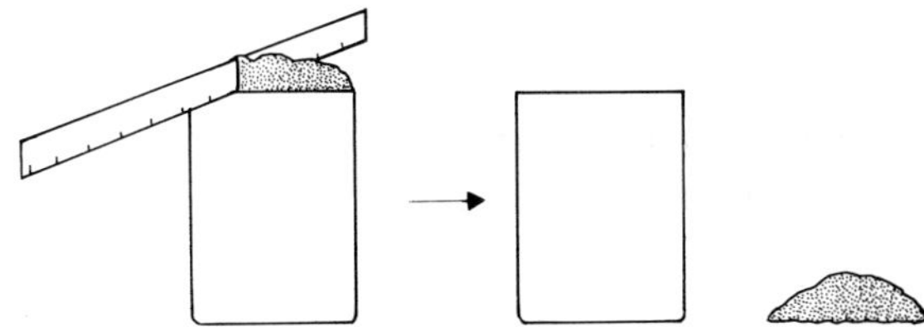

6. Empty the tin of soil into a one litre measuring cylinder that contains exactly 500 ml of water.
7. Stir until all the air bubbles are removed.
8. Read the new level in the measuring cylinder.

$$\frac{(\text{volume of tin} + 500) - \text{new level}}{\text{volume of tin}} \times \frac{100}{1}$$

$=$ percentage air in soil.

Which type of soil would you expect to contain most air: a sandy soil or a clay soil? . . . Q.7

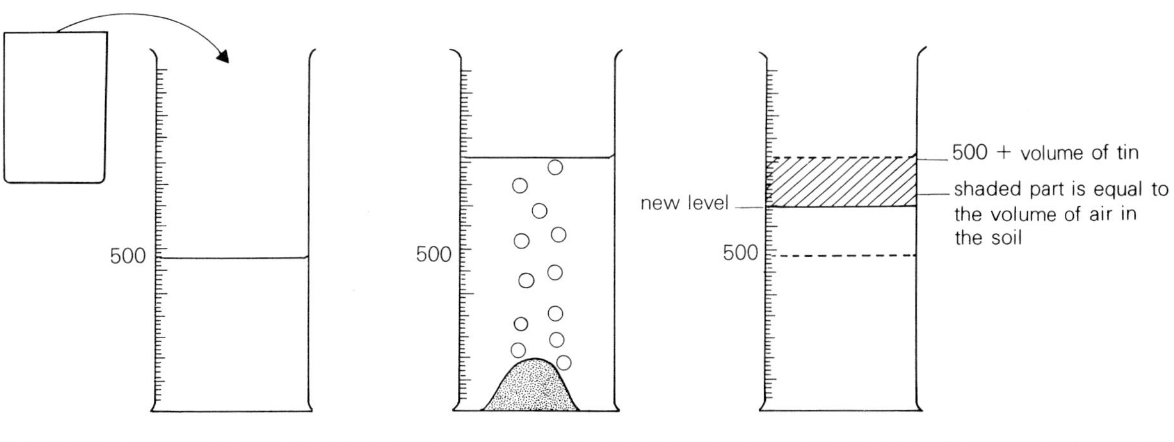

Experiment 1.7
To show the presence of mineral salts in soil

1. One-third fill a 250 ml beaker with top soil, and add an equal volume of distilled water.
2. Thoroughly stir the contents of the beaker, using filter paper that has been wetted with distilled water, and filter two or three times.
3. Place a clean watch-glass over a beaker of gently boiling water, add the filtered water to the watch-glass a little at a time, and allow it to evaporate.
4. Arrange a control by setting identical apparatus alongside and evaporating distilled water from a watch-glass.
5. Examine both watch-glasses. The first watch-glass will have a coating of mineral salts over its surface; the control watch-glass will be clean.

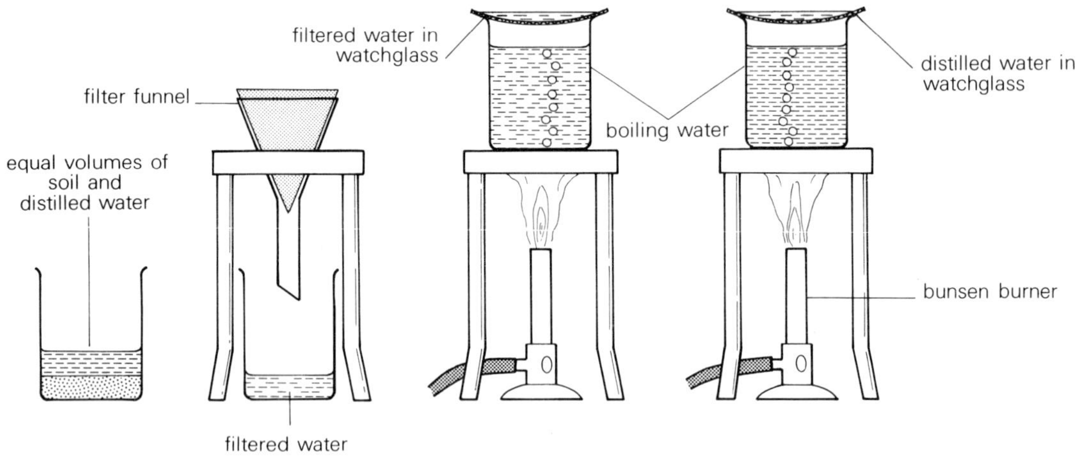

Having worked this far you should now know that soil consists of a mixture of the following:

1. Tiny fragments of rock
2. Water
3. Mineral salts
4. Air
5. Humus
6. Bacteria

Soil structure

In practice, the rock particles in a fertile soil group together to form crumbs. This crumb formation and the resulting pore space is called the *structure* of the soil. A well-structured soil will consist almost entirely of crumbs.

What effect will crumb formation have upon the air content of a clay soil? . . . Q.8

A soil with a good structure (i.e., a high proportion of crumbs) will drain more freely, warm more quickly and provide a much better environment for soil fauna and plant roots. A soil with a good structure is therefore much more productive than a badly structured one.

Under a well-managed grassland the structure of the soil gradually improves. In arable soils badly timed cultivations can destroy the structure of the soil, reducing its fertility. In general the addition of organic material (compost, manure, etc.) will improve the structure of the soil.

Task 1.2

1. Crush a small quantity of dry topsoil in a pestle and mortar and sprinkle a little onto a microscrope slide.
2. Sprinkle a little uncrushed topsoil onto a second slide.
3. Using the lowest possible magnification, view the two slides.
4. Draw diagrams of the crushed and uncrushed soils to show any differences observed.

Different types of soils have different properties: one soil type may produce a good crop of wheat, yet may be unsuitable for carrot production. A beautiful border of azaleas and heathers may be grown in a soil in which lupins and carnations fail. Try the following experiments to compare the properties of a sandy soil with those of a clay soil (if there is only one soil type available, use a set of soil sieves to separate the sand from the clay in the available soil and perform the experiments with these).

Experiment 1.8
Permeability of soil to water

1. Place two funnels in two retort stands with measuring cylinders underneath (as shown in the diagram).
2. Plug each funnel with a little glass wool.
3. About half-fill one funnel with clay soil and put an *equal volume* of sandy soil in the other.
4. Almost fill both funnels with water.
5. Collect the water that runs through the soils in two measuring cylinders over a given period of time. During the time period, keep the water topped up in both funnels to avoid any pressure difference.

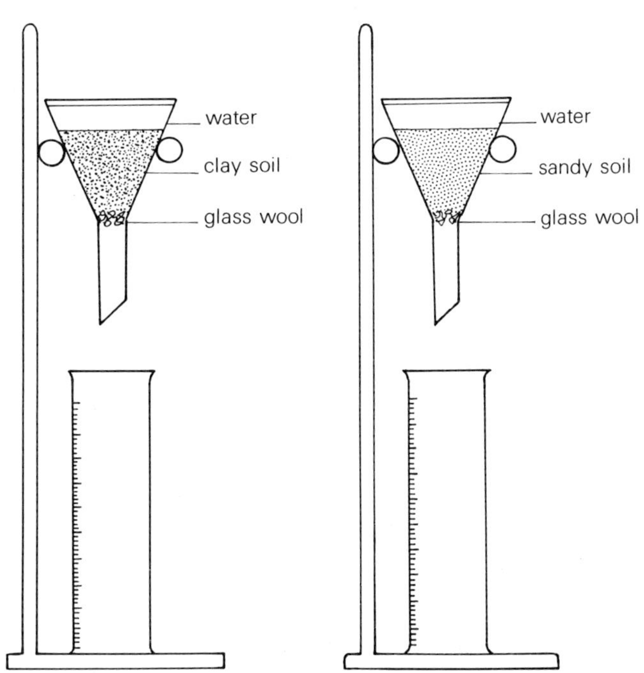

Experiment 1.9
To compare the rise of water in sand and clay soils

1. Thoroughly dry 2 kg of each soil type.
2. Sieve both soils to remove stones and large particles.
3. Take two 600 mm lengths of 30 mm glass tubing, plug one end of each with filter paper.
4. Fill one tube with clay soil and the other with sandy soil, tapping gently to obtain even packing.
5. Clamp the tubes vertically in two stands with a metre rule in between them.

6. Lower the end of the tubes into a trough of water and start a stopwatch.

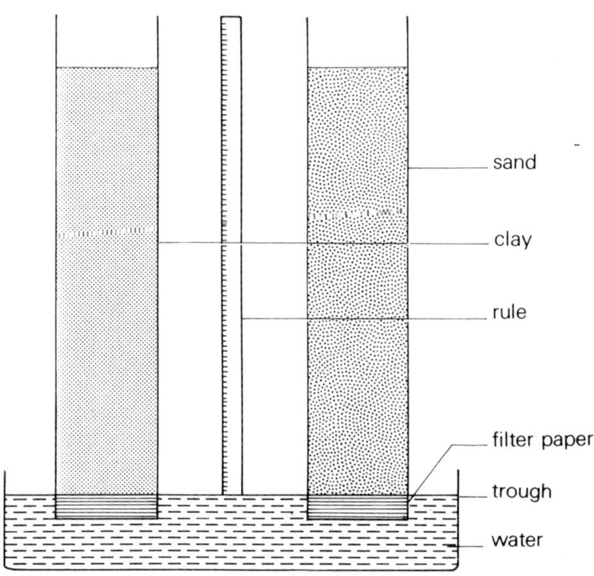

7. Read and record the heights of the water in each tube every five minutes for the next half-hour.
8. As the water rises more slowly increase the time interval between the readings.
9. Take the final reading the following day and plot the results on a graph (it may look something like the one in the diagram).

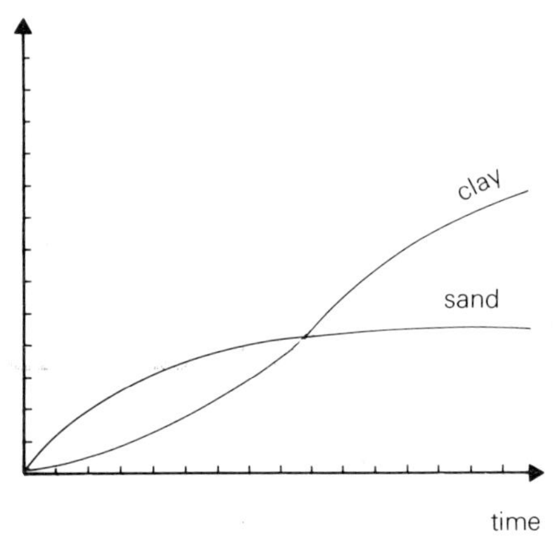

A graph of height of water against time

Note: The water rises up the tubes by *capillary action*.

Experiment 1.10

Using the experiments described earlier in the chapter the comparative amounts of water, humus and air can be found in sand and clay soils.

Clay soil in July, after two weeks without rain

Clay soils shrink as they dry – causing cracking. This can be demonstrated in the laboratory by making a paste from a clay soil and spreading it to a depth of about 5 mm over a piece of card:

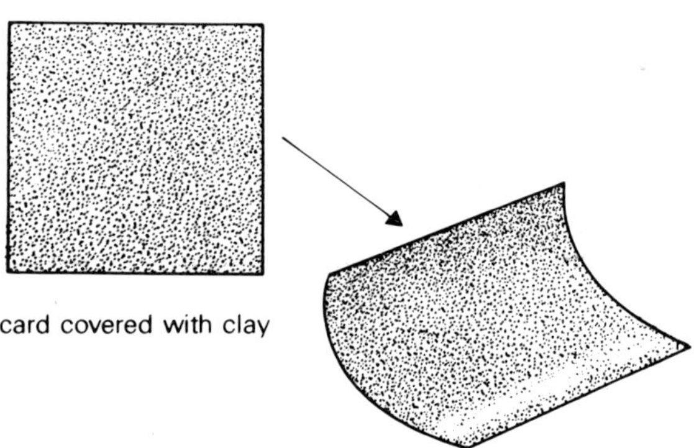

As the soil dries, the card curls up due to the shrinkage of the clay.

Comparison between a sand and clay soil

	Clay	*Sand*
Particle size	Very small	Large
Humus content	Usually high	Usually low
Water content	High	Low
Air content	Low	High
Plant nutrients	High	Low
Temperature	Cold – slow to warm in spring	Warms (and cools) quickly
Anchorage for roots	Provides good anchorage	Poor anchorage
Drainage	Poor – swells when wet preventing passage of water	Drains freely
Cultivation	Difficult, often sticky a *heavy* soil	Easily cultivated a *light* soil

Soil formation

The process of soil formation began millions of years ago when rocks first appeared on the surface of the earth, and it is still going on. Many different processes: physical, chemical and biological, break down rocks into sands, silts and clays and mix in organic material to form a soil.

A Processes which break down rock

1. *Uneven heating of rock*
   If boiling water is poured into a thick glass bottle, the inside of the glass expands before heat can be conducted to the cold outside parts; this causes stresses within the glass and the bottle breaks. Similarly in nature, hot sun on some types of rock can cause cracking and flaking.

2. *Expansion of water upon freezing*
   The glass bottles in the photograph opposite were filled with water and placed in a deep freeze cabinet. As the water froze, it expanded, shattering the bottles. Rainwater enters rock fissures, and as it freezes exerts pressure which may break off pieces of rock.

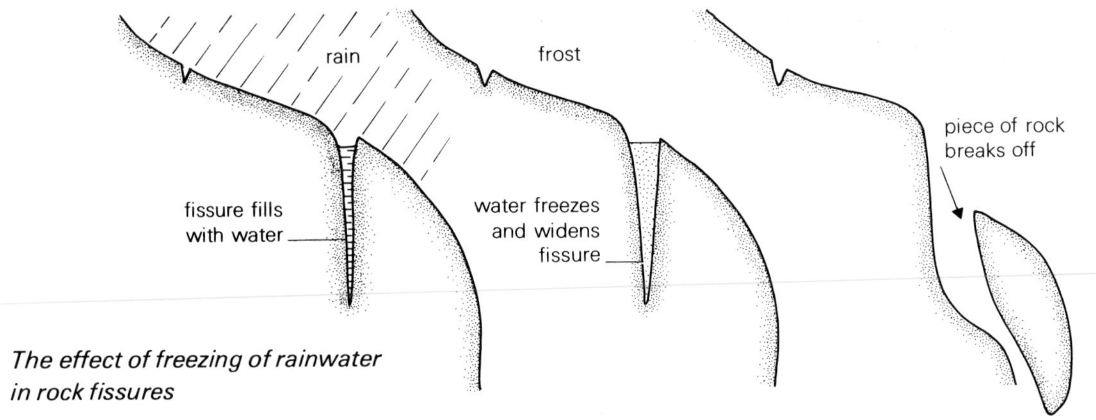

The effect of freezing of rainwater in rock fissures

3. Glaciers (rivers of ice) wear away the rocks they flow over; in addition boulders frozen into the glaciers rasp away the underlying rock.

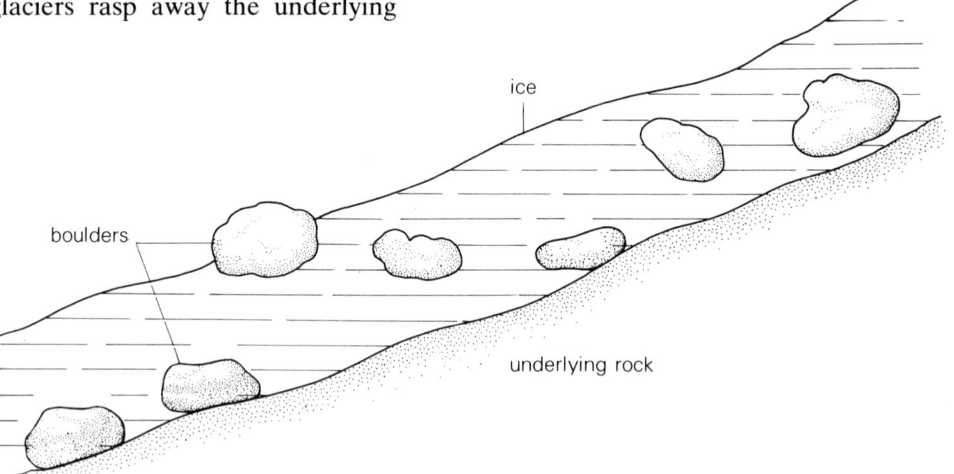

4. Seas pounding, and tides and rivers flowing tumble rocks together, wearing them away. Stones in a stream are often smooth and round due to the action of water over long periods of time, wearing them away. The fragments broken off will have been deposited somewhere down stream. Fast moving water also carries fragments of rock and deposits them in areas where the water slows, these deposits form the basis of a soil.

Are the four processes mentioned so far physical, chemical or biological? . . . Q.9

Each time a rock is broken, more surface is exposed, upon which weathering agents can work: this accelerates the process.

5. Rainwater contains a little dissolved carbon dioxide and is slightly acid, this acid reacts chemically with some rocks (e.g., limestone) and gradually breaks them down.
6. Some types of rock react chemically with atmospheric oxygen and water causing powdering or flaking (a process similar to the rusting of iron).
7. Plants and animals produce chemicals, some of which cause rock to decay.

B Processes which add organic material to soils

1. Dead plants and animals lie upon the surface and decay. The products of composition are washed into the soil by rain.

2. Earthworms pull dead leaves and other dead plant material from the surface into their burrows. Worms ingest a lot of soil with their food and the inorganic parts of the soil are thoroughly mixed as they pass through the digestive tract (see Book 1).
3. Plant roots grow down into the soil; when the plant dies they remain and decay.
4. Since civilisation began man has dug or ploughed organic manures into the soil.

Some soils are formed from the rocks they overlie.

topsoil
subsoil
rock particles becoming smaller
underlying rock

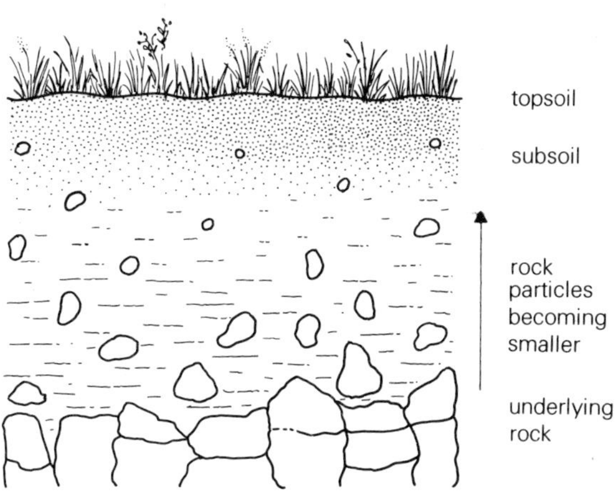

Topsoil derived from its underlying rock

Other soils are formed from rock particles that have been transported many hundreds of kilometres from the parent rock by wind or water (see illustration below).

Sand dunes at the seaside are an example of soils being formed from transported material. As the blown sand slowly increases the area of land, vegetation prevents further drifting and the sand gradually becomes soil. The area where the trees are growing was once beach. If the plants were removed the very sandy soil would soon be eroded (blown or washed away). The soil beneath the trees is known as a *podzol soil*.

Soils formed from transported material: sand dunes

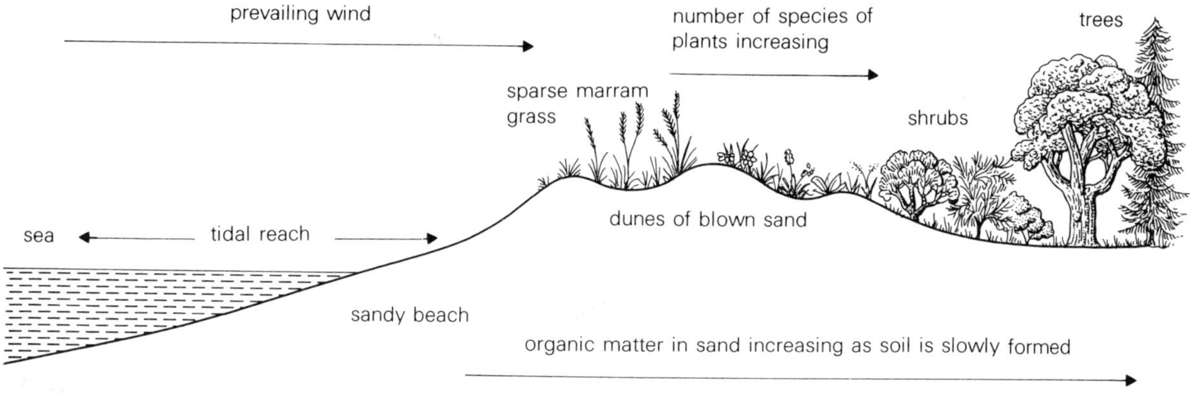

prevailing wind
number of species of plants increasing
trees
sparse marram grass
shrubs
dunes of blown sand
sea
tidal reach
sandy beach
organic matter in sand increasing as soil is slowly formed

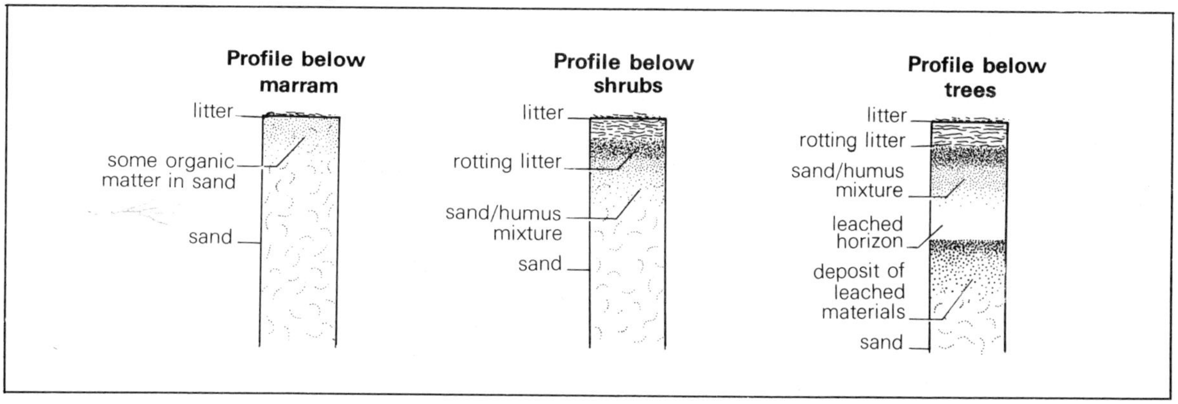

Profile below marram
litter
some organic matter in sand
sand
Profile below shrubs
litter
rotting litter
sand/humus mixture
sand
Profile below trees
litter
rotting litter
sand/humus mixture
leached horizon
deposit of leached materials
sand

Drainage

A soil cannot support a worthwhile crop if excess water cannot flow away. In a badly drained soil the air spaces fill with water and the soil becomes waterlogged. Badly drained soils have the following disadvantages:

1. Soils which contain a lot of water take a long time to warm and are consequently cold in spring: this slows the germination of seeds and the growth of plants.
2. Wet soils contain little air: this inhibits root development and soil animal respiration.
3. Certain plant diseases flourish in wet soils, e.g., *club root* see page 71.
4. The feet of livestock and the wheels of machinery destroy the structure of a wet soil, turning it into an unproductive mud (this process is called *poaching*).
5. Some weeds (rushes, sedges, etc.), which are unpalatable to the grazing animal, thrive in wet soil.
6. Wet soils contribute to some animal diseases e.g., *foot rot* and *liver fluke* (see Book 3).
7. Wet soils are difficult to cultivate.
8. Crops of potatoes, sugar beet, etc., are difficult to harvest from wet soils.

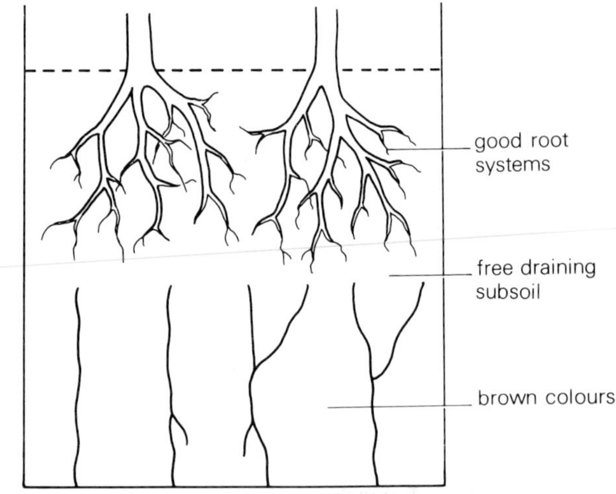

Soil profile of a well drained soil

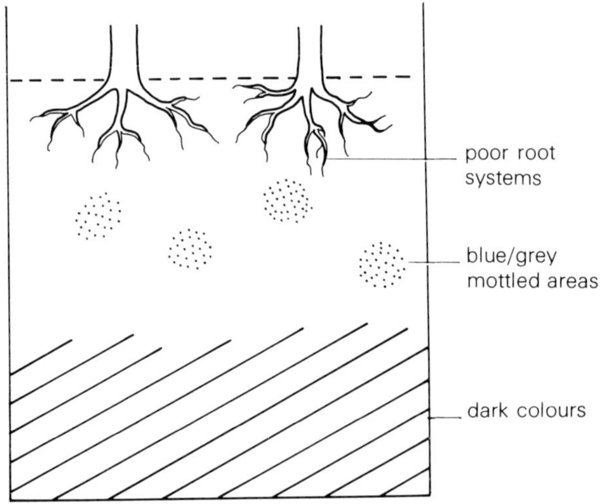

Soil profile of a badly drained soil

Years of cultivation by heavy machinery can form a compacted layer just below the depth of cultivation. This layer becomes impervious to water, causing the soil above to become waterlogged. This pan can be broken with a special deep cultivator called a 'sub-soiler'. This implement is best pulled by a crawler tractor as tracks apply less pressure to the soil than wheels do.

Where waterlogging is caused by impervious top and sub-soils the soil can be improved by drainage. Drains are laid under the depth of normal cultivation and the water is channelled to natural streams and rivers. Although farmers have been draining their land for over one hundred years there are still 3.5 million hectares of land in England and Wales that require draining.

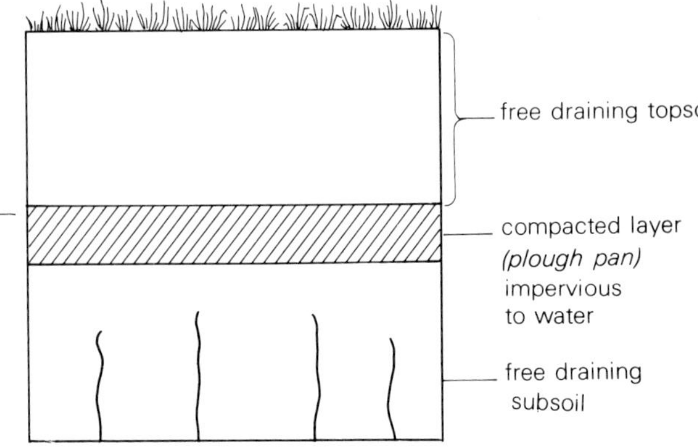

Section through a soil, showing the 'plough pan'

A subsoiler

Very large machines are used to cut ditches and lay tile or plastic pipes in the bottom of drains; these pipes are covered with a porous material (large stones, or clinker from power stations) and the top soil is then replaced.

Note: the feeder drains run across, not down the slope; they are usually about 15 metres apart but this distance varies according to the soil type.

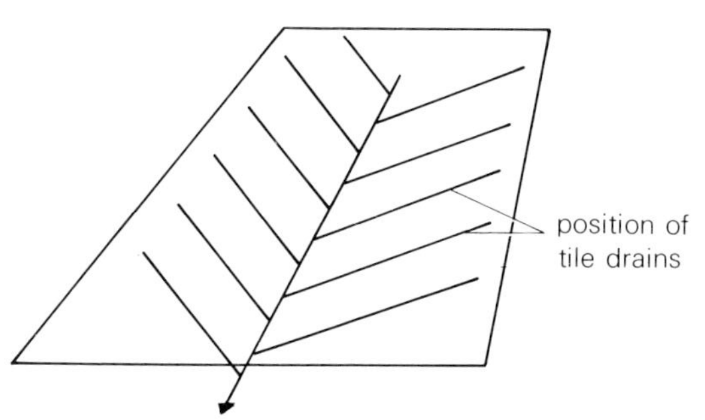

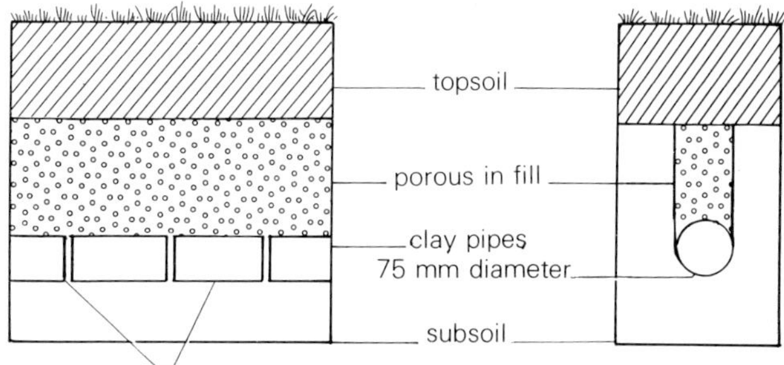

Mole drains

The effectiveness of tile draining is increased by using a special plough, called a mole plough which makes tunnels in the soil, just above the pipes. In clay soils these mole drains last up to ten years.

The mole plough produces a circular channel 75 mm in diameter.

The action of a mole plough

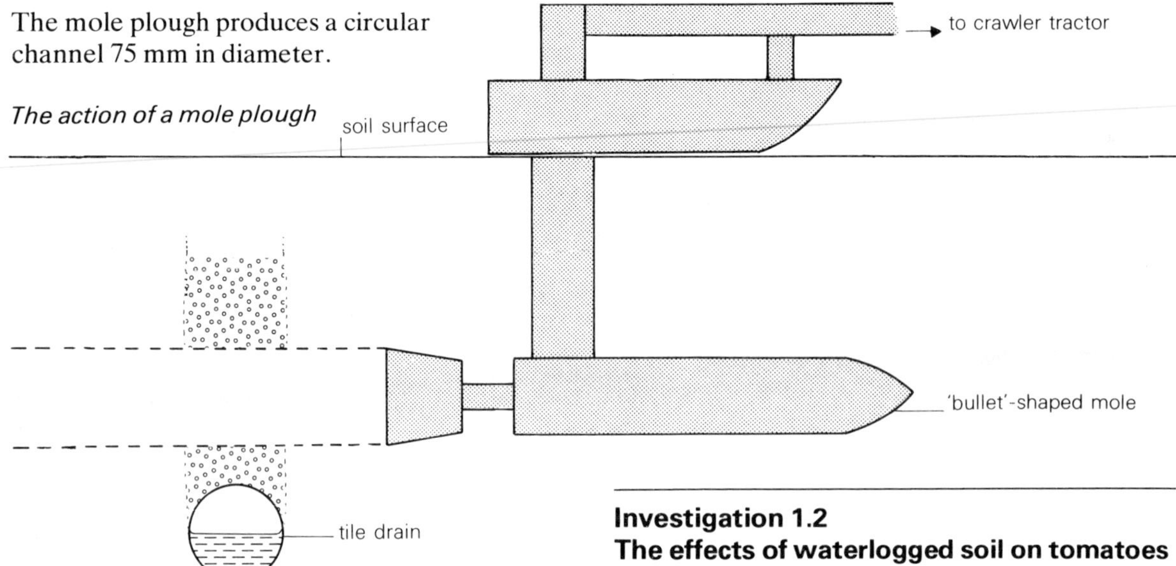

Draining a small area of land

The simplest way to drain a small area (e.g., an allotment) is to dig a number of soakaways.

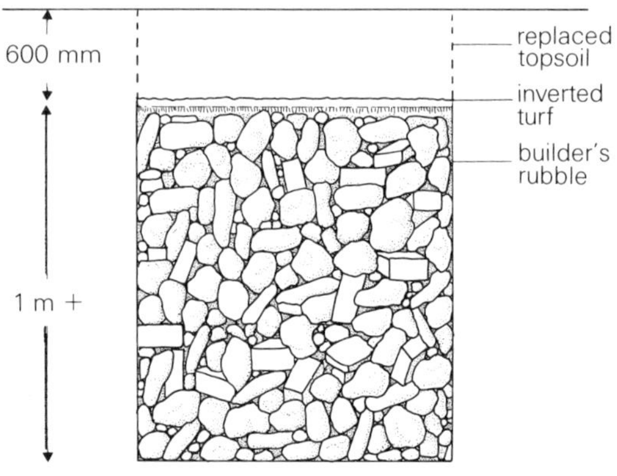

Cross-section of a soakaway

A large hole is dug and filled to within 600 mm of the top with builders' rubble. The rubble is covered with a layer of inverted turf before the topsoil is replaced.

Investigation 1.2
The effects of waterlogged soil on tomatoes

One week ago, these plants were almost identical – the plant on the right has been waterlogged for four days

1. Select two tomato plants (growing in 125 mm pots) similar in growth and development.
2. Submerge one pot in a bath with the water level just over the top of the pot.
3. Four days later remove the plant from the bath and allow it to drain.
4. Examine the plants daily during the next ten days and record any differences you observe.

Note: if tomato plants are not available, pot grown peas may be used for this investigation.

A machine for draining soils

Water table

In many areas, if a deep hole is dug, it will fill with water to a certain level: this level is the *water table*; it is not fixed but rises and falls according to the seasons. The water table can be defined as the *level in the soil, below which all available spaces are filled with water.*

Low water tables have no effect upon soil moisture. But, if the water table is high some water may be lifted into the topsoil by capillary action. A clay soil will raise water 800 mm above the water table and a sandy soil will raise water about 400 mm above the water table.

The water cycle

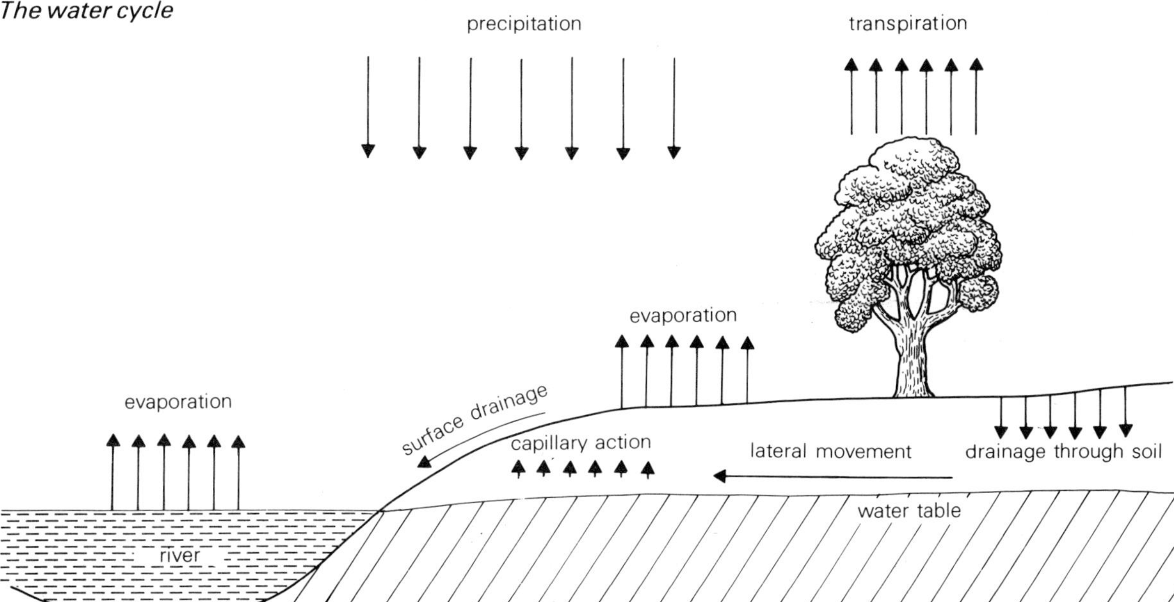

Soil temperature

The soil derives its heat from the sun, the sun's rays pass through the atmosphere and warm the soil (the air is warmed by contact with the soil). Only some of the sun's energy is used in warming the soil, the rest is used in other ways as the diagram shows:

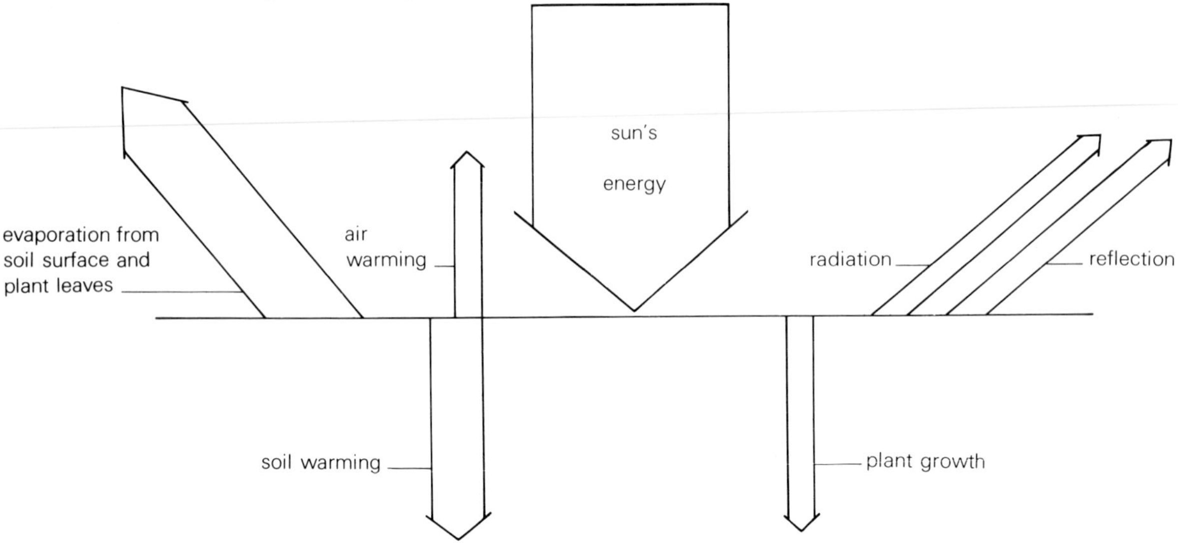

Soil is a very poor conductor of heat – lower layers are usually at very different temperatures to the surface layers:

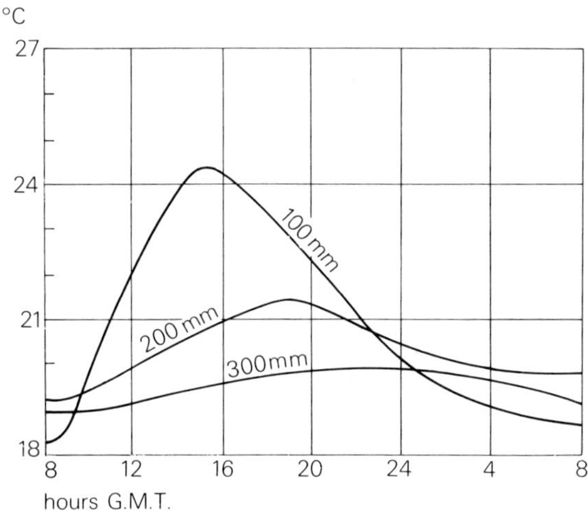

A graph to show the temperature variations of a soil at various depths, during a sunny day in August

At what time did the soil 100 mm deep reach its highest temperature? . . . Q.10

What was the highest temperature reached by the soil 200 mm deep? . . . Q.11

Factors affecting soil temperature

1. Direction of slope of the ground

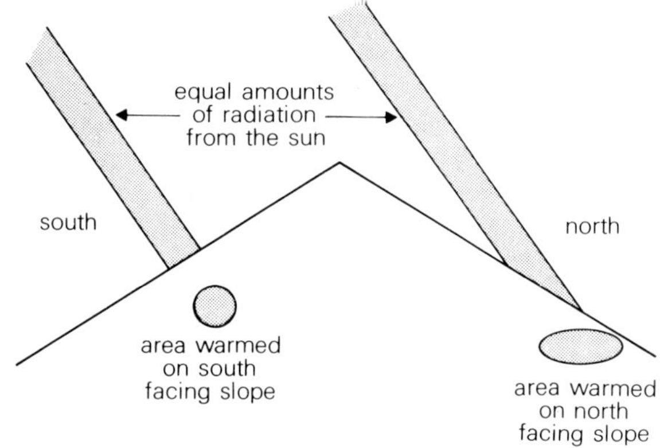

The same amount of radiation warms a smaller area of soil on the south slope than the north slope (as shown above) making the south facing slope warmer than the north facing slope. This effect is often increased as south slopes are sheltered from cold north winds.

Which slopes will be warmer in New Zealand, north or south? . . . Q.12

2. Water content

Wet soils warm more slowly than dry soils, as much of the incoming heat is used to warm up the soil water.

3. The colour of the soil

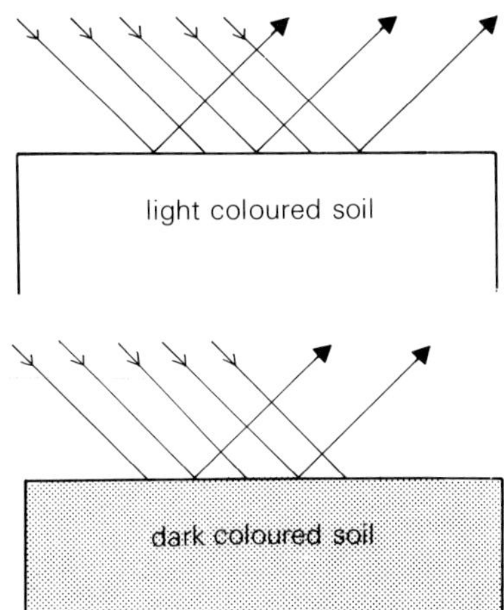

A light-coloured soil reflects a larger proportion of the incoming radiation than a dark soil; however a dark soil radiates more energy than a light one.

4. Cropping

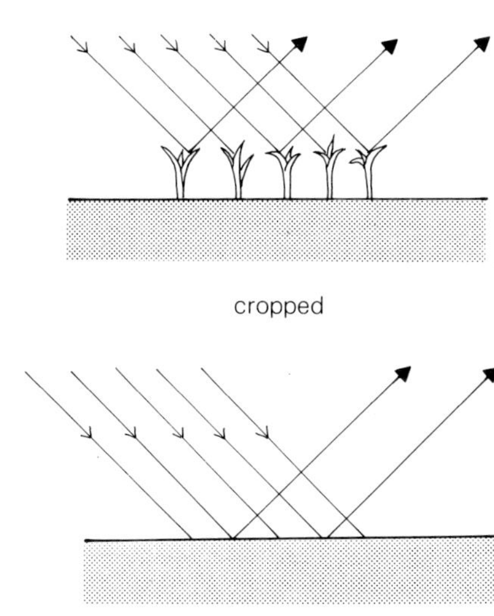

A cropped soil reflects more energy than a bare one.

Soil reaction

Solutions are either acid, alkaline or neutral. Soil water is a solution containing many different chemicals and as such it is either acid, alkaline or neutral, depending upon the amount of calcium that is present. Acidity is measured on a pH scale.

The pH scale

The pH scale begins at 0 and ends at 14:

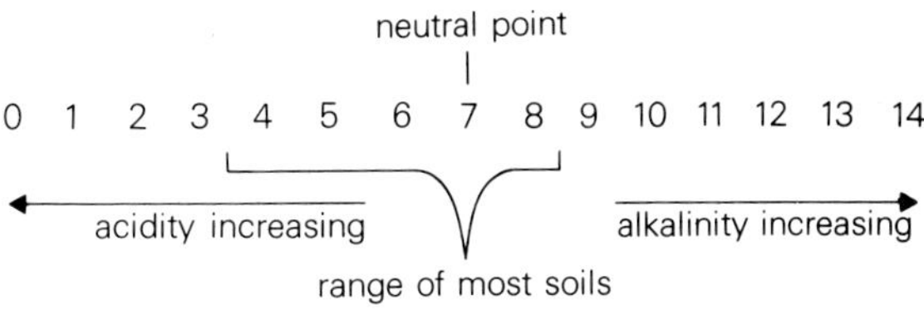

The pH scale is not linear – it is logarithmic, this means that pH 3 is *ten times* more acid than pH 4 which is *ten times* more acid than pH 5, and so on.

In the U.K. many soils tend to become acid as calcium is leached from them (*leached* = washed out of the soil by rain and removed with the drainage water). Calcium is also removed from the soil by the growing plant.

Harmful effects of a very acid soil (low pH)

1. Bacteria become less active releasing smaller quantities of plant nutrients into the soil.
2. At pH values less than 5.7, *Rhizobium* bacteria do not form nodules on the roots of legumes (see Book 3).
3. Earthworms do not live in soils with pH less than 4.5.
4. Crop yields are reduced.
5. Some substances which are toxic to plants are released into the soil.
6. Brassicas (cabbage family) become infected with the fungus disease *club root* (see page 71).

Harmful effects of a very alkaline soil (high pH)

1. Humus is broken down too quickly.
2. Some important nutrients become unavailable
3. Conditions are favourable for the disease *potato scab*.

Different plants have different pH requirements

calcifuges (lime hating plants) → conifers, heathers, azeleas, rhododendrons; fine lawn grasses

calcicoles (lime loving plants) → brassicas, legumes; carnations, spinach

crop	most crops fail	conifers, heathers, azeleas, rhododend-rons	fine lawn grasses	top and soft fruit	most crops thrive	brassicas legumes	carnations spinach	most crops fail
pH of soil	3	4	5	6		7	8	9

The chart above shows the pH requirements of certain plants.

At what soil pH do most plants thrive? . . . Q.13

Experiment 1.11
To test the pH of soil under a lawn using barium sulphate tubes

A barium sulphate tube is a glass tube, 200 mm long, with two marks towards one end. Stoppers are provided for each end of the tube. The soil sample is collected, with a soil auger by the following method:

The auger is used to collect cores of soil, all the same length (i.e., depth) from ten sites selected at random (the auger is screwed into the soil to the required depth and pulled straight up without turning, the sample of soil is caught in the 'thread'). The cores are thoroughly mixed and a sample is taken from this mixture.

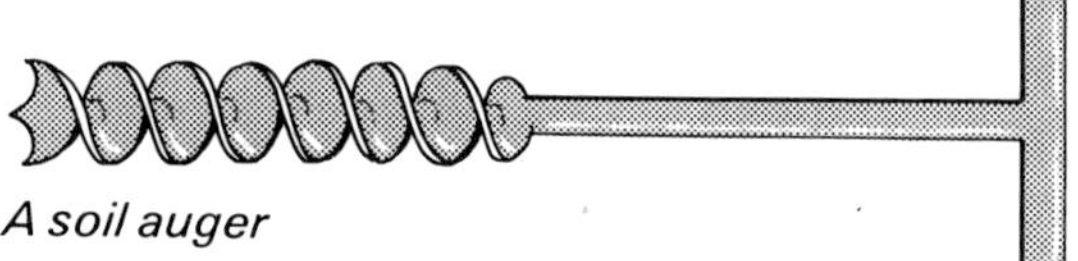

A soil auger

1. Stopper the bottom of the barium sulphate tube and put in approximately 5 ml of the soil sample.
2. Add distilled water to mark A (as shown on the diagram opposite).
3. Carefully pour in Universal indicator solution until the level rises to mark B.
4. Add 2 ml of barium sulphate solution and stopper the top.
5. Invert the tube a number of times to mix the contents.
6. Stand in a test tube rack whilst the contents settle and the liquid clears.
7. Compare the colour of the liquid with the indicator colour chart, obtain the best colour match and read the pH from the chart.

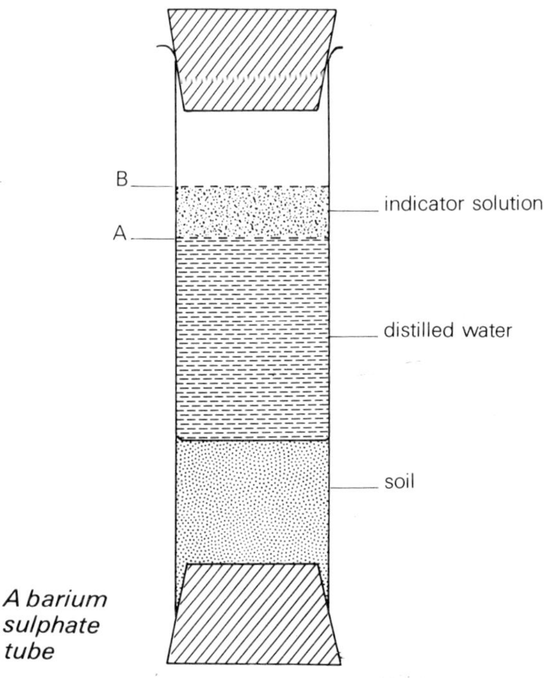

A barium sulphate tube

Note: the barium sulphate helps the liquid to clear quickly.

Correcting soil acidity

The pH of acid soils can be increased by adding lime. Natural limestone or chalk rock is quarried, crushed and sieved giving a compound consisting of 95% calcium carbonate. This is spread on the surface of the soil and either left for the rain to wash in (e.g., on grassland) or worked into the soil with cultivating machinery. The quantity of lime applied varies with soil type and pH level: a normal application is 5 tonnes per hectare (500 g/m^2). There is a time lag of several months between applying lime and pH increase; autumn is therefore the best time to apply lime – improving the soil for the following season.

Lime must *never* be added at the same time as organic manures, or rapid and wasteful breakdown of the manure will occur and the plant nutrients lost.

Lime improves the structure of clay soils by increasing the proportion of crumbs: this increases the pore space of the soil, making it lighter and easier to cultivate.

Beneficial effects of liming a soil

1. Lime supplies calcium to the soil (calcium is an essential plant nutrient).
2. Lime speeds the breakdown of organic matter releasing plant nutrients.
3. Lime makes conditions favourable for earthworms and beneficial soil bacteria.
4. Lime removes some harmful substances from the soil solution.
5. Lime reduces the numbers of some pests (e.g., slug, wireworm, leatherjacket).
6. Lime makes conditions unsuitable for the fungus disease club root.
7. Lime improves the structure of clay soils by flocculation.

Harmful effects of liming a soil

1. Lime creates conditions suitable for the disease potato scab.
2. Too much lime causes rapid and wasteful breakdown of soil humus.

Experiment 1.12
To show the effect of lime on the structure of clay soil

1. Place about 100 ml of clay soil in each of two glass jars A and B and two-thirds fill with water (as shown in the diagram).
2. Cover each jar and shake vigorously until the water is clouded with a suspension of clay particles.
3. Add 50 ml of lime water to jar A.
4. Add 50 ml of distilled water to jar B.
5. Allow the jars to stand and observe the clay suspension in each. Crumbs of clay will be seen to form in jar A which quickly sink, clearing the water. This is known as *flocculation*. There is no flocculation in jar B, and the water remains clouded for many hours.

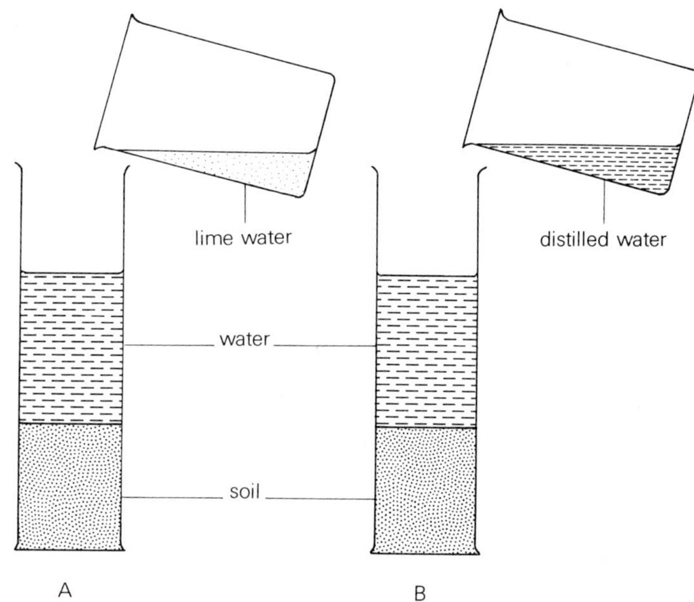

Questions: Soil

1. Write single sentences to answer the following questions.
   (a) What is a soil profile?
   (b) What do you understand by soil texture?
   (c) Why is the soil sample heated over a waterbath in the soil water experiment?
   (d) Which soil is described as light sand, chalk or clay?
   (e) Is soil a good conductor of heat?
   (f) What scale is used to measure acidity?
   (g) In what way is an excess of lime bad for the soil?
   (h) How does a clay loam differ from a silt loam?
   (i) For what purpose are soil sieves used?
   (j) What soil type has extremely small mineral particles?

2. (a) What is humus?
   (b) Why is a high humus content desirable in a mineral soil?
   (c) Describe an experiment to determine the amount of humus in a soil sample.
   (d) What steps could a gardener take to increase the humus content of his soil?

3. Briefly describe the soil type on the school farm or garden, or on any other *one* site which you have studied. State any *two* problems which you associate with clay soil. How can the physical properties of clay soil be improved?

4. (a) Name the constituents of a sample of fertile soil.
   (b) Describe how you would carry out a physical analysis of a sample of soil.
   (*W.M.E.B.*)

5. (a) Name a type of soil which allows water to drain freely and one type which does not drain freely.
   (b) List three ways in which the water retention properties of a soil can be increased.
   (c) *Either* explain *fully* an experiment that soil contains living organisms *or*, with the aid of a diagram describe one method you have used to collect soil animals.
   (*S.R.E.B*)

6. (a) Describe how you would determine the the volume of air in a soil sample.
   (b) State the results you would expect to obtain with
   (i) a sandy,
   (ii) a clay soil, and account for them.
   (c) State the importance of air to soils.

7. (a) Why is lime important to farmers and gardeners?
   (b) Describe how you would carry out a soil test to find the pH value of your soil.
   (c) Name four plants which thrive in acidic soils and four plants which thrive in alkaline soils? (*W.J.E.C.*)

8. (a) State *two* ways in which an application of lime benefits a clay soil.
   (b) Describe an experiment, which you would conduct in *either* the garden *or* the classroom, in order to demonstrate *one* way in which an application of lime would benefit clay soil. (*W.M.E.B.*)

9. (a) What is meant by the pH scale and why is the pH scale useful to the farmer/gardener?
   (b) Give details of any test you have carried out to determine the pH of a soil sample.
   (c) How would you raise the pH of the soil in your garden? (*W.Y. & L.R.E.B.*)

10. *Soil*
   A tin of volume 100 cm^3 was filled with soil A. The soil was emptied into a measuring cylinder of water, raising the level of water from the 200 cm^3 mark to the 270 cm^3 mark.
   (a) Why was the final reading at the 270 cm^3 mark?

(b) The experiment was repeated with a different kind of soil, B; this time the water level at the end was 290 cm^3. Which soil is a sandy soil, and which a clay soil?

Soil A.

Soil B.

(c) Describe one experiment which you carried out during your study of soil.

Include in your answer

(i) the equipment used,
(ii) the method used,
(iii) what you observed,
(iv) an example(s) of the results you recorded,
(v) conclusions.

(S.R.E.B.)

2 Vegetable culture

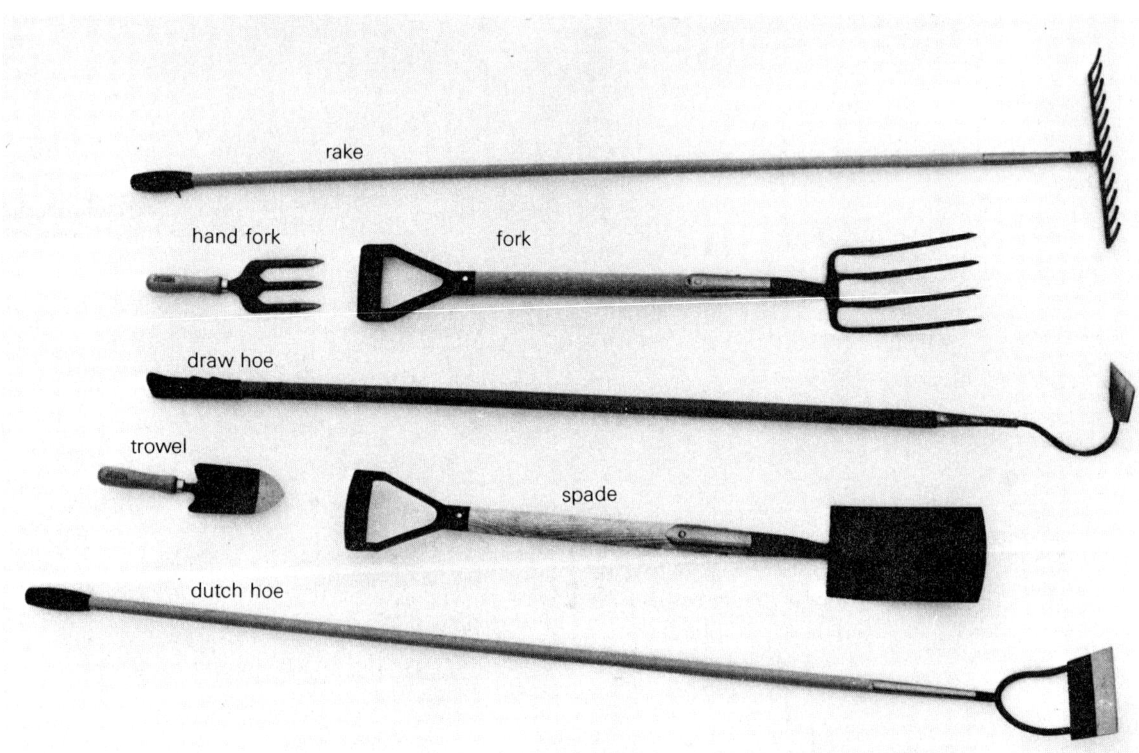

The tools in the photograph above are the only ones required to grow most vegetables and flowers.

Spade

The spade is used for digging, trenching, mixing soils, spreading lime, skimming weeds from the surface and many other operations. The blade is designed in such a way that the bottom edge remains sharp during use, the length of the blade (usually 225 mm) is called a 'spit'. If misused, the handle breaks where the wood and metal join: a spade should never be used like an axe and only limited pressure should be exerted on the handle when the blade is in the ground.

Fork

The fork is used for digging, usually in spring on soils that were dug by spade the previous autumn. The fork is also used to loosen compacted soils, for removing the roots of perennial weeds, harvesting potatoes and root vegetables, lifting (digging up) large plants and moving manure and compost.

Why is the spade not used to harvest potatoes? . . . Q.1

Dutch hoe

The dutch hoe is used to control seedling weeds.

The hoe is pushed to and fro in the top 10 mm of soil in a series of short (200 mm) strokes, cutting off germinating weeds at ground level. The operator moves backwards, taking care not to step on the crop plants and the weeds are left on top of the soil between rows.

What will happen to these weeds? . . . Q.2

The action of the dutch hoe leaves a thin layer of loose soil on the surface which reduces soil water loss by evaporation.

Use of the dutch hoe

Draw hoe

The draw hoe is used to loosen the top 50 mm of soil and to kill weeds in between rows of plants. The draw hoe is always used to earth up potatoes (see page 37) and other plants.

Use of the draw hoe

Rake

The garden rake is used to level the soil, to prepare a *tilth* (structure of the surface soil), to draw a *drill* (shallow trench) for sowing seeds and to firm the soil above them.

The rake is not used to remove large lumps of soil – it is pushed and pulled across the surface with the handle fairly low, soil is pulled from the high areas and deposited in the hollows. This operation levels the soil and improves the tilth.

Use of the garden rake

Trowel

The trowel should be used whenever a small hole is required in which to plant seedlings, bulbs or potatoes. Some gardeners use a dibber for this purpose: this is not recommended as the dibber may damage the structure of some soils by compacting the area immediately around the plant or bulb. The trowel (or hand fork) is also used for lifting small plants.

Garden line

A garden line completes the list of essential equipment, and is used for obtaining straight lines in the garden.

Tool care

Most garden tools are manufactured from mild steel which rusts very easily. Tools must be cleaned after use and stored in dry conditions. If a tool is not likely to be used for a few weeks the bright metal parts will keep in good condition if smeared with oil.

Safety

Gardens tools are *dangerous if used incorrectly*. Tools must never be carried on the shoulder nor must they be laid flat on the ground (not even for a few minutes).

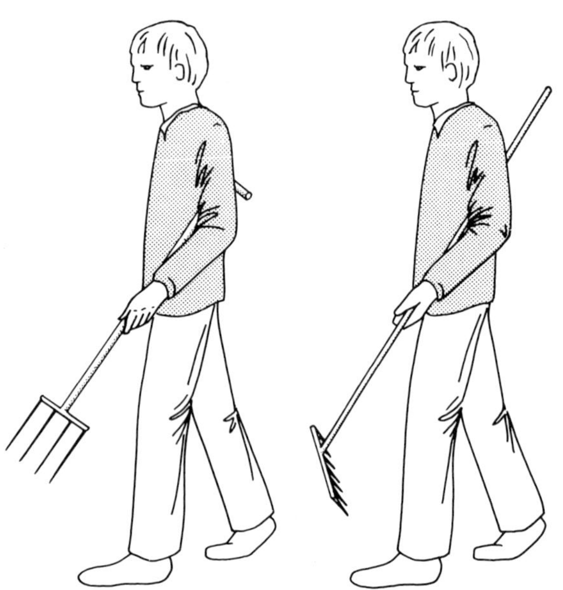

The correct way to carry garden tools

Why is it dangerous to carry a spade on the shoulder? . . . Q.3

Why is it dangerous to lay a tool flat on the ground? . . . Q.4

Digging

The first operation in preparation for crop production is to dig the soil, i.e., to turn over the surface layer of soil. Ideally soils should be dug when they are below field capacity, otherwise the digger's feet will poach the soil and cause some damage to its structure. The reasons for digging are:

1. Digging leaves a bare surface, burying weeds and the remains of the previous crop; the roots and rhizomes of perennial weeds can also be removed.
2. Digging increases the air content of the soil by loosening it up.
3. Digging allows organic matter to be buried in the soil where it will decay and produce nutrients for the succeeding crop.
4. Digging creates conditions where a tilth is easily produced.
5. Autumn digging exposes more of the soil to frosts, this has the effect of causing clods in a heavy soil to crumble

Why does frost cause clods of clay to crumble? . . . Q.5

Single spit digging

This method turns over the top spit, and creates suitable conditions for the production of most crops:

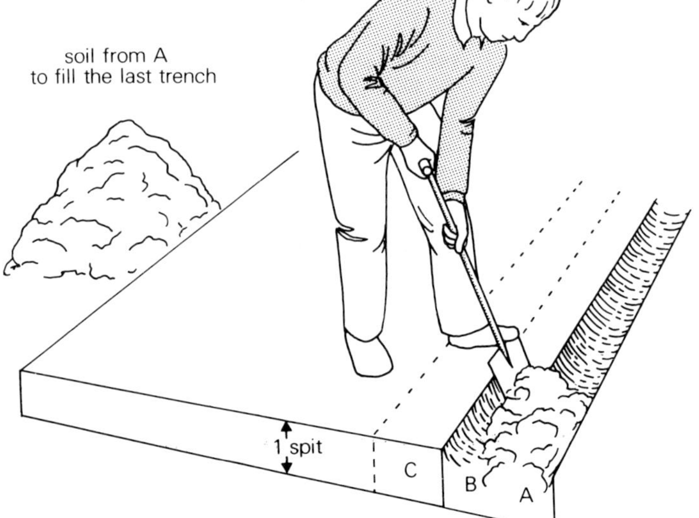

1. Dig trench 'A' one spit deep and 250 mm wide; place the soil from this trench at the far end of the plot.
2. Working across from one side to the other, turn the soil from 'B' into 'A', making sure that the spade is vertical and reaches maximum depth each time. This will fill 'A' and leave a trench at 'B'.

3. If the plot is to be manured, spread manure in the bottom of 'B' before turning 'C' into 'B'.
4. When the end of the plot is reached, fill the last trench with the soil from 'A'.
5. Leave the plot to settle for a week or so before planting.

Bastard trenching

Bastard trenching is similar to single spit digging except that the bottom of each trench is forked with a garden fork before it is filled. Care must be taken not to raise any subsoil to the surface. This method of digging breaks up the second spit of soil which assists drainage, and the rooting of such crops as parsnips and potatoes.

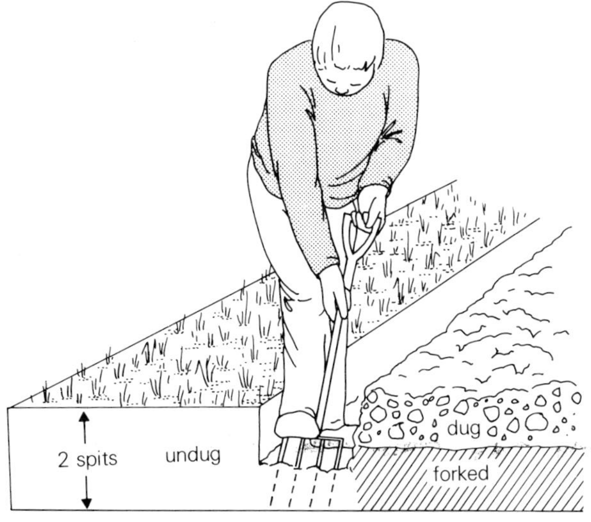

Double digging

This method ensures that the soil is fully worked to a depth of two spits without mixing the two layers together:

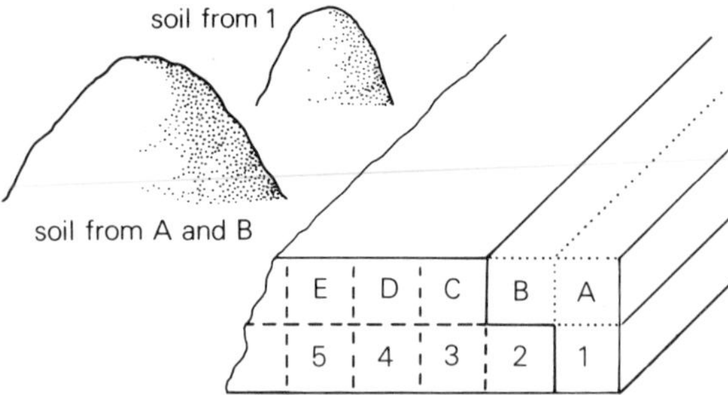

1. Soil is taken from 'A' and 'B' and put at the far end of the plot.
2. Soil is taken from '1' and put at the far end of the plot in a separate heap.
3. The plot is dug in the following sequence: '2' into '1'; 'C' into 'A'; '3' into '2'; 'D' into 'B' and so on.
4. When the end of the plot is reached soil from '1' is used to fill the lower trench and soil from 'A' and 'B' is used to fill the wide trench above.

Double digging requires considerable skill and should not be attempted until the single digging technique has been completely mastered.

Preparing a tilth

A few weeks after digging (or a few months in the case of autumn dug soils) the surface soil is broken down and levelled to obtain a fine tilth in which seeds will germinate. The weather and soil surface must be dry for this operation, which consists of the gardener raking the plot over a number of times. The combined action of feet and rake breaks up lumps of soil and leaves the surface with the tilth to suit the crop. The greater the number of times the soil is raked, the finer the tilth. The compaction of the soil that occurs during this operation helps to conserve the soil moisture. *Note*: if fertiliser is to be applied it is spread evenly over the surface before the tilth is prepared.

Sowing

Sowing small seeds in the open ground

1. The line is stretched taut across the plot.
2. The corner of a rake is used to draw a shallow drill along the line (if the line is moved during this operation it is restored to its original position by lifting 300 mm in the centre and allowing it to fall):

3. A pinch of seeds is taken and sprinkled *as thinly as possible* along the drill; a second and third pinch may be required depending upon the length of the row. The operator in the photograph is dropping seeds very slowly by tapping the packet with his forefinger:

4. The seeds are covered lightly using the teeth of the rake:

Small seeds must not be buried too deep, but should have a minimum of 10 mm of soil over them to prevent the germinating seed from drying out.

5. The soil above the seeds is firmed with the head of the rake:

6. Footprints are raked out before moving the line to the next row.

Sowing large seeds in the open soil

Large seeds are sown in the same way as small seeds except that the drill is drawn deeper, and the seeds sown individually, with a certain distance between each one. Large seeds should not be buried very deep – a covering of 25 mm of soil is sufficient for the largest seed.

Peas are sown in a trench 200 mm wide and 20 mm deep; the seeds are scattered in the bottom of the trench with some 30 mm between them. Before being covered, the seeds are pressed gently into the soil to prevent their spacing from being disturbed.

Thinning

Small seeds are usually sown too thickly to allow the seedlings enough space for correct development. When they are large enough to handle, the surplus plants are pulled out, leaving *single* plants with enough space to mature.

Making the trench

Sowing the seeds

Covering the seeds

Transplanting

Some vegetables (e.g., Brassicas) are moved from the seed bed in the early stages of growth and planted in their final positions:

(a) Put the line taut across the plot.
(b) Using a trowel, dig a hole alongside the line.
(c) Put the plant in and holding at the correct depth, fill the hole with soil.
(d) Firm the soil.

Investigation 2.1
To find the optimum distance to allow between rows of lettuce

1. Prepare a fine tilth.
2. Sow a row of lettuce seed.
3. Move *one end* of the line 600 mm and sow a second row.
4. Sow several more rows, moving one end of the line only.
5. When the seedlings are large enough to handle, thin along each row to 150 mm apart.
6. When the plants in the row are touching, remove every other plant (these may be used for salads).
7. Leave the remaining plants to heart.
8. Compare the plants that have been grown too close together with those that have had sufficient space.
9. Use the results of your observations to decide upon the best distance to allow between rows of lettuce.

Will your results apply to all varieties of lettuce?
. . . Q.6

Organic manures

Plants remove nutrients from the soil and use them to form leaves, stems, flowers, fruits and seeds. Animals feed on plants and the same nutrients are used to form bones, muscle and other tissues. When plants and animals die, their tissues decay and the nutrients return to the soil.

In nature a state of balance exists – nutrients are returned to the soil at similar rates to their removal. By cropping soils man upsets this balance and depletes the soil of nutrients, e.g., consider one chemical element – calcium, an essential component of teeth and bones: in the U.K. man obtains much of his calcium by drinking milk:

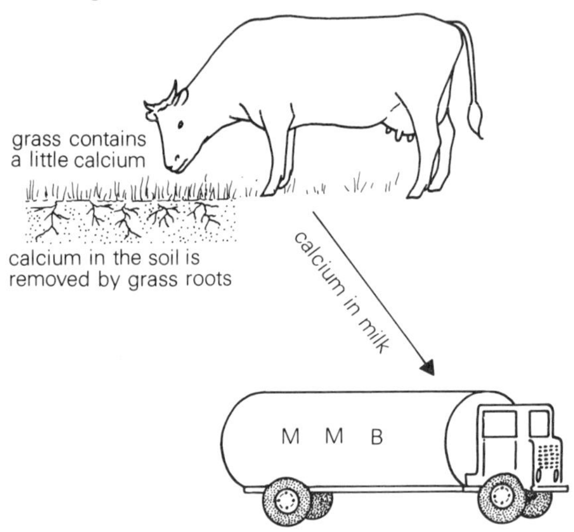

Thus as the farmer sells milk, the soils in his fields are gradually losing calcium; the same is true for other plant nutrients. Farmers and gardeners must replace these nutrients or their soils will become progressively less productive. Substances applied to the soil to supply nutrients are called manures or fertilisers. There are two groups of fertilisers – *organic* and *inorganic* (see Book 3). In addition to supplying plant nutrients, organic manures increase the humus content of the soil, improving its structure and water capacity. Farmyard manure (animal droppings and urine mixed with straw), spent hops (brewery waste) wool shoddy (waste from woollen mills) and compost (from the compost heap) are examples of organic manures.

The compost heap

All garden and household organic waste can be composted except very woody material (fruit-tree prunings), diseased plants (Brassicas with club root), roots of perennial weeds, and clippings from lawns recently treated with weed killers.

Various containers for compost

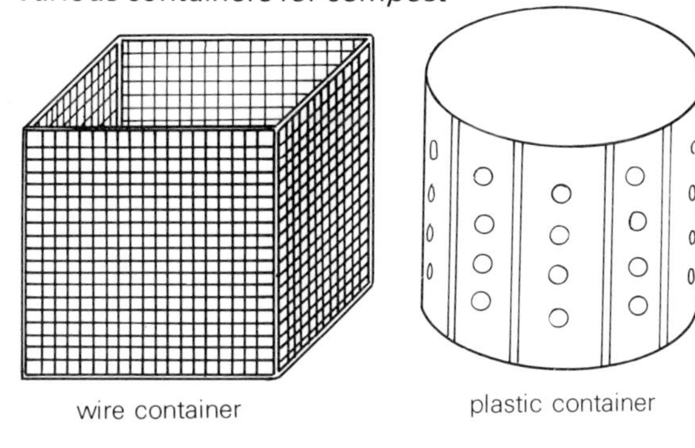

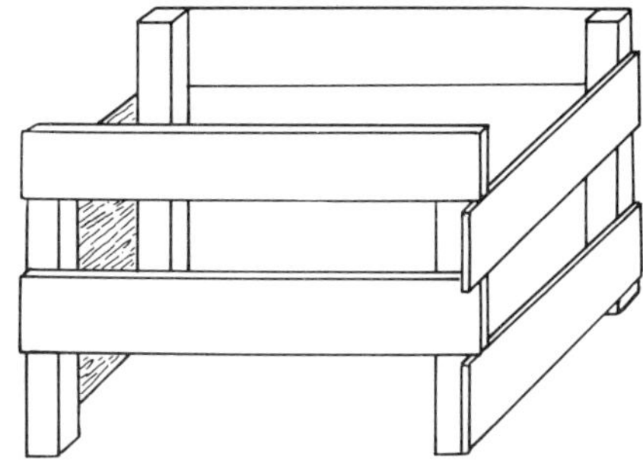

wooden posts with planks

wood front

bricks with air spaces

The waste material may be piled up without support, or it may be held in a specially constructed container of wood, brick or plastic: in either case the walls are designed to allow air to enter the heap.

The heap is built up in layers as grass clippings, crop waste and weeds become available. This organic material is broken down into a friable compost by the action of bacteria – a thin layer of topsoil spread over each layer will increase the numbers of bacteria; these will multiply more rapidly if a little nitro-chalk or sulphate of ammonia is sprinkled over each layer (one handful per barrow-load of waste). Bacteria require moist conditions, so very dry material must be watered when added to the heap.

Investigation 2.2
The effect of soil, air and fertiliser on the decay of organic matter

1. Obtain 80 kg of lawn clippings and divide into four equal parts.
2. Put each part into a polythene garden refuse bag as follows:
   A Seal the bag with string to exclude the air.
   B Leave open and pierce holes with a knife all around the sides.
   C Fill in 150 mm layers, spreading a handful of topsoil over each layer. Leave open and pierce holes to admit air.

D Fill in 150 mm layers, spreading 50 g of nitro chalk or sulphate of ammonia and a handful of topsoil over each layer. Leave open and pierce holes.

3. Insert a soil thermometer into each bag, in such a way that the bulb is approximately in the centre.
4. Read and record the temperature twice daily and plot your results on graph paper.

Note: heat is produced as bacteria break down the lawn clippings; the level of bacterial activity will therefore be indicated by the temperature.

Which sack, 'A', 'B', 'C' or 'D' would you expect to reach the highest temperature? . . . Q.7

Vegetable production

(*Note:* Chapter 3, *Pests and Diseases of Plants,* should be studied before attempting to grow vegetables).

Vegetables are grown in straight rows across the plot; this allows even spacing and easy weed control. To avoid depleting the soil of particular nutrients and building up concentrations of soil-borne pests and diseases, the various crops are grown in different parts of the garden each year; this is known as *crop rotation* and has been practised in this country for hundreds of years. There are a number of different rotations, usually involving periods of three or four years. An example of a *three year crop rotation* is:

Year 1		Year 2
onions, legumes, lettuce, leeks	*Section A*	brassicas
brassicas	*Section B*	potatoes and root crops
potatoes and root crops	*Section C*	onions, legumes, lettuce, leeks

Task 2.1

Draw plans showing the arrangement of the crops in years 3 and 4, in the three year crop rotation described.

Using this crop rotation, how could a gardener ensure that potatoes are not grown in the same soil more often than one year in six? . . . Q.8

Potato (*Solanum tuberosum*)

Potatoes grow wild in South America; they were brought to Europe by the sixteenth century explorers and by the end of the eighteenth century had become an important part of the diet of most Europeans. Modern potatoes yield more food per hectare than cereals, but they do not store well; they also contain a large proportion of water (78%) which makes their transport expensive. Potato tubers become green and poisonous if exposed to light. Growers talk about *early*, *late*, *ware* and *seed* potatoes: these terms are explained below.

Early potatoes are tubers of quick maturing varieties lifted before the skins have become firm (e.g., Arran Pilot and Pentland Javelin).

Late potatoes are tubers of other varieties left in the ground until they have reached maximum size and the skins have set (e.g., Maris Piper, Majestic). They are sometimes called *main crop* potatoes.

Ware potatoes are graded tubers sold for human consumption.

Seed potatoes are specially grown disease-free tubers which are planted for crop production. *Note*: 'seed' potatoes are *not* seeds they are *stem tubers*.

Growing early potatoes

Care of seed

Potato plants and tubers are destroyed by frost, so they must be kept at temperatures above 0°C; 7°C is ideal for storing tubers. In January, seed potatoes are taken from store and placed in a light warm shed, in stacking trays which are designed to allow light to reach all tubers. The buds develop into strong green shoots; this process is known as *chitting*, and well chitted tubers produce an earlier and heavier crop than unchitted ones.

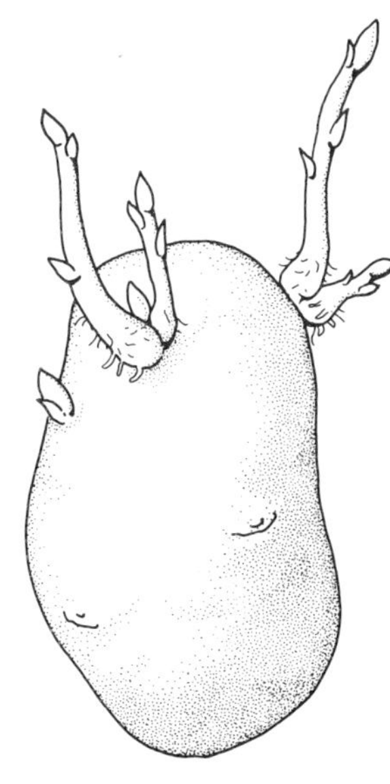

Sprouted potato tuber

The soil

Almost any well drained soil will grow potatoes; it is worked deeply in autumn when organic manure is dug in at the rate of 2–5 kg/m². In spring 40g/m² of complete fertiliser is spread over the surface and a coarse tilth is prepared. Soil of pH 6 is desirable (as high pH values favour the development of the potato scab organism); this is achieved by ensuring that potatoes are the last crop in the rotation before lime is applied.

Planting

Holes are dug, along a garden line, with a trowel to a depth that will allow 50 mm of soil above the tubers. One tuber is placed in each hole with the shoots uppermost, and the hole is then filled by crumbling soil into it:

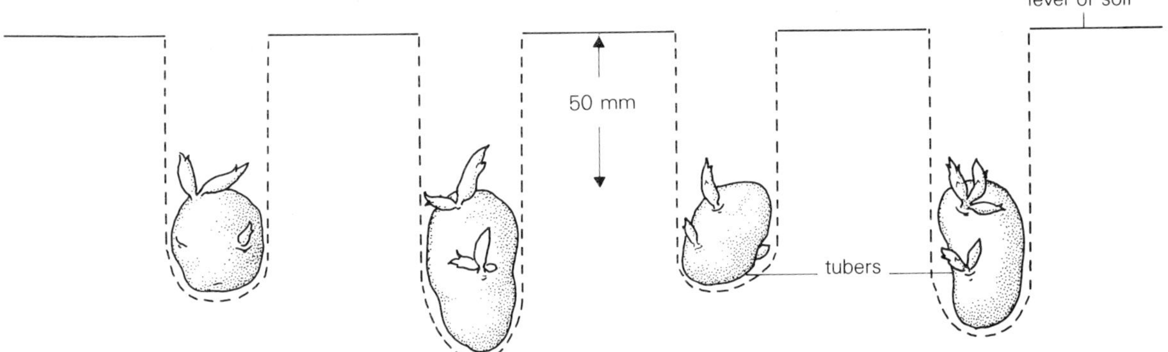

Cultivation

When the potato plants are about 100 mm high, a draw hoe is used to cultivate the soil between the rows – this kills weeds and loosens soil for

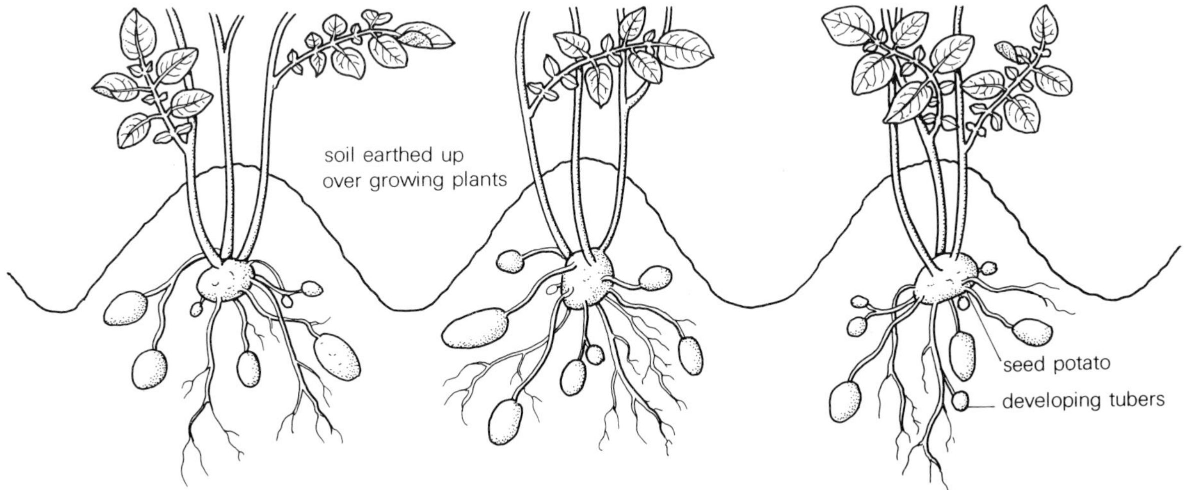

earthing-up. Soil is drawn, from between the rows, over the growing plants – this protects the developing tubers from sunlight (sunlight turns potatoes green making them inedible).

Harvesting
New potatoes are eaten with the minimum delay after harvest. When the tubers reach the size of small hen's eggs the whole plant is lifted with a garden fork, the tubers collected and the haulm (leaves and stems) is taken to the compost heap.

Maincrop potatoes

Maincrop potatoes are increasingly grown only as a farm crop, although they can be grown in a garden in a similar way to early potatoes but with increased spacings, more manure, and more disease and pest control. Maincrop potatoes are not lifted until the tubers are mature and their skins are firm. Most of the maincrop is stored in special buildings with a controlled environment, although satisfactory storage can be achieved in an outside clamp, especially if the tubers are treated with Technazene powder which delays sprouting.

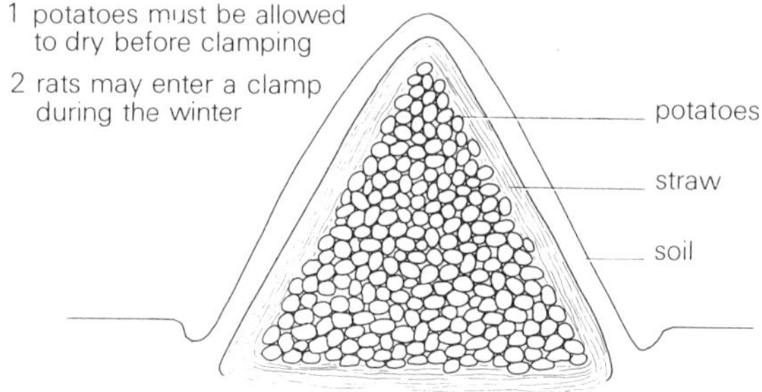

Section through a potato clamp

Potato crop spacings

	Distance between the plants	*Distance between the rows*
Early	250 mm	600 mm
Maincrop	400 mm	900 mm

Catch cropping
Early potatoes are harvested long before the end of the growing season. The land where the potatoes have grown may be used to produce another crop (e.g., lettuce, radish or swede). This second crop is called a *catch crop*.

Jerusalem artichokes

A row of Jerusalem artichokes in August – tubers were planted 300 mm apart in early April

The only other stem tuber to be grown in this country for culinary purposes is the Jerusalem artichoke (*Helianthus tuberosus*). Tubers planted in spring produce plants two metres tall; the new tubers are lifted in winter as required. A row of Jerusalem artichokes can be used to screen an unsightly area – the ones in the photograph are screening a garden shed. Although this plant is hardy (withstands frost) a lot of hot sunshine is required to induce flowering and its flowers are seldom seen in this country.

Onions (*Allium cepa*)

The second most important culinary vegetable is the onion which, together with related species, has been eaten by man for over 5000 years. There are three methods of growing onions:

1. Onion plants are raised in the greenhouse and planted into the onion bed in April or May, according to the season and locality.
2. Onion seeds are sown in the open soil and thinned out as they grow.

3. Onion sets are planted individually in rows 15 mm apart, in the onion bed. (Onion *sets* are very small onions which are grown in the summer, are stored at 24°C throughout the winter and are sold in spring for replanting.) Each set grows into one large onion. Spring onions are grown by method (2), above. The seeds of the variety 'White Lisbon' are sown thickly, and the crop is pulled before the bulbs begin to swell.

The soil

If worthwhile crops of onions are to be obtained, the soil must be well supplied with nutrients and have a pH of not less than 6.5. The onion bed is dug in autumn and 5 kg/m² of organic manure is incorporated. In spring, 20 g/m² of a complete fertiliser is spread over the surface and raked-in very lightly. The bed is then consolidated by thorough treading, and raked again, very lightly disturbing only the top few millimetres of soil.

Sowing

Seeds are sown as thinly as possible in a very shallow drill, or onion sets are planted with just the tip of the bulb showing. Rows should be 250 mm apart.

Planting shallots (onion sets should be planted in the same way)

Covering shallots

Cultivation

Regular dutch hoeing, as shallow as is practical, supplemented by hand weeding around the plants, controls weeds – an essential part of onion culture. Onions being grown from seeds are thinned to 75 mm, and the thinnings used as spring onions.

10 g/m² of a complete fertiliser is sprinkled over the surface two or three times during the growing season (this practice is called *top dressing*). In common with all vegetables, onions require water: the bed should be irrigated when rainfall is low (a small application of water is of no use, as it will evaporate – sufficient water *must* be applied to allow the wetting front to reach the moist soil underneath). Flower buds that appear during the growing season are broken off.

Harvesting

At the end of the growing season, the tops of the onions are bent over to allow the sunshine to ripen the bulbs. Shortly afterwards, the bulbs are lifted and left on the surface to dry; in wet seasons a cradle, made by stretching a net horizontally between four posts, may be used to dry the crop.

Storing

Onions will keep until the following season, as long as they are kept in a cool frost-free place where air can circulate around the bulbs. This is achieved by tying the onions in 'ropes' around a string and suspending the ropes from a hook:

Shallots

The shallot is the same species as the common onion; it is usually used for pickling, keeping firm and crisp in spite of its immersion in vinegar.

Culture
Shallots are grown from bulbs and are the first vegetable to be planted in spring. As soon as soil conditions allow, part of the onion bed is raked, and the shallot bulbs are planted 150 mm apart in rows with 250 mm between them; the tips of the bulbs should just be visible when the work is complete. The crop is kept weed-free and single bulbs produce leaves and divide into some fifteen new bulbs. Shallots are harvested in July, good shaped bulbs are selected for the following year's crop and the others are used.

Leeks (*Allium porrum*)

The leek is an elongated cylindrical bulb which is blanched (kept white) by deep planting, thus excluding the light. It is a popular vegetable with a very long season (September–May) and is available when there are few other fresh vegetables on the market.

The soil
The soil is dug and manured in autumn and forked over the following spring, a week or two before planting.

Planting
Although leeks can be produced from seeds sown in the open ground, plants are usually raised in the greenhouse to extend the growing season (see illustration below):

Cultivation
Weeds are controlled and the soil aerated by regular hoeing.

Storage
Leeks are not stored, as they are very hardy and can be lifted as required throughout the winter.

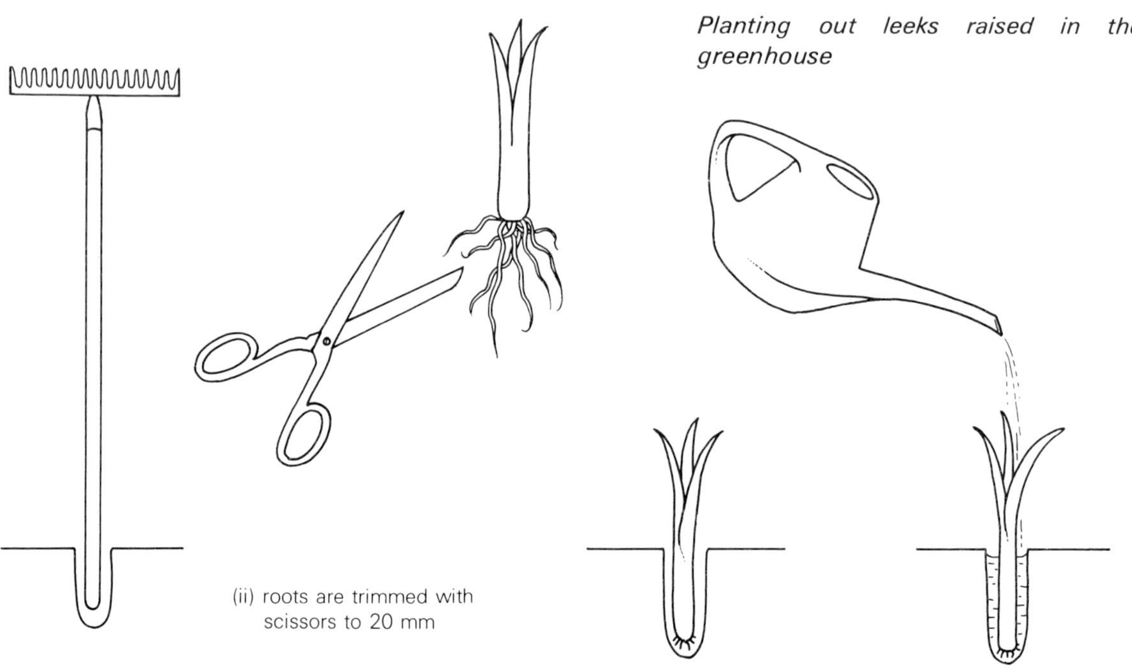
Planting out leeks raised in the greenhouse

(i) holes, 100 mm deep and 200 mm apart are made with a rake handle

(ii) roots are trimmed with scissors to 20 mm

(iii) one plant is placed in each: *note* that the hole is *not* filled with soil

(iv) each hole is filled with water

A leek lifted in the snow

The legumes

Beans, peas and related crops have been a source of protein in man's diet for thousands of years; there is evidence that broad beans were grown by Iron Age man in Britain and other parts of Europe.

The garden pea (*Pisum sativum*)

The many varieties of garden pea can be divided into two main groups: *smooth-seeded* (e.g., Feltham First, Meteor) which are extremely hardy, and the more delicate *wrinkled-seeded* varieties (e.g., Onward, Kelvedon Wonder). In most districts the smooth-seeded peas are best for growing in schools as they can be harvested before the summer holidays. In later districts, peas can be sown in small compressed peat pots, and grown in the classroom window until soil conditions allow them to be planted in the open ground.

The soil

Peas require a soil with a high pH (6.5–7) and a good moisture reserve; the latter is often achieved by preparing a trench across the plot where the peas are to be grown:

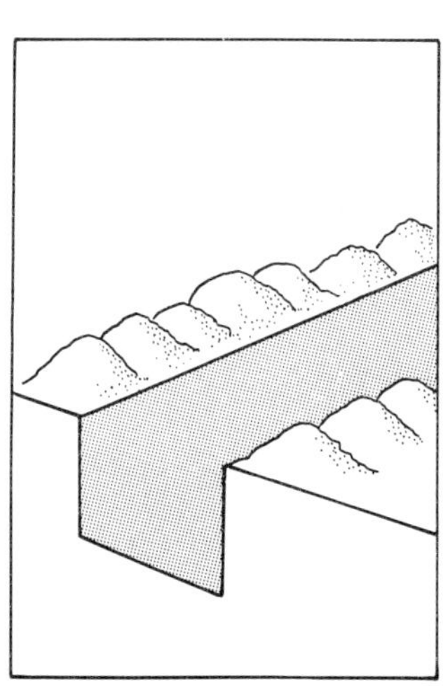

(i) a trench, one spit deep and 400 mm wide, is dug across the plot

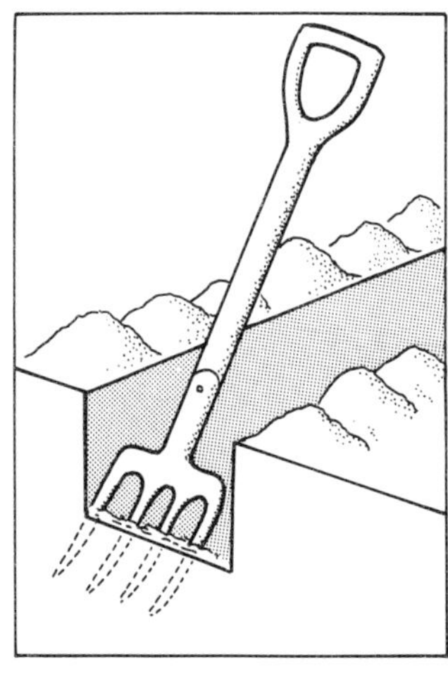

(ii) a heavy dressing of farmyard manure or compost is dug into the bottom of the trench

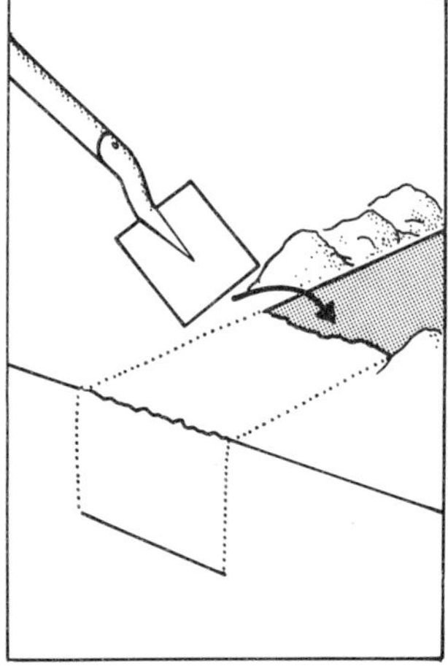

(iii) the top soil is replaced and left to settle for as long as possible before the crop is sown

An application of 50 g/m² of complete fertiliser is raked into the top 10 mm of soil.

Sowing
The seeds are sown as described on page 33. Germination time is reduced if the seeds are soaked in water for a few hours before sowing. Immediately after sowing a few lengths of black cotton are stretched taut 50 mm above the soil, to prevent birds eating the peas as they germinate:

sticks pushed into soil
50 mm
black cotton
row of peas

Support
The pea is a climbing plant, producing tendrils on the ends of its leaves. Many dwarf varieties are grown without support, but the taller varieties (750 mm and over) are supported with plastic netting or twiggy sticks:

Note: when two rows of peas are grown side by side, a path of at least one metre must be allowed between the rows.

plastic net supported on a frame
row of peas

Support for peas

Peas at three stages of ripeness

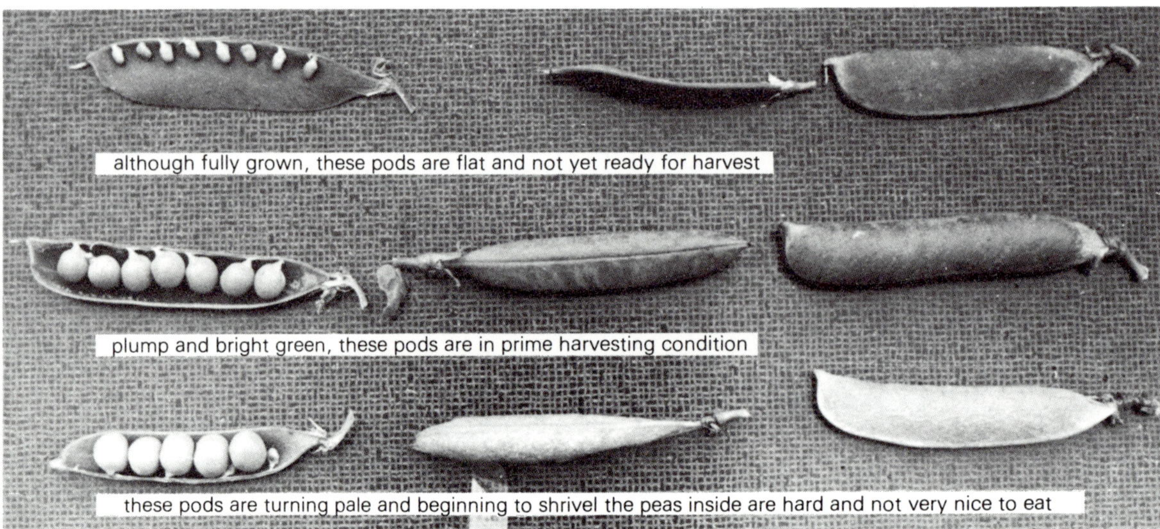

Cultivation
No cultivation is necessary after sowing except inter-row hoeing for weed control.

Harvest
Peas are harvested as soon as the pods are full. If left on the plants, the flavour quickly deteriorates as the seeds ripen. Two hands are used when harvesting: one to hold the stem, and the other to remove the pods; in this way the plant is not disturbed and more peas will mature.

How are peas stored? . . . Q.9

Crop succession
A row of peas produces edible pods for only two weeks. A succession of these vegetables is obtained by making a sowing every two weeks during April and May. Different varieties, sown on the same day, may mature at different times.

Runner bean (*Phaseolus coccineus*)

This plant is a South American perennial, but, as it is killed by frost, it is only grown as an annual in this country. The bright red flowers give it the name 'scarlet runner' although there are white-flowered varieties. Climbing to heights of over two metres the runner produces fruit from bottom to top, giving a very large crop from a small area of land.

Soil
Runner beans have similar soil requirements to peas, except that they require even larger reserves of moisture and, unless the soil is very deep and fertile, trenching is essential.

Support
Sticks or nets are usually positioned before the crop is planted: a row of 'wigwams' or a double row of 2 m canes is erected. If, as is usual, one plant is grown up each cane, the canes are positioned 250 mm apart with 1 m between the rows.

Planting
The sowing time for runner beans varies widely according to local conditions. Where the last spring frosts occur before the end of May, beans can be sown in the open ground during the middle of that month, if soil temperatures are 10°C and over. In later districts, seeds are germinated individually in 90 mm pots, and planted out when the danger of frost has passed.

Cultivation
Except for weed control, cultivations are unnecessary. The crop requires copious amounts of water and deficiencies in rainfall are made good by irrigation.

Harvest
Unlike the other legumes, runner (and french) beans are grown for the pods, and these must be harvested regularly before the seed begins to swell.

Inter-cropping
In between the two rows of bean supports it is possible to grow a row of quick maturing crops, such as lettuce or radish. These crops will develop and be harvested before the runner beans cover the canes and exclude the light.

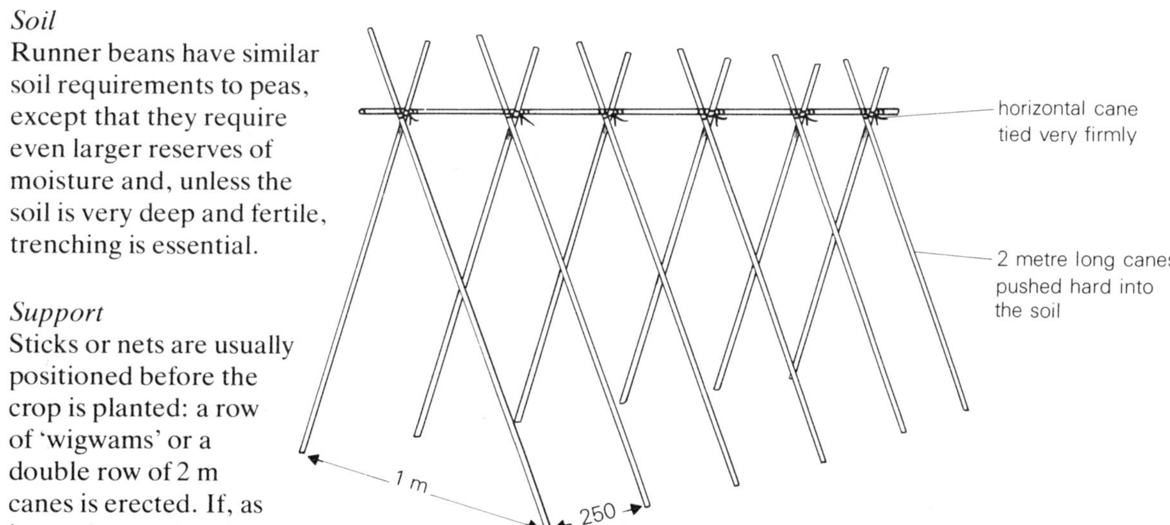

Support for runner beans

Investigation 2.3
To find the maximum thickness of supports the runner bean will climb

Make a collection of 2 m poles and pipes of various diameters (e.g. plastic water pipes, conduit tubing, thick bamboo, etc.). Arrange the collection vertically in a row across the garden, allowing 300 mm between each, the thickest at one end, graduating to the thinnest (a taut length of nylon string supported top and bottom) at the other. When the danger of frost is over, plant one runner bean plant at the bottom of each support.

Observe during the summer and record observations and results.

Broad bean (*Vicia faba*)

Broad beans are very hardy and can be sown in autumn, to overwinter in small plants, in the milder areas of the British Isles.

Soil
Any well manured soil will produce a satisfactory crop of broad beans providing it is not acid.

Sowing
Early spring sowings are made to avoid summer attacks of black fly. Seeds are sown in single rows, with 20 mm between each seed. As the seeds germinate, mice often dig them up and eat them: this can be prevented by soaking the seeds in paraffin for 30 minutes before sowing. January sowings under cloches using the variety 'Aquadulce' can be made when weather conditions allow.

Support
A post is driven into the soil at each end of the row, and two lengths of garden twine are stretched between the posts either side of the row, one string 30 mm high and the other 60 mm high.

Cultivation
The dutch hoe is used to control seed growth. When the first beans are forming, the tops are removed to prevent black fly attack.

Removal of broad bean tops

Harvest
Broad beans do not deteriorate as quickly as peas – the pods remain in good condition for two weeks. The pods are gathered when full, and before they become so ripe that the skins are tough:

A broad bean pod at the best stage of development for picking

The Brassicas

The nine vegetables below are all cultivars of one plant species – the biennial wild cabbage – *Brassica oleracea*. This fact can be demonstrated by leaving the vegetables in the ground to flower – the spikes of yellow flowers have exactly the same structure, regardless of which of the nine vegetables it grew from. Brassicas are best grown in a well consolidated fertile soil, pH 6.5–7.0.

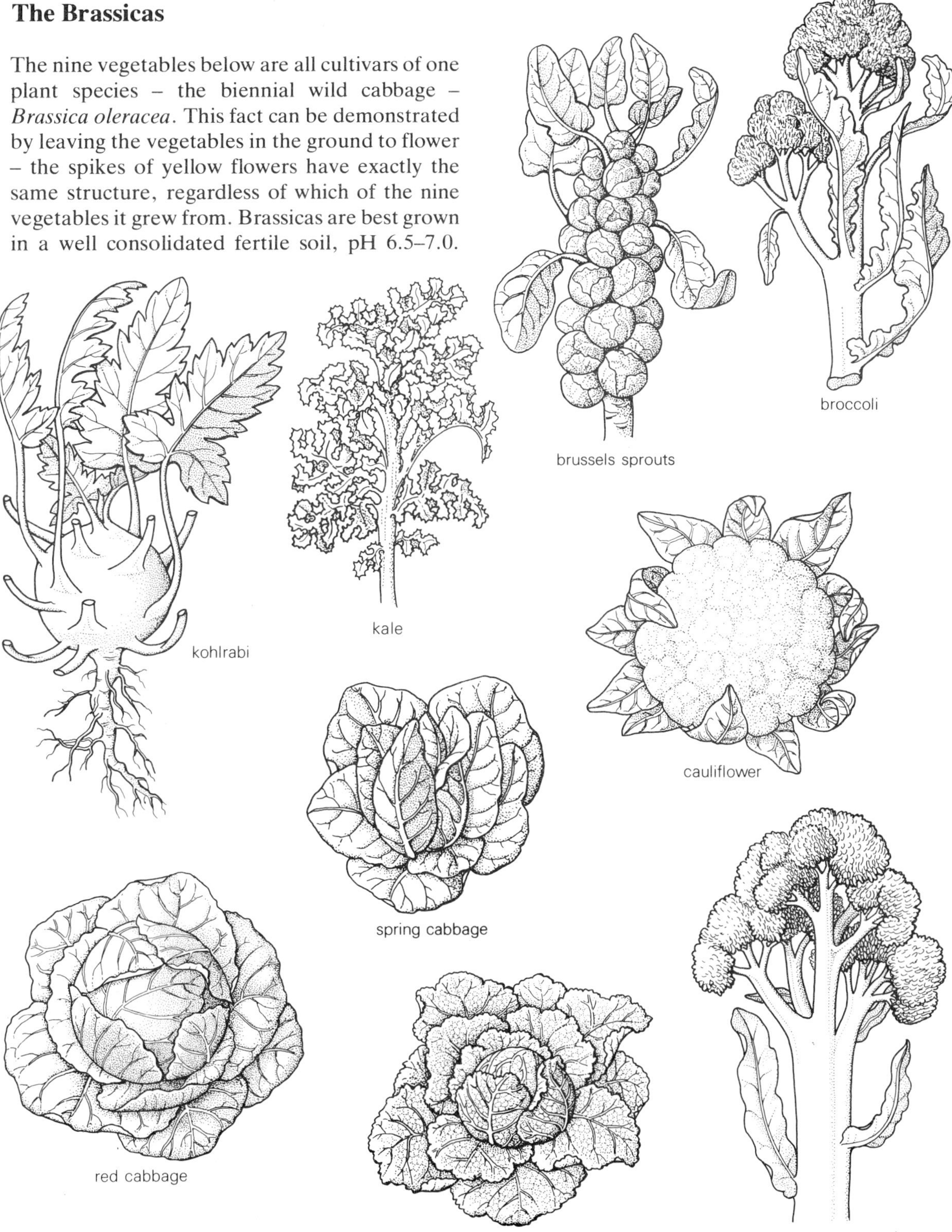

Brassica Information Chart

Plant	Sowing Date	Harvest Date J F M A M J J A S O N D	Distance between plants (mm)	Distance between rows (mm)	Notes
Cabbage	Spring for summer use Summer for autumn and winter use		450 450	450 600	A cabbage is an enlarged terminal bud. There are many varieties, some suitable for summer use, and some suitable for winter use. Information on available varieties is obtained from seed catalogues.
Red cabbage	March/April		600	600	Used chiefly for pickling.
Spring cabbage	15 July – 15 August according to the locality		300	400	Spring cabbage varieties are all pointed, transplanted in October and overwinter as small plants. Closer plantings may be made if unhearted cabbages are to be harvested.
Savoy	May		450	600	Savoy cabbages are usually transplanted in July on ground that has produced a previous crop (e.g. lettuce or early peas).
Brussels sprouts	Mid March to mid April		750	750	It is essential to have very firm ground for brussels sprouts, or loose buttons are produced. Sprouts are harvested from the bottom of the plant as they become ready.
Cauliflower	Under glass – January Outside – March – April		400 – 600 according to the variety	600 – 750	A cauliflower curd is a dense mass of white undeveloped flower buds. Plant leaves are folded over to protect developing curds from the sun.
Broccoli (winter cauliflower)	Mid April to mid May		600	600	Different varieties mature at different times; a selection of varieties is grown to obtain succession. Severe frost may kill this crop.
Purple sprouting	April		750	750	Clusters of purple flower buds are gathered. A very hardy crop.
Calabrese	April		600	600	This plant is susceptible to frost. Clusters of green flower buds are gathered for freezing or canning.
Kohlrabi	April/May		150	300	Seeds are sown in rows where the plants are to develop. The crop is thinned to 150 mm and the swollen stems are eaten before they are fully grown (i.e. when they are the size of a tennis ball).

Plants are either purchased or raised in a seedbed and transplanted to their final positions when about 70 mm high.

Task 2.2

Refer to the Brassica information chart and plan a plot of Brassicas to give a continuous supply of green vegetables throughout the year. Include in your plan the sowing dates for each variety.

Two more Brassicas – turnip and swede

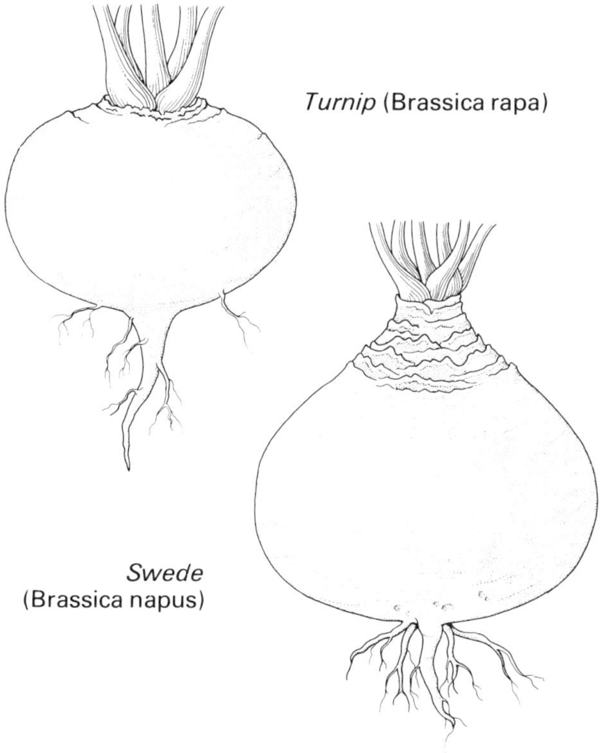

Examine the diagrams of swede and turnip above. How can a turnip be distinguished from a swede? . . . Q.10

Swedes and turnips are important agricultural crops and are grown extensively in allotments and gardens. Although these vegetables are referred to as roots, the vegetables consist of a hypocotyl, swollen with a large food store. The hypocotyl is the tissue above the root that grows to push the cotyledons above the soil as the seed germinates:

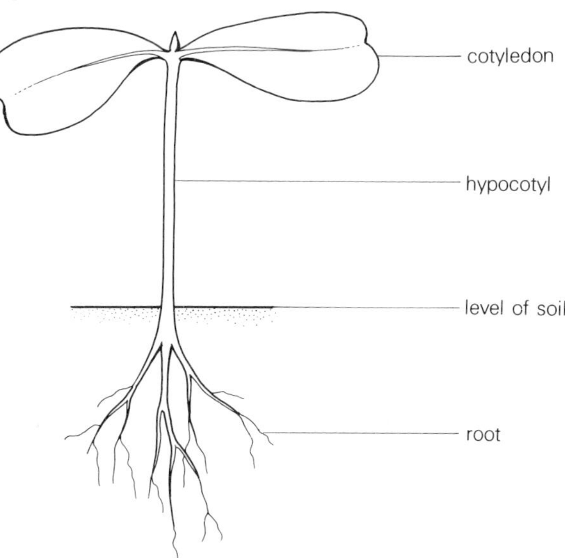

Soil
A satisfactory crop of swedes and turnips will grow in most soils, as long as the soil is not too acid and it has not been freshly manured.

Seed sowing
After raking to a fine tilth the seeds are sown as thinly as possible in rows 300 mm apart. Turnips are usually sown every three weeks from April until July to give a succession of young 'roots' as old 'roots' become tough. Swedes are best sown in June and make a useful catch crop after early potatoes.

Cultivation
Regular dutch hoeing between rows controls annual weeds. As the plant becomes large enough to handle, they are thinned first to a distance of 70 mm and later to 200 mm.

Harvest
The whole plant is pulled up, after loosening with a fork, and the tops are twisted off to be used for compost.

Store
Turnips lifted in late autumn can be clamped in the same way as potatoes. Swedes are not often harmed by frost and can either be clamped or left in the soil and dug-in winter as required.

The umbelliferous root crops

Carrot (*Daucus carota*)

The wild carrot is a biennial plant which grows in grassy places. It has a small, tough, pale, tap root most unlike the garden carrot. Carrots are rich in vitamin A and have a high sugar content which gives them a sweet taste.

Soil
Good well drained soil, free from fresh manure and stones, is necessary to grow straight unforked roots.

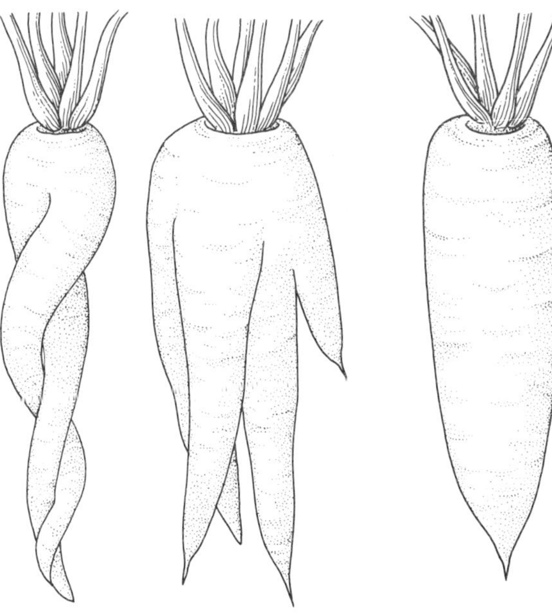

Carrots grown in freshly manured soil *Carrot grown in sandy, stone-free soil*

Sowing
A very fine tilth is prepared as carrot seed is extremely small; rows, 200 mm apart are sown as thinly as possible. Carrot seed is available in pelleted form and if this form is used much thinner sowing is possible. Pelleted seed was developed to allow farmers' machinery to sow seeds individually at the correct spacing, removing the need to thin such crops as sugar beet, swede and mangels. Each seed is encased in a sphere of material about 4 mm in diameter. As the material absorbs water, it crumbles, allowing the seed to germinate.

Cultivation
Dutch hoeing is necessary for inter-row weed control. Carrots are thinned twice, once to a distance of 20 mm, and later to 100 mm, the latter thinnings being used. After thinning, loose soil is consolidated by treading and the crop is watered as one of the carrot fly control measures.

Harvest
Carrots are lifted as required and the tops are composted. Maincrop carrots are lifted in October for winter use.

Storing
Carrots are treated with great care as bruised roots will not keep, they are clamped like potatoes, or packed in boxes of sand and left in a frost-free shed. If not lifted, carrots will keep well in the soil as long as they are protected from frost, by a layer of straw, or similar material.

Parsnip (*Pastinaca sativa*)

Wild parsnip, from which the cultivated forms have been bred, are very common in England and Wales; in Scotland the 'wild' parsnips are probably escapees from gardens.

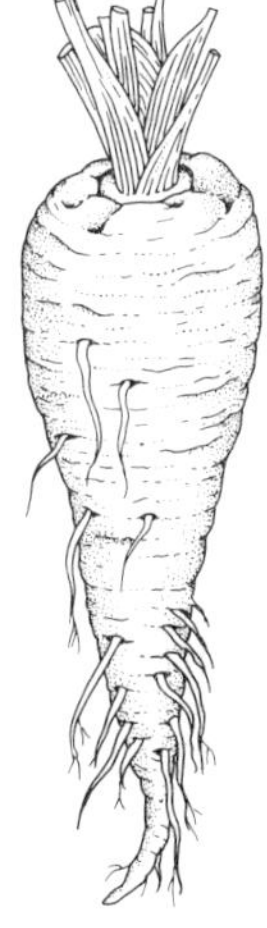

A parsnip

Task 2.3

Dig up a wild parsnip (easily recognised by its distinctive smell, hollow ridged stem and large leaves) and compare the tap-root with a cultivated parsnip.

Soil
Deep, rich, friable loam soil, free from stones and fresh manure, is necessary for parsnip production.

Sowing
Seeds are sown in March as soon as soil conditions allow; two or three seeds are sown in groups every 250 mm along the garden line.

Cultivation
Weed control is achieved by the regular use of the dutch hoe. When the seedlings are large enough, the best one is left at each station and the others pulled up and discarded: if two seedlings are left together neither one produces a satisfactory root.

Harvesting
Parsnips are left in the ground until required and are then dug up with a fork, care being taken not to break the tap-root. If any of the crop remains in March it is lifted to prevent it from starting growth.

What type of growth would an unharvested parsnip produce? . . . Q.11

Salad crops

Lettuce (*Lactuca sativa*)

By far the most important salad crop is lettuce, which, although composed of over 90% water (with the exception of the variety 'salad bowl'), is an important source of vitamin A.

Garden lettuce form a large terminal bud or heart, cabbage lettuce form spherical heads, and cos lettuce form larger upright heads:

Left: Vertical section of a cos lettuce

Right: Vertical section of a cabbage lettuce

The soil
Most fertile soils produce satisfactory crops of lettuce. Ideally manure is dug-in during the autumn and the ground is left 'rough' until April.

Sowing
A very fine tilth is prepared and the seeds are sown thinly, as near to the surface as possible, in rows 300 mm apart. For household use a part of a row is sown every other week from April until July to maintain a succession of lettuce throughout the summer.

Cultivation
The soil is cultivated regularly to control weeds and maintain a tilth around the plants. When the first true leaves have formed, the plants are thinned to 150 mm; a second thinning is carried out by removing (and using) every other plant as required, the remainder are left to heart. Lettuce requires regular watering in dry seasons.

Harvesting
The hearted plants are cut as near to the ground as possible with a knife, and rain-splashed outside leaves are removed and discarded.

Lettuces must be protected from sparrows, especially early in the season – strands of black cotton (see page 42) or cages of small mesh chicken wire may be used. The two lettuce plants in the photograph were almost identical before a sparrow fed from the plant on the right.

Sparrow damage to lettuce

Beetroot (*Beta vulgaris*)

Soil
Beetroot can be grown in most soils, but freshly manured ground should be avoided. Crops on poor soils can be improved by raking 100 g/m^2 of complete fertiliser into the seed bed.

Sowing
Sow the seed clusters 25 mm apart, in shallow drills 300 mm apart.

Cultivation
The fruits of beetroot cluster together into seed balls – each ball contains several seeds. Although the 'seeds' in the packet may be sown individually, the crop germinates as small clusters of seedlings – care should be taken when thinning the crop (to 150 mm) that only single plants are left. Weed control by hoeing is also necessary.

Harvesting
Beetroot are pulled up, as required, when the roots are large enough for cooking. Tops are twisted off, as this causes less sap loss than cutting.

Storage
As for carrots.

Radish (*Raphanus sativus*)

Radishes are ideal for school use as they take only five weeks to mature and can be sown any time from April to September. The flowers produced by unharvested plants can be used for pollination experiments and flower structure study.

Soil
A crop of sorts can be grown in almost any soil, but the best quality roots are grown in well drained soils with a high water and humus content, broken down to a fine tilth.

Sowing
Seeds may be sown thinly in shallow drills *or* the seeds can be sprinkled thinly and evenly over a small area of soil and gently raked into the soil with a garden rake. This latter method of sowing is known as *broadcasting* and is widely used for sowing lawns and agricultural grasses.

Harvesting
No cultivations are required – the plants are pulled up when their roots are large enough to eat.

Mustard (*Sinapis alba*) **and cress** (*Lepidium sativum*)

The seedlings of these two plants are eaten when about 50 mm tall, before the true leaves appear. Tall seedlings are obtained by sowing the seeds more thickly than is normal for most other plants. Although mustard and cress can be grown outside, it is not very practical as rain can splash the crop and contaminate it with mud. The small plastic trays (punnets) of mustard on sale in greengrocers' shops are usually rape (*Brassica napus*) seedlings (rape is an agricultural crop (see Book 3)).

Investigation 2.4
To find the most suitable method of growing mustard in the classroom

Think of several different ways of growing mustard. Some examples are given below (plant pots may be used instead of seed trays):

seed tray

covered with transparent plastic film.

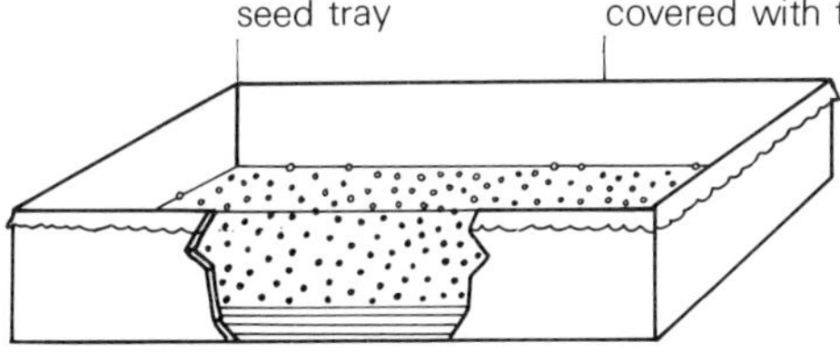

layers of soaked paper towels, with seeds sprinkled on top

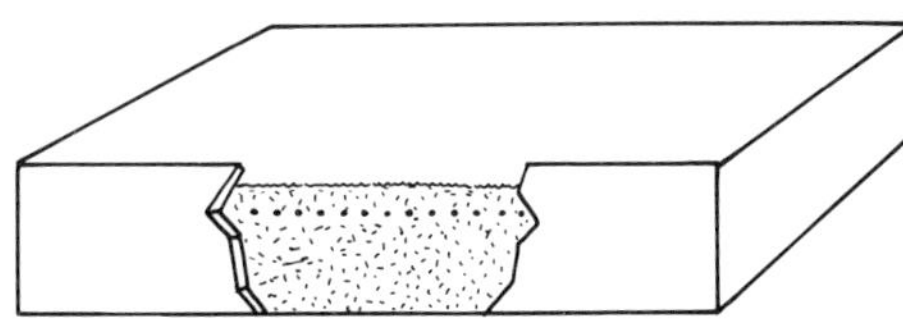

wet sawdust, seeds 5 mm deep

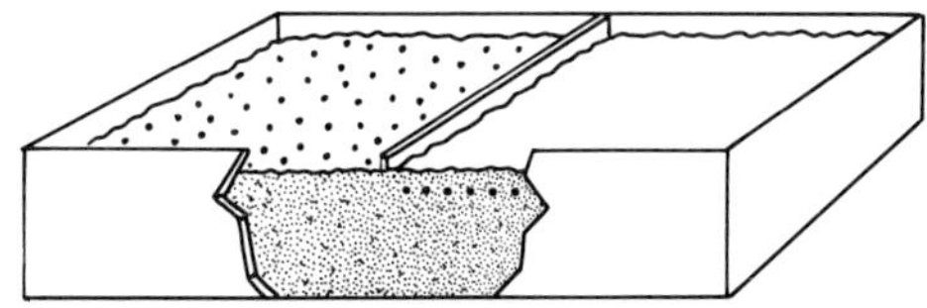

moist peat, one half of the box has seeds on the surface, the other has seeds 5 mm deep

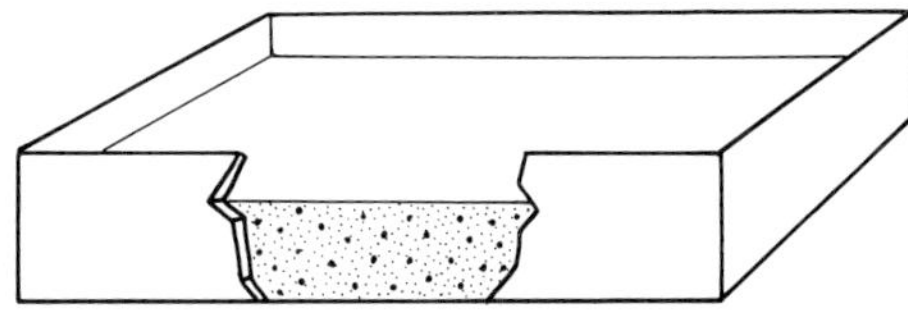

wet sand and seeds mixed, and tray half filled with the mixture

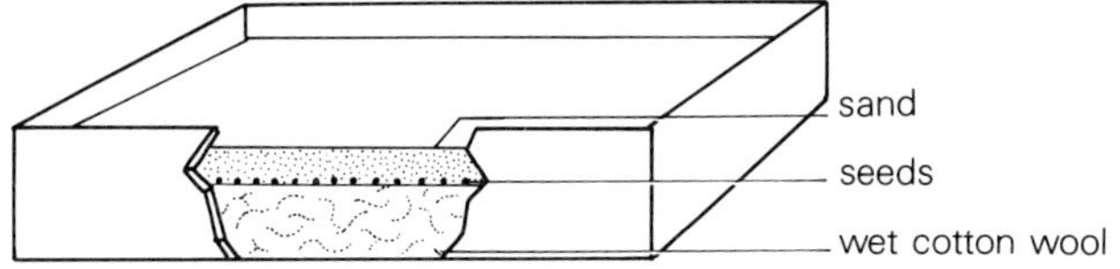

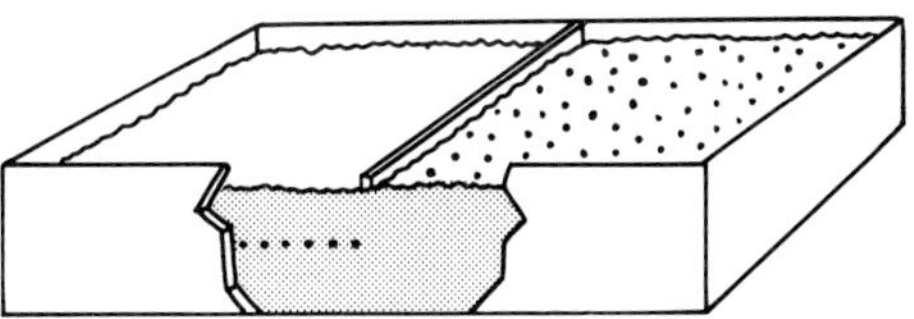

John Innes compost half sown with seeds on the surface, half sown with seeds 10 mm deep

Set up as many of these methods as possible and leave them in a warm room to grow.

Harvest the crops by cutting with scissors as they become ready and write a report about each method stating its advantages and disadvantages (include reports of methods that failed and say why they were unsuccessful).

Comparison of growth of mustard seeds in different environments (Investigation 2.4)

Investigation 2.5

Take a small seed tray and fill it with moist peat. Sow half the tray with mustard seeds and the other half with cress seeds; note and record the date. Leave the tray on a warm window-sill and water with a fine rose as necessary. Harvest each crop as it matures and record the dates,

Using the results of this investigation say how mustard and cress could be grown to mature on the same day.

Task 2.4

Use a pestle and mortar to thoroughly crush about 25 g of mustard seeds. Remove the husks by sieving with a fine sieve. Mix the remaining flour to a smooth paste with a little water.

What is the paste you have just made? . . . Q.12

Gourds

Marrows, courgettes and pumpkins, collectively known as gourds, belong to the single species *Cucurbita pepo*. The annual plants are half hardy with large leaves, and hollow stems which are bristly to the touch. The single sex flowers are large and yellow; fruit does not form if the flowers are unpollinated. Marrows and pumpkins require a lot of space, as trailing varieties produce stems several metres long; they are very useful to fill an odd corner.

Growing gourds

In late April or early May:

1. Fill a 100 mm plant pot with John Innes seed compost.
2. Using a sharp knife chip a little of the testa from a seed (this will reduce the germination time).

3. Insert the seed into the compost, pressing it in 10 mm or so; water well.
4. Invert a polythene bag over the pot and seal with adhesive tape.
5. Place on the window-sill of a warm room or put into a greenhouse (20–25°C).
6. When the cotyledons appear, remove the bag and water as necessary.
7. After the danger of late frost is over, plant-out in a previously prepared bed.
8. Use a ploche or cloche for the first few nights to protect the young plant, helping it to acclimatise to the colder condition.
9. Keep weed free and water generously. (*Note*: it is better to grow three or more plants, as more flowers will improve the pollination rate.)
10. Harvest courgettes when they are 150–200 mm long. If left, courgettes will grow as large as marrows.
11. Harvest marrows and pumpkins when fully grown by twisting the fruit from the stem.
12. Marrows and pumpkins will keep for several months in a cool, dry frost-free atmosphere.

Herbs

All the vegetables mentioned in this chapter are grown to supply man with energy and vitamins to maintain his health and vigour. Herbs are aromatic plants grown to flavour other foods and increase their palatibility. As herbs are eaten in small quantities they are only grown in small quantities in a sunny position in the kitchen garden:

The herb garden above consists of 600 mm × 600 mm concrete slabs arranged like a chess board, this gives small areas of soil to grow various herbs and allows them to be collected without walking upon the earth.

Herb	*Culture*	*Use*	*Notes*
Borage (*Borago officinalis*)	Sow seeds in May and thin to 150 mm.	Young leaves added to iced drinks.	First leaves ready for picking in eight weeks.
Caraway (*Carum carvi*)	Biennial; grown from seeds; sown in April or September.	Foliage used in stews and salads; 'seeds' (actually fruits), used to flavour cakes.	This plant seeds itself each year if some fruits are left unharvested.
Chives (*Allium schoenoprasum*)	Sow seeds in March; perennial, the clumps can be divided and planted elsewhere.	Onion-flavoured leaves chopped and added to egg and cheese dishes.	
Lavender (*Lavandula spica*)	Raise a single plant from seed sown in May.	Flower collected and dried for use in sachets placed in wardrobes and clothes drawers.	Perennial bush.
Mint (*Mentha spicata*)	Plant rhizomes in a large bottomless bucket sunk into the soil, this will prevent the plant from spreading over the entire herb garden.	The leaves are chopped, scalded and added to vinegar to flavour lamb, purple sprouts, etc.	There are many different flavoured mints.
Parsley (*Petroselinum crispum*)	Biennial, grown from seed which has been soaked; seed requires light to germinate. Leave on the surface and cover with a ploche, remove when seedlings appear. Thin to 150 mm.	Chopped leaves are added to white sauce and served with fish and gammon. Mixed with other herbs to make poultry stuffings. Garnishing for sandwiches, potatoes, etc.	May be grown in pots on window-sills.
Rosemary (*Rosmarinus officinalis*)	Single plant grown from seed is all that is required to produce a dwarf perennial bush.	The needle-like leaves are inserted into lamb joints before cooking.	Single plant can be purchased for little more than the cost of a packet of seeds.
Sage (*Salvia officinalis*)	Perennial evergreen bush grown from seed sown in March, or from cuttings.	Leaves are widely used in stuffing for poultry and pork, usually blended with onion.	Best grown in warm, dry conditions.
Thyme (*Thymus vulgaris*)	Low-growing shrub, grown from seed sown in late spring. Requires warm, light soil.	Leaves are used to flavour stews, stuffings and sauces.	One of the most popular herbs.

Questions: Vegetable culture

1. Write single sentences to answer the following questions:
   (a) Why is the dutch hoe unsatisfactory for controlling perennial weeds?
   (b) What is a 'spit'?
   (c) From what is garden compost made?
   (d) Which vegetable has the scientific name *Solanum tuberosum*?
   (e) What name is given to the shallow trench in which seeds are sown?
   (f) Why are shallots grown?
   (g) How can pea seeds be protected from birds?
   (h) What pH value ought a soil to have that is to grow Brassicas?
   (i) How long do radish take to mature?
   (j) What effect does chipping the testa of a marrow seed have?

2. Describe how you would set up a small herb garden. Use the following headings:
   (a) Choice of plants
   (b) Propagation
   (c) Preparation of site
   (d) Planting
   (e) Care after planting.

3. Describe the growing of leeks using the following sub-headings:
   (a) Production of the plants
   (b) Preparation of the ground
   (c) Manuring
   (d) Planting
   (e) Cultivation during the growing period
   (f) Harvesting. *(W.M.E.B.)*

4. (a) What are the main benefits to be gained from adopting a rotation in a vegetable garden?
   (b) Naming the crops, suggest a suitable rotation which takes full advantage of the benefits you have described in (a) above. *(S.E.R.E.B.)*

5. (a) What are the symptoms of a poorly drained soil?
   (b) How does poorly drained land affect plant growth?
   (c) List and describe all the ways in which drainage can be improved on a horticultural holding.

6. Give details of how you would raise any vegetable of the cabbage family from seed to maturity.
   Use the following headings to help you in your answers:
   (a) Preparation of seed bed
   (b) Choice of seed and method of sowing
   (c) Transplanting, method and distances between plants.
   (d) Culture during growth
   (e) Pest and weed control
   (f) Harvesting. *(W.Y. & L.R.E.B.)*

7. Describe the culture from selection of seed to maturity and harvesting of *one* of the following crops: potatoes, carrots, parsnips, leeks. Use the following headings:
   (a) Preparation of the plot (cultivating, manuring, fertilising)
   (b) Choice of seed, and any special treatment of the seed before planting
   (c) Planting: distances between rows and plants, or raising of seedlings
   (d) Culture during growth: thinning, transplanting, cultivations, feeding
   (e) Pest and weed control
   (f) Harvesting
   (g) Storage.
   Credit will be given for names of varieties grown and an indication of the times of year for planting and harvesting, the cost of the seed, the anticipated yield and financial benefit. *(A.L.S.E.B.)*

8. Describe the growing of carrots using the following sub-headings:
   (a) Preparation of the ground
   (b) Suitable variety
   (c) Method of sowing and distance between seeds and rows
   (d) Cultivation during the growing period
   (e) Pests and disease control.

   (*W.M.E.B.*)

9. You are given a packet of a new variety of summer lettuce. Describe in detail how you would compare the new variety with two *named* varieties which are familiar to you.

10. Describe with words and diagrams how root vegetables may be stored for early spring use.

11. How can (a) annual, and (b) perennial weeds be kept under control in the vegetable garden?

3 Pests and diseases of plants

In all food chains, plants are the primary producers and provide the whole of the energy for the animal kingdom. Man is only one animal species amongst thousands and he has to compete with other life forms for his food. Any organism which feeds on man's crops is considered to be a pest or disease. The more man learns about the pests and diseases which affect his crops, the better he is able to control them. In the school garden some plants should always be left untreated (or unprotected) to provide specimens for study, examples of damage and effectiveness of control measures.

During the last few decades, man has made increasing use of chemicals in pest control. There are great dangers in the indiscriminate use of many chemicals currently available; these dangers include:

1. Killing natural predators which would otherwise assist control.
2. Reduced yields by killing pollinating insects.
3. Introducing dangerous chemicals into the food chain with disastrous effects upon top carnivores.
4. Breeding pest strains which are resistant to the chemicals being used.
5. Killing beneficial soil organisms.
6. Leaving a residue of poison in the part of the crop that is to be consumed.
7. Operator's health affected by contact with toxic chemicals.

Where control can be effected by good husbandry, these methods should be practised, and chemicals should only be used if there are no other methods available. The manufacturers' instructions must be read and strictly observed, including *all* safety precautions. Dust and sprays must not be inhaled and hands should be thoroughly washed after using pesticides.

The insect pests

Large cabbage white butterfly (*Pieris brassicae*)

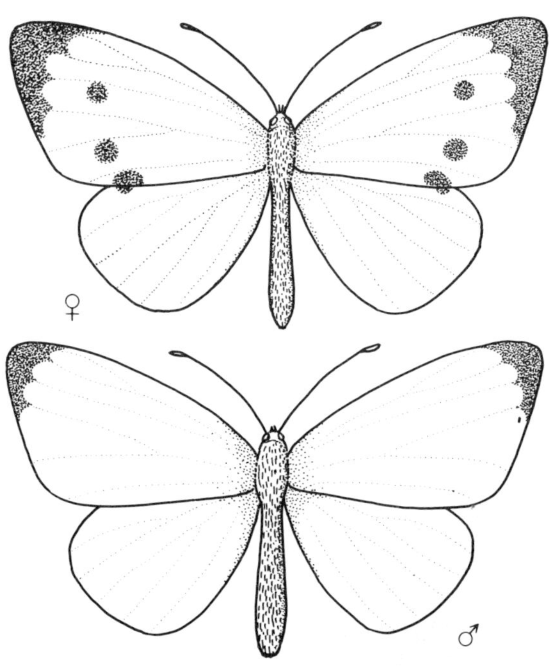

Large cabbage white butterfly (female, top; male, bottom)

The larvae of the large cabbage white butterfly feed on the leaves of cabbage, brussels sprouts, cauliflower and other Brassicas, often reducing them to a skeleton. In addition to loss of leaf, and the resulting reduction in growth, the excrement of the caterpillars spoils the appearance of the vegetables, making them unfit for consumption.

Life cycle

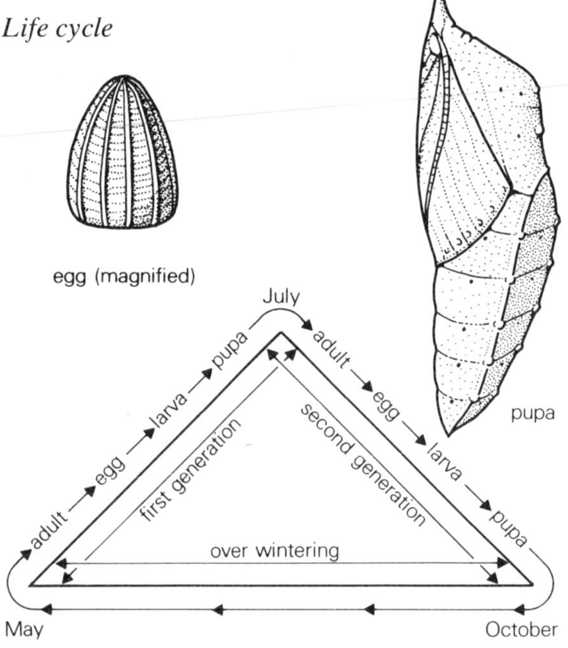

After mating, the females lay yellow pointed eggs, in clusters of 20–100, on the underside of cabbage leaves. Unlike the ladybird eggs, they are not smooth but have a sculptured pattern over their surface. After ten days or so the caterpillars emerge, consume their egg shell and begin feeding in groups on the plant leaves. During the growing period the yellow and black larvae moult four times before reaching a length of 40 mm, a process that takes about thirty days. On reaching full size the caterpillar crawls to a sheltered spot – the side of a shed or fence – and spins a silken support before changing into a pupa. Two or three weeks later the pupa changes into an adult and the life cycle continues.

The pupae of the second generation are more numerous than the first generation, why is this? . . . Q.1

In some years, thousands of cabbage white butterflies migrate from the continent to the South of England; these migrations are now less common due to a virus disease which kills this insect in its larval stage.

Caterpillars of the large white butterfly, feeding on a cabbage leaf

Control
In gardens, the cabbage white caterpillar can be controlled by picking-off eggs and larvae by hand. This method is impractical for commercial growers – they obtain considerable control by siting their crops in exposed positions, as cabbage white butterflies seek sheltered areas in which to lay their eggs. Young caterpillars can be destroyed by dusting with derris dust or trichlorphon. Dusting is most effective when the air is still and the plants wet with dew.

Leatherjackets (*Tipula paludosa*)

Leatherjackets are the larvae of crane flies (daddy long legs), they live in the soil and feed on the underground parts of plants. Unlike many insect larvae they have no distinct head and no legs, they are grey/black in colour with soft bodies and very tough skins – hence their name.

Leatherjackets feed just below the surface, destroying not only roots but also the underground parts of stems, often leading to the death of the plant, particularly in the seedling stage. At night, in warm damp weather, leatherjackets feed on the surface, cutting off young plants at ground level. Most types of plants are attacked, including Brassicas and many herbaceous plants. Large plants are weakened rather than killed – strawberries may be seen wilting as a result of root loss.

Leatherjackets are an extremely serious pest of cereals, grass and other farm crops, they are troublesome in new gardens and those which are neglected and weed-infested for the latter part of the year.

Life cycle
Crane flies emerge in the late summer; in the evening they are often attracted by light into houses, and are easily identified by their long legs.

After mating, each female lays about 300 small, oval black eggs, depositing them in the soil, with the aid of her pointed abdomen. About two weeks later the eggs hatch into minute grubs

Leatherjacket (crane fly larva)

Adult crane fly

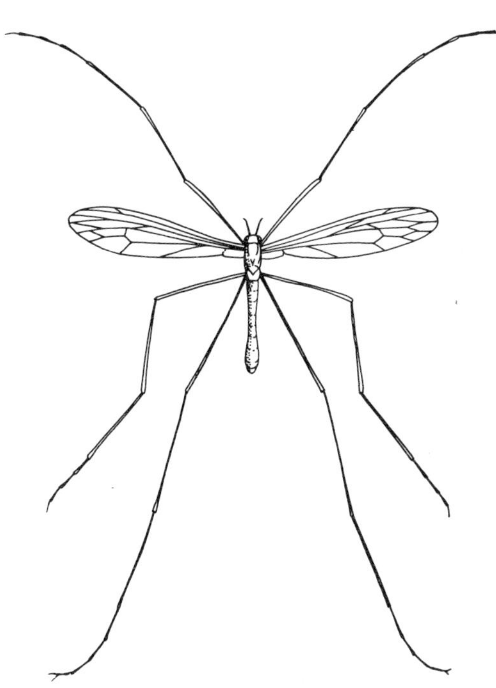

Life cycle of the crane fly

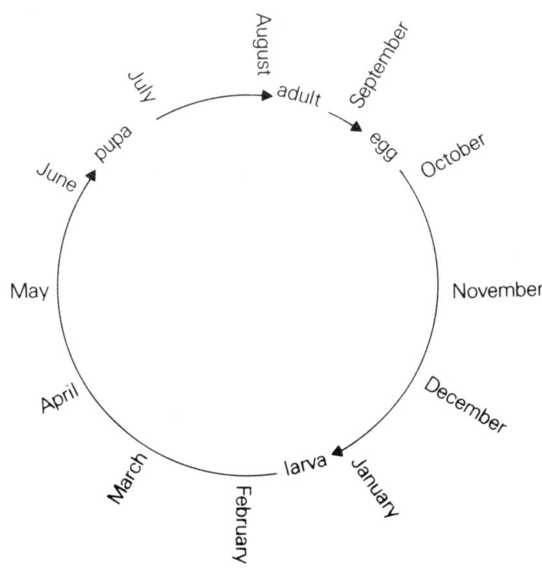

which begin feeding on plant roots. They continue feeding during winter and spring, reaching full size (40 mm) by mid June. When fully grown, the larvae change into pupae which remain in the soil for about eight weeks, at the end of this period the pupae push themselves partly out of the soil and the adults emerge.

Control

In late autumn, when the leatherjackets have grown large enough to eat, starlings and rooks feed on them, reducing their numbers considerably; the numbers available to predators can be increased by cultivating and so exposing more insects. On lawns, good kills can be obtained by watering thoroughly in the evening and covering with a tarpaulin – in the morning the tarpaulin is removed and leatherjackets on the surface can be swept up and destroyed. Infested new gardens should not be planted until the leatherjackets have pupated (mid June). After the first year, if kept weed-free, there should be no further trouble.

Why does a weed-free garden have less leatherjackets than a weedy one? . . . Q.2

Farmers spread bran mixed with gamma BHC over the fields in the late evening, during the night leatherjackets surface and eat the poisoned bait. Slug pellets may be used in a similar way in gardens.

Colorado beetle (*Leptinotarsa decemlineata*)

This beetle was first found in Colorado in 1923 when it left its normal diet of wild buffalo burr for the settlers' potatoes. It quickly spread across the whole of the American continent. In 1922, Colorado beetles appeared in the French port of Bordeaux and have since spread across Europe as far as the river Volga. The Russians are trying to prevent any from crossing this river – railway wagons are fumigated in giant tunnels, and lorries are quarantined before being allowed to cross from West to East.

The English Channel, together with the vigilance of the Ministry of Agriculture has kept the beetle from becoming endemic in the U.K. Colorado beetles have been reported in the U.K. since 1901, usually carried in ships or hovercraft. In some years, as many as 400 beetles are reported but these are individuals and not breeding colonies. Between 1901 and 1980 the Ministry dealt with 140 breeding colonies.

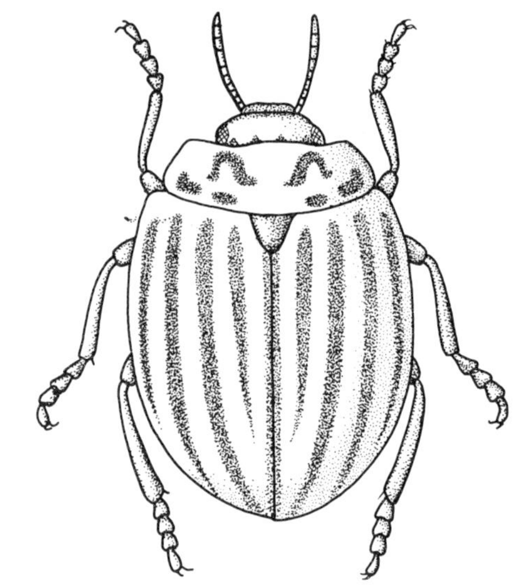

Adult Colorado beetle (see also colour photograph on cover)

The adult is 10 mm long with distinctive black and yellow stripes on its wing cases.

Larval stage of the Colorado beetle

The larvae are brown when hatched but soon turn bright pink with two rows of black dots along each side.

Both beetles and their larvae feed on potato leaves. As the materials for tuber growth are manufactured in the leaves, loss of leaves means loss of tubers; in a bad attack the whole field can become a mass of leafless stems and the crop a total failure.

Life cycle

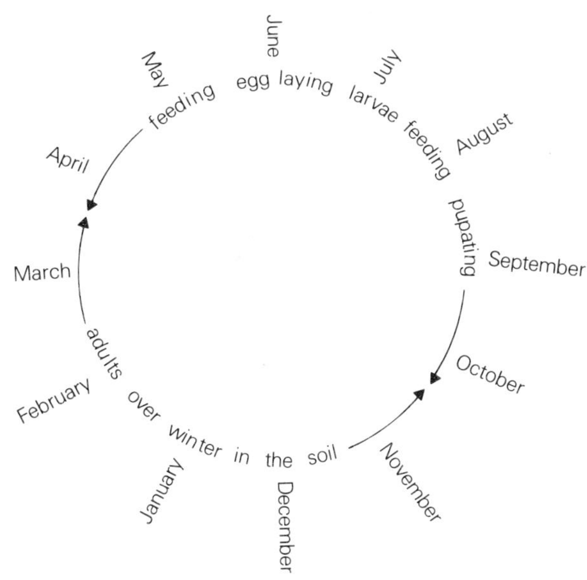

Adult beetles overwinter in the soil at depths of 300 mm. In spring, as the soil warms, beetles work their way to the surface and fly in search of potato plants, where they lay orange/yellow eggs on the underside of the leaves. During the summer, the female may lay as many as five hundred eggs. The larvae hatch within a few days and begin feeding on the potato leaves – first they bite holes and later feed around the edge of the leaf, giving it a saw-like appearance. It takes only three weeks for the larvae to become fully grown; they climb down the plant, burrow into the soil and pupate. Two weeks later, pupae change to adults, which either emerge or burrow deeply into the soil to over-winter, depending upon the season. In autumn all adults burrow into the soil, where they spend the winter.

Control

Pheasants are the only natural enemy which Colorado beetles have, except for heavy rain which washes some larvae from the plants. In the United Kingdom any kind of control is prohibited by law. If beetles are found they must be sent to the Ministry of Agriculture (Harpenden, Herts.), who will deal with the outbreak and make sure that total eradication is achieved.

Black bean aphid (*Aphis fabae*)

Description

'Blight', 'green fly' and 'black fly' are common names given to hundreds of different sucking insects called *aphids*. The size, shape, feeding method and life cycle are similar for all aphids, but different aphid types attack different species of plants. The black bean aphid has been chosen for study in this book as it is typical of most aphids and is usually available before the end of the summer term, on broad beans, runner beans, spinach, fat-hen, poppy and dock (it also infests the farm crops sugar beet and mangels).

There are two forms of aphid – one winged and one wingless. The bodies are brownish-black, with the legs somewhat lighter in colour. When viewed through a hand lens, the eyes can be clearly seen, and two small spikes at the base of the abdomen – the cornicles. When the insect is not feeding, the proboscis is folded underneath the body.

A wingless aphid

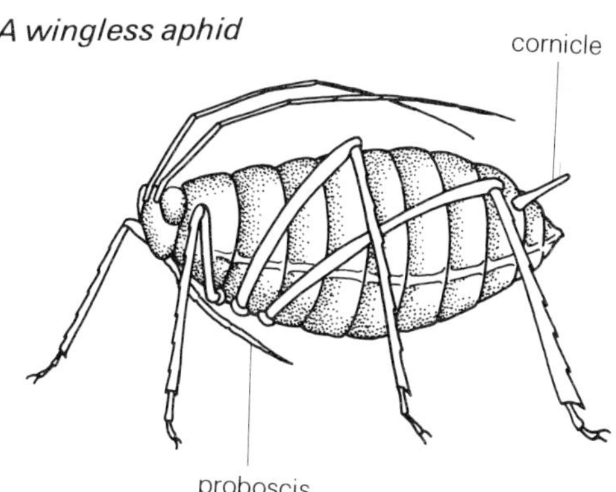

A winged aphid

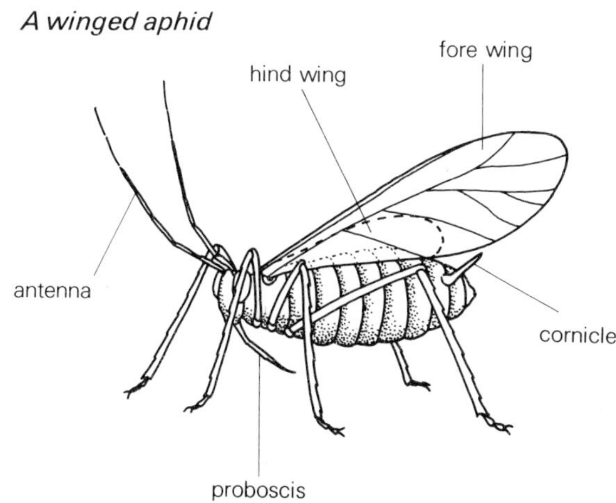

Black bean aphids on a broad bean plant

Damage

Infestation begins at the growing tips of plants, and the aphid feeds by sucking sap from the plants. Aphids reproduce very rapidly – a single aphid can give rise to one million in one month, and as numbers increase plants are injured by loss of sap. Aphids move down the plants and damage the flowers and young fruits, preventing their development. In a severe attack, a broad bean crop may fail completely.

Why are aphids more likely to feed near the growing tips?
. . . Q.3

Life cycle

The black bean aphid over-winters as an egg on spindle trees and snowball trees. In early spring, the eggs hatch into wingless females which feed on the buds and leaves of the trees. Without mating, the wingless females produce a generation of winged females – these fly away and colonise the summer host plants.

Life cycle of the black bean aphid

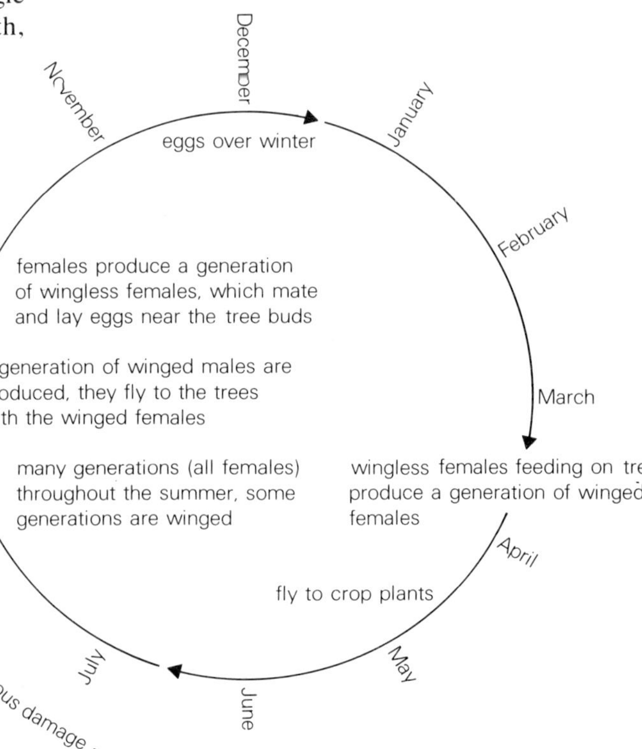

Throughout the summer, the females produce many generations of wingless females, the young being born alive in the shape of miniature adults (nymphs). When individual plants become heavily infested, a generation of winged females is produced; these fly away to form new colonies. In late autumn, a generation of winged males and winged females is produced which fly back to the spindles and snowball trees. The females give birth to a generation of wingless females which mate and lay shiny blacks eggs near to the tree buds; these eggs overwinter.

Control
Broad beans sown under ploches or cloches early in the year usually fruit before an aphid attack becomes serious. Very early unprotected sowings are less likely to be attacked than later sowings. Attacks are less likely if the growing tips are removed when the plants are over one metre high.

Why does removal of broad bean tops reduce the incidence of aphid infestation? . . . Q.4

Ladybirds and their larvae together with the larvae of some species of hover fly feed on aphids and help control their numbers. If insecticide dusts and sprays are used to kill aphids there is a danger of destroying predators as well. Sprays containing gamma BHC are more effective against predators than against aphids and should therefore be avoided. If chemicals have to be resorted to, the best material is probably derris dust, as this is not persistent, and is less harmful to the user than many substances currently available. Spraying should be carried out late in the day to reduce the risk of killing pollinating honey and wild bees – without these insects there will be no crop.

Some insecticides are absorbed by plants and move through the tissues (so poisoning the aphids' source of food); this type of insecticide is called *systemic*.

Three weeks must elapse between using a systemic insecticide and harvesting a crop. Why is this? . . . Q.5

Task 3.1

Collect the top of a broad bean plant which is infested with aphids (if broad bean is not available, aphid colonies may be found upon a large range of plants, e.g., rose or cabbage). Take the specimen to the classroom and answer the following questions:

1. What colour are the insects?
2. Are the insects evenly spread over the plant? If not which parts of the plant do they prefer?
3. Cut a square hole, side 10 mm, in a piece of paper. Place the paper over a thickly populated area and count the number of aphids in the square.
4. How many winged specimens can you find?
5. Are the majority of the aphids feeding?
6. Aphids moult as they grow, can you find any cast skeletons?
7. Using a hand lens examine one individual, how many legs does it have?
8. How many parts are there to its body?
9. Draw a diagram of the aphid's head to show the relative size of the eyes.
10. How long are the antenna compared with the total length of the body?
11. Identify the proboscis and draw it on your diagram.
12. Draw the abdomen, showing the position of the cornicles.

Carrot fly (*Psila roase*)

Description
The carrot fly is about 8 mm long with a black body and reddish-brown head; it has a single pair of transparent wings which span 12 mm. The larvae, when fully grown, are creamy-white cylindrical grubs 9 mm long.

Damage
Carrot fly larvae feed on the roots of carrots, parsnips, celery and parsley. First generation larvae are present when the plants are small – at this stage carrots are often killed by loss of root, causing gaps to appear in the rows; plants that

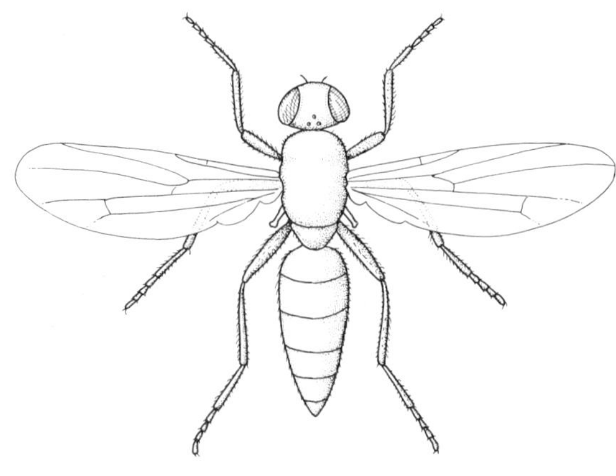

Adult carrot fly

Carrot fly larva

survive an attack wilt and the leaves appear reddish coloured. Second generation larvae are present when the tap-roots have developed, the larvae tunnel into these roots, causing the unsightly brown markings typical of this pest. Damage becomes progressively worse during the autumn, and the whole crop may be unsuitable for human consumption.

Life cycle

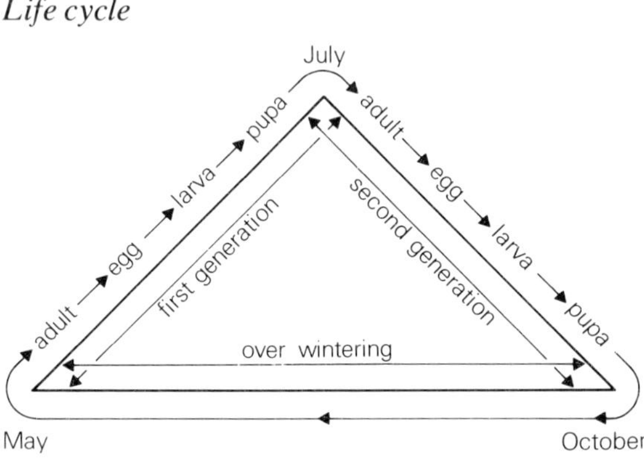

White, oval eggs about 1 mm long are laid singly, or in groups, in loose soil near to the host plants. Seven days later, tiny white larvae hatch, burrow into the soil and begin feeding on the roots. When fully grown, the larvae develop into yellowish-brown *puparia*, which collect close to the tap-roots. Pupae of the first generation develop into flies in two or three weeks; pupae of the second generation remain in the soil until May of the following year.

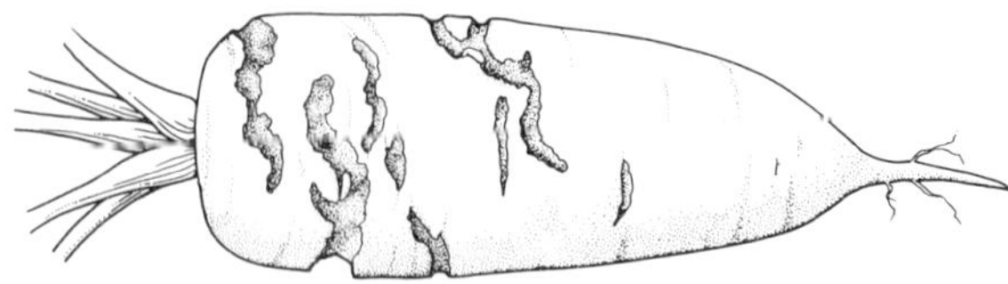

Damage to a carrot, caused by the action of carrot fly larvae

Control

Carrot flies shelter in hedges and weeds, leaving this shelter to lay eggs, when attracted by the smell of disturbed carrots. Control of weeds, especially nettles, deprives the flies of some shelter. Carrots sown in exposed positions will be less liable to attack than carrots sown in sheltered places. Late sown (June) carrots will not be damaged by first generation flies. Thinning rows of carrots makes attack more likely for two reasons:

1. The smell of disturbed carrots attracts the flies.
2. The earth is loosened enabling the fly to position her eggs where they are most likely to succeed.

If carrots are sown very thinly, thinning is unnecessary (the use of pelleted seed assists in obtaining correct spacing of seeds). If thinning has to be done, the operation should be carried out late in the evening, all thinnings should be removed, and the soil should be trodden firmly alongside the rows, which should then be thoroughly watered.

Why does treading and watering after thinning reduce the risk of carrot fly damage? . . . Q.6

Where carrot fly damage is known to be present, the roots should be lifted as soon as possible, as damage would otherwise get progressively worse. Some control can be obtained by coating the seeds with gamma BHC powder (strictly following the manufacturer's instructions), before sowing; coating seeds with a pesticide or fungicide is known as *seed dressing*.

Cabbage root fly (*Erioischia brassicae*)

In spring and summer Brassica plants are often seen wilting. If a wilting plant is lifted, small white maggots may be found feeding on the roots and burrowing into the stem: these maggots are the larval stage of cabbage root fly.

Life cycle

At about the same time as cow parsley begins to flower, adult flies emerge from the soil where they have overwintered as pupae. After mating, the females lay white eggs in the soil near to the stems of Brassicas; the eggs are about 1 mm long and can be found by careful searching. A few days later the eggs hatch into tiny legless larvae, which move to the Brassicas and begin feeding upon their roots. Three weeks later the fully grown (8 mm long) larvae leave the plants and crawl 30–40 mm through the soil, before forming pupae. Two to three weeks later the second generation of adult flies emerge to continue the

Life cycle of the cabbage root fly

Investigation 3.1

During April or May when the cow parsley is coming into flower, purchase fifty cauliflower plants and transplant them into freshly dug soil; do not apply any chemicals to either the roots or the soil. In most areas and in most seasons some of the plants will be seen wilting within a few weeks – lift a wilting plant and examine the root for feeding larvae. Three or four weeks later, dig the soil from around an infected plant and search for pupae (these are about 6 mm long and reddish brown in colour).

One-third fill a large glass jar with moist soil and put in the pupae, covering with 20 mm of soil. Cover the jar with an insect-proof net and leave it in a warm room; two or three weeks later adult flies will emerge.

Which state of the life cycle of the cabbage root fly have you not seen during this investigation? . . . Q.7

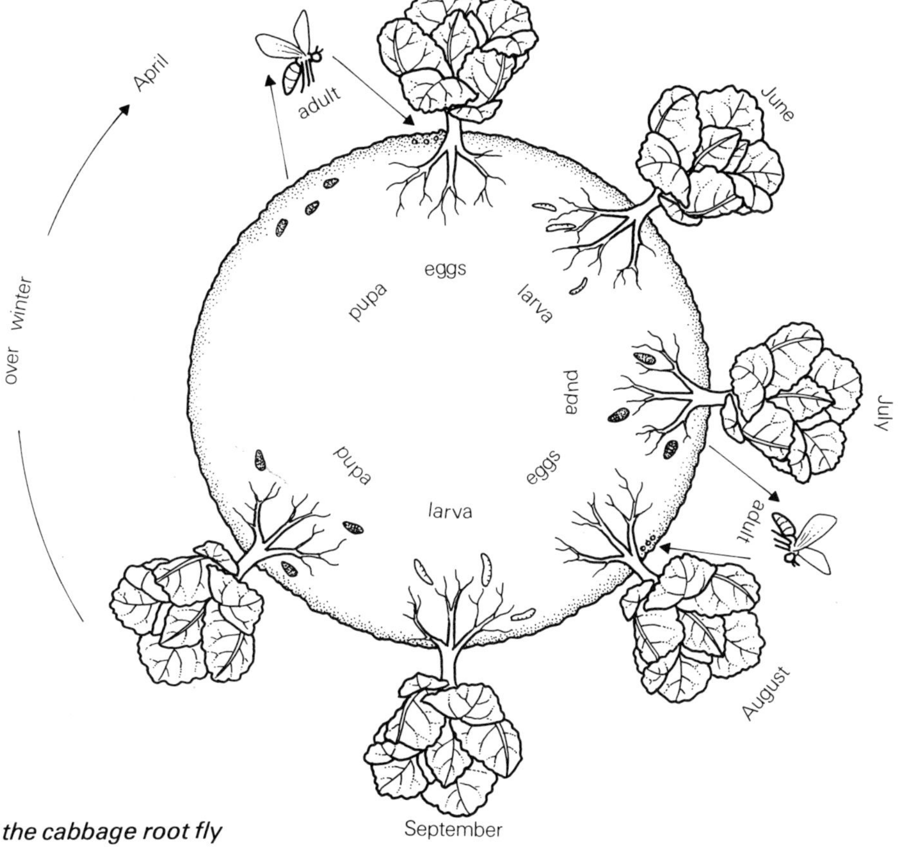

The cabbage in the centre of the photograph shows stunted growth, brought about by the action of cabbage root fly larvae in the roots

life cycle: pupae from the second generation remain in the soil throughout the winter to produce the first generation the following year (in the warmer parts of the U.K. there may be a third generation).

Damage

Cabbage root fly larvae are feeding on the roots of the plant in the centre of the above photograph. Young Brassica plants often fail to withstand a root fly attack and die; larger and more established plants survive root fly attack, but yield from these plants will be reduced, and cabbages and cauliflowers will be smaller. The quality of swedes and turnips is impaired by the

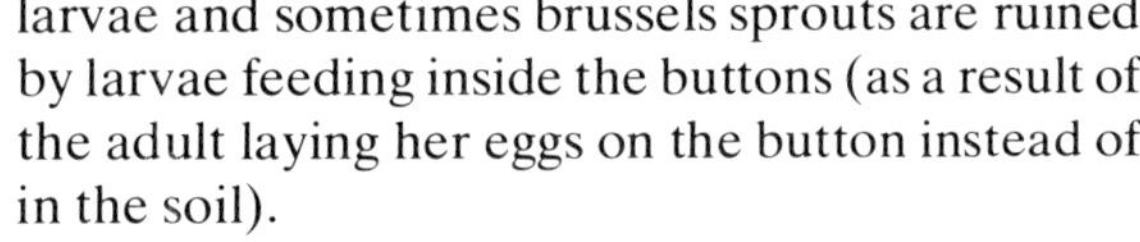

larvae and sometimes brussels sprouts are ruined by larvae feeding inside the buttons (as a result of the adult laying her eggs on the button instead of in the soil).

Control

First generation flies cause most damage – if transplanting is avoided at the time of their emergence, a measure of control is achieved. Circles of foam rubber carpet underlay (150 mm diameter) placed on the soil, snugly around the stems of transplants, prevents eggs from being laid in the soil around the plants – eggs laid on the mats may dehydrate and die. If plants under attack are given plenty of water, the effects of root damage are reduced as the plants are less likely to suffer from water stress.

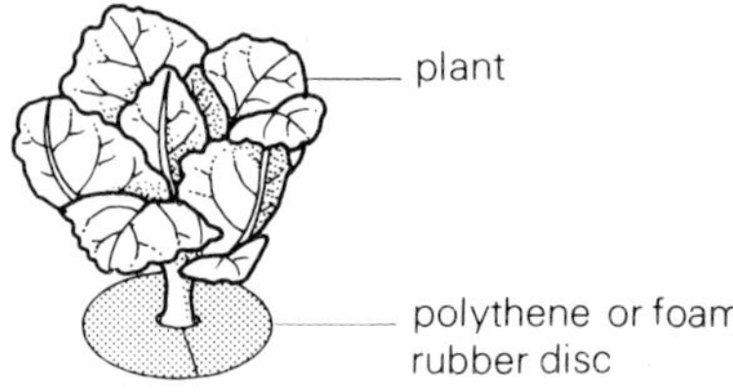

Cabbage transplant protection against attack by cabbage root fly

A cauliflower plant lifted from an infected row. The roots of the plant have been eaten by the larvae of the cabbage root fly; note the stunted growth of the damaged plant, and the small larvae nearby

Calomel dressings applied to the roots of transplants for the control of club root, give some protection against cabbage root fly. Chemicals are not effective against larvae feeding on the roots – control depends upon killing either eggs or emerging larvae, and must therefore be applied around the base of each plant within four days of transplanting. Garden insecticides (bromophos or gamma HCH) can be used strictly according to manufacturers' instructions, or a good puff of derris dust at the base of each transplant may help. Indiscriminate use of insecticides has led to the development of resistant strains of cabbage root fly, upon which chemicals have little effect – these strains are widespread in most areas of the United Kingdom south of Carlisle.

Beneficial insects

The insects described in this chapter so far are pest species. In nature, the populations of these species are kept within reasonable bounds by other creatures which prey upon them or which parasitise them. Many insects in fields and gardens are beneficial to man's activities, and without them pests would soon reach epidemic proportions. Six of the most common beneficial insects are described below:

Rove beetle or devil's coach horse
(*Staphylinus olens*)

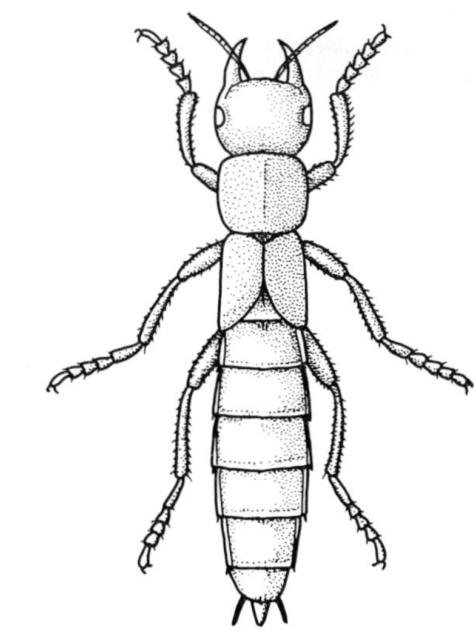

Adult rove beetle

This beetle is common in garden soils; it is an active hunter, feeding upon a wide range of soil inhabitants, including many pest species. Rove beetles and their larvae destroy considerable numbers of cabbage root fly pupae. The devil's coach horse dislikes sunlight and dry places – it probably feeds on the surface at night.

Ichneumon fly (*Ophion luteus*)

There are over 1850 species of these sun-loving insects in the United Kingdom. The females lay many eggs, placing each one singly on or in the body of a caterpillar. The egg hatches into a larva with strong biting mouthparts, and the larvae

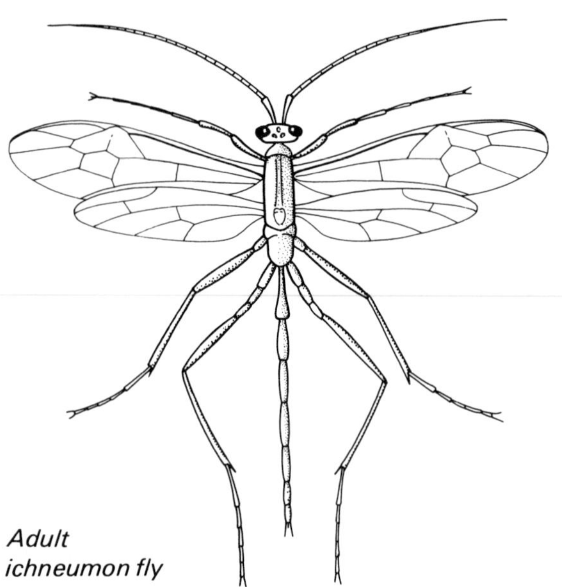
Adult ichneumon fly

devours the contents of the caterpillar, pupates and emerges as an adult. The adult males die in the autumn, the females hibernate and emerge the following spring.

Hover fly (*Syrphus balteatus*)

These wasp-like flies are often numerous in summer; they are easily recognised by their ability to remain stationary in the air. Eggs are laid near to aphid colonies, and the larvae hold aphids aloft and suck out the body contents. Some larvae destroy as many as 800 aphids in this way, before they pupate.

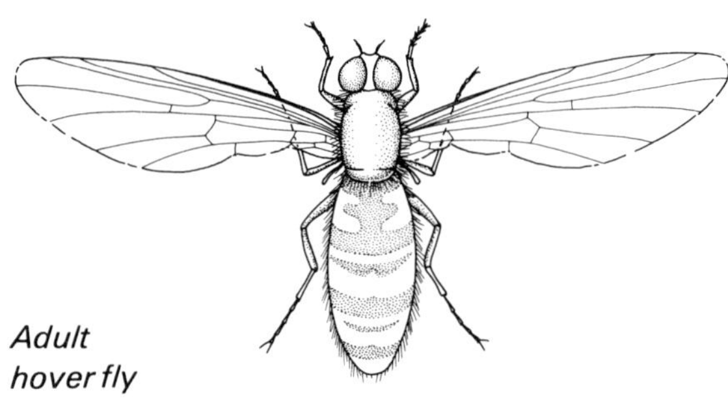
Adult hover fly

Black-kneed capsid bug (*Blepharidopterus angulatus*)

This insect lays eggs in the bark of apple trees, the eggs overwinter and hatch in spring, producing a

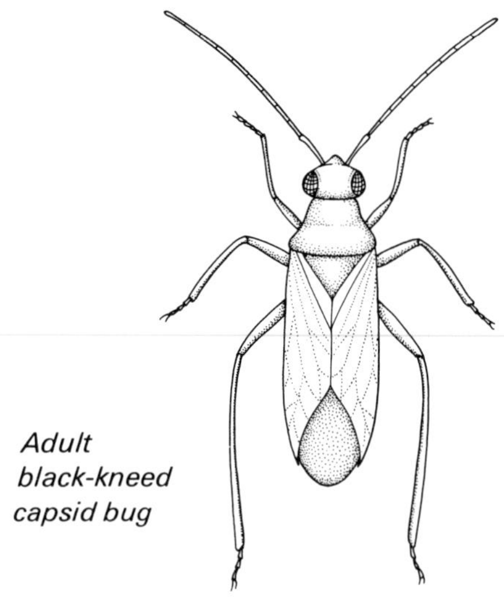
Adult black-kneed capsid bug

nymph. Nymphs and adults feed upon red spider mite (a fruit-tree pest) by inserting their proboscis into the spider mite and sucking it dry. Female black-kneed capsids have been known to kill 4000 red spider mites in one season. *Note*: some capsid bugs, e.g., the apple capsid and the common green capsid are serious pests of apple trees and soft fruit bushes.

Green lacewing (*Chrysopa carnea*)

Adult green lacewing

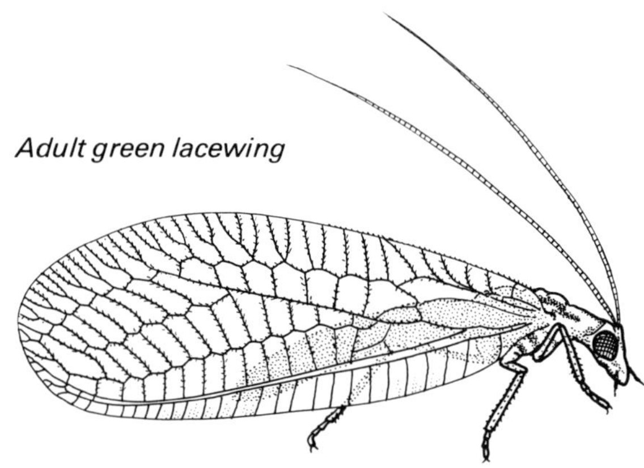

The green lacewing passes the winter as a larva in a silk cocoon or as a hibernating adult. In spring the females attach eggs to leaves with fine stalks. Larvae and adults feed on aphids and often frequent farm and garden crops; the larvae are difficult to see as they cover their backs with the empty shells of aphids.

Ladybird (*Adalia bipunctata*)

One of 44 different species, 43 of which are carnivores. Adults hibernate during the winter, in groups of up to 70, under tree bark, in hollow stems and other places. In April and May they emerge and lay over 100 eggs on the underside of leaves. Both adults and larvae feed on aphids, the larvae consuming some 20 aphids each day. Ladybirds are not very effective at controlling black fly on broad beans, as they prefer eating the aphids on stinging nettles.

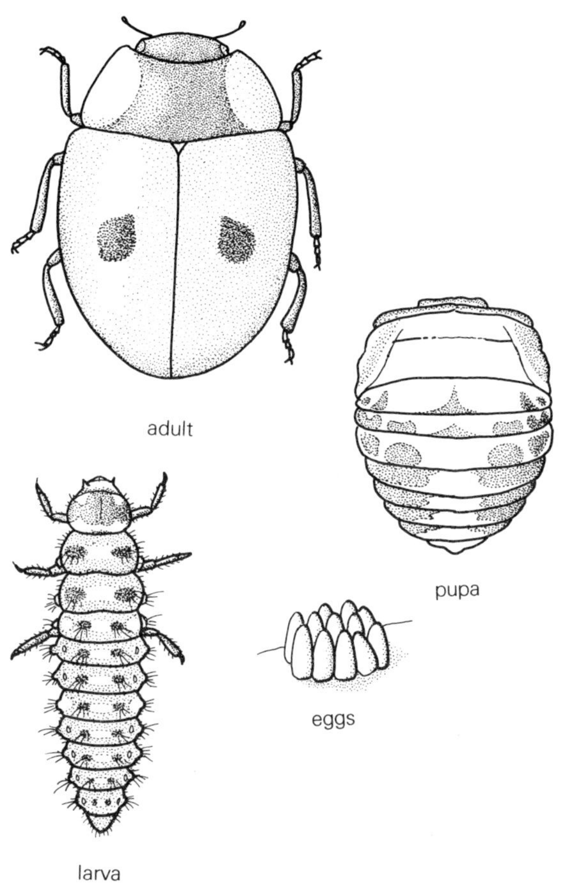

The developmental stages of the ladybird

Which of the six beneficial insects described are predators and which are parasites? . . . Q.8

Nematode pests

Potato cyst eelworm (*Heterodera rostochiensis*)

Description
Sometimes called potato root eelworm, this organism is an extremely small unsegmented worm, pointed at both ends; it belongs to the large group of roundworms called the nematodes. The eelworm is invisible to the naked eye; it moves through the soil with a thrashing movement, and feeds only on the roots of potatoes and tomatoes.

Potato cyst eelworm is perhaps the most serious pest in the soils of temperate climates (i.e., climates cooler than tropical and warmer than arctic); it infests most arable land, gardens and allotments.

Damage
Eelworm causes serious reductions in potato yields – when infestation is heavy the crop may fail completely. Bare patches and patches of stunted growth appear in potato fields, while in gardens growth is uneven, with some plants failing to produce any worthwhile tubers.

Life cycle
Newly hatched larvae enter the root of the potato and begin to feed upon it. As they develop within the roots their sex is determined, some becoming females, but more becoming males. The females feed and become so fat that their bodies burst the root, leaving their heads inside the root feeding, and their bodies outside. The slender males leave the root and fertilise the females. The fertilised female's body swells into a complete sphere, packed tightly with some five hundred eggs; this tough ball of eggs is called a *cyst.* Cysts are 0.5 mm in diameter and in August and September, can just be seen with the naked eye, as small white spheres on the roots of freshly dug potato plants. Left in the soil, the cysts darken and become detached from the root.

The cysts of potato eelworm remain in the soil for periods of up to ten years; each year some 10% of the eggs in the cyst hatch, and the larvae

Cysts of the potato cyst eelworm on the roots of a potato plant (Courtesy of C. C. Doncaster, Rothampstead Experimental Station)

enter the soil in search of potato roots. If a potato is growing near by all the eggs hatch and the larvae move towards the potato and begin feeding upon its roots.

Control

Cysts are spread from infected areas whenever soil is moved; wind, water, tractor tyres, garden tools, boots and seedling transplants all spread cysts to areas that may not have grown potatoes. One method of control is to keep soil movement to a minimum by adopting strict standards of hygiene.

Granules containing a *nematocide* (chemical which kills nematodes) are available to market growers. The granules are worked into the soil and release poisons which destroy larvae and eggs. There are often 25 000 000 cysts in one hectare – chemicals only destroy part of these. Plant breeders are attempting to produce varieties of potatoes in which eelworms cannot complete their life cycles, e.g., Maris Piper, Ulster Glade (maincrop) and Pentland Javelin (early) are effective against certain strains of eelworm.

The most effective method of control is to have a long rotation, and grow potatoes in the same area only one year in six. This method prevents the build-up of heavy infestations of cysts, as long as any 'weed' potatoes are promptly removed in years when other crops are being grown.

Which potatoes will leave the heaviest infestation of eelworm cysts, 'earlies' or 'maincrop'?

. . . Q.9

Task 3.2

1. Take a handful of soil from an area that has been used to grow potatoes.
2. Drop it into a beaker three quarters full of water and stir.
3. Pour the top of the water with the floating debris into a filter lined funnel.
4. When the water has drained from the funnel examine the ring around the top of the filter paper with a low power microscope.
5. If potato eel worm cysts are present they will be seen as almost spherical shapes. Once located by the microscope they can be seen with the naked eye as dark specks about 0.5 mm in diameter.

Fungal diseases

Club root (*Plasmodiphora brassicae*)

Club root is a disease of Brassicas caused by a fungus which, unlike any described so far, does not form hyphae or a mycelium.

Cabbage, cauliflower, brussels sprouts, radish, swedes and turnips are the vegetables most commonly infected; in the flower border wall-flowers are attacked, and also some weeds, e.g., shepherd's purse and charlock.

Symptoms of the disease
The first sign of the disease is wilting during periods of hot sun. Later infected plants appear weak and sickly, and often die completely. When lifted, the roots show tumour-like growths similar to those in the photograph opposite – at first these growths are firm, but later they decay into a foul-smelling brown mass. When cut through with a knife, the inside of a tumour appears brown and mottled.

Life cycle
Club root spores remain in the soil for several years; they germinate into a tiny organism which moves through the soil and enters the root of a host plant. Inside the plant, the fungus increases and the plant reacts by growing tumours in which further growth is made. The fungus forms millions of spores which enter the soil as the tumours decay in autumn.

Control
Club root flourishes in badly drained acid soils. Drainage and lime application to correct these faults, together with a long rotation for susceptible crops is often sufficient to control the disease. Weeds liable to be infected must not be allowed to grow, or they will nullify the effect of the long rotation. Any infected plant should be lifted and burnt before it rots and releases spores.

What is the likely effect of putting diseased roots on the compost heap? . . . Q.10

Cauliflower plant infected with club root

The disease is often introduced into gardens by purchasing infected transplants. Although it is an offence to sell diseased plants, purchased plants should be inspected for signs of club root swellings. Good control is obtained when transplanting healthy plants in suspect soil, by dipping the roots in a fungicidal paste, made by mixing 25 g of pure calomel with half a litre of water, before planting.

Potato blight (*Phytophthora infestans*)

This disease destroyed the potato crop in Ireland in 1846, causing a famine from which over one million people died. Blight is caused by a fungus which is parasitic on the leaves and stems of potatoes and tomatoes.

Damage
Brown patches appear on leaves and stems; at first these patches show the typical circular shape of fungal growth. Underneath the leaves are fine white threads of the fruiting bodies, which shed millions of spores into the air. In warm, moist conditions the fungus quickly spreads over the whole plant, reducing it to a rotting brown mess.

Weight of potato tubers in one hectare of maincrop potatoes

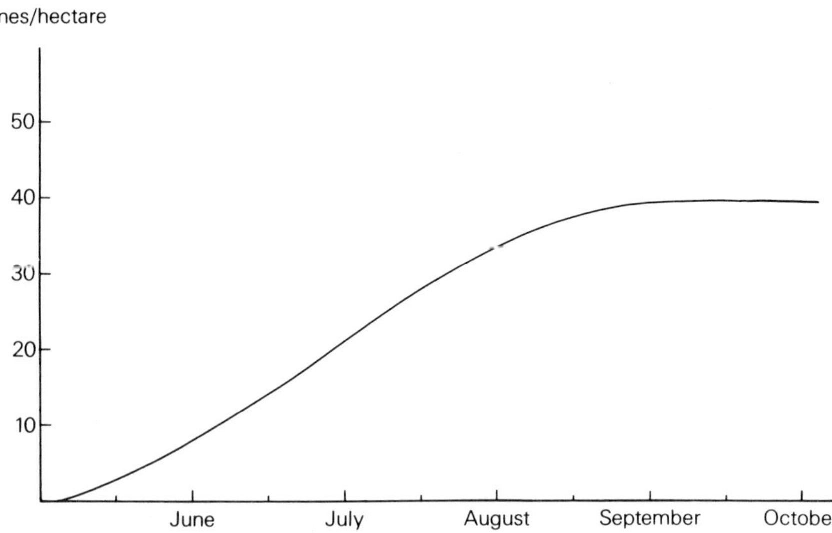

Plants in the immediate area become infected and within two or three weeks the disease can spread over a whole field.

When leaves and stems of the plant are destroyed there is no further growth of tubers. The loss in yield caused by potato blight depends upon the time of year the disease strikes:

Reading from the graph, if the haulm is destroyed in July, the yield will be 20 tonnes – a loss of 20 tonnes; if the haulm is destroyed in August the yield will be 30 tonnes – a loss of 10 tonnes. In fact, the loss may be much greater than this as many of the tubers may be too small to sell.

Spores which come in contact with tubers, either by washing through the soil or as the tubers are lifted, cause the inside to go mottled-brown, under a slightly depressed area on the surface.

Life cycle

Potato blight overwinters in diseased tubers, which left in the soil, or planted as 'seed', grow and produce diseased shoots in which the fungus grows and sheds many millions of spores – the source of infection. In warm, wet conditions, if a spore settles on potato foliage, it will germinate and grow into the tissue of the leaf. Inside the leaf the fungus grows very quickly and forms fruiting bodies on the underside, which shed millions of spores into the air. Potato blight cannot be cured – the only control methods available are prevention, this is achieved in two ways:

1. Avoid sources of infection by careful harvesting followed by rogueing any weed potatoes as they appear the following season. Make sure that no diseased potatoes are placed on the compost heap, where they may grow and become a source of infection. *Plant only certified potato seed.*
2. Spraying the growing crop with a fungicide when conditions favour blight growth. This coats the leaves with fungicide, which will kill any spores as they germinate. Repeat the spraying every two weeks to protect new growth and replace fungicide that has been washed off.

Blight is likely after a continuous period of forty-eight hours with temperatures in excess of 10°C and the relative humidity above 75%; these periods are known as *Beaumont periods.* Warnings of likelihood of blight are given over the radio and television during Farmers' programmes when Beaumont periods occur.

Growers use organo-tin compounds (i.e., a manufactured organic compound containing tin) to protect haulm against blight, sprayed over the crop at the rate of 200 litres per hectare from the air or from ground machines. Gardeners can make a fungicide called Bordeaux mixture by mixing 10 g of powdered copper sulphate with 12.5 g of hydrated lime and applying this as a dust, or mixed with one litre of water as a spray. Dusting should take place when the foliage is wet with dew.

Tubers can be protected from spores by very good earthing-up. Many tubers are infected during lifting by being in contact with spore-bearing foliage – this source of infection can be avoided by delaying harvest until the haulm has been dead for at least two weeks.

Potato scab (*Streptomyces scabies*)

Scab is a fungus disease of potatoes caused by the soil-borne organism *Streptomyces scabies*. The organism invades the tubers, which respond by growing scabs, effectively preventing entry into the flesh of the tuber. Scabbed tubers are perfectly good to eat, all infection being removed with the peel. The appearance of the tubers is spoiled, however, and if more than half the skin is affected they are considered unsaleable.

Scab is favoured by dry, alkaline soils deficient in humus, and control can be achieved by avoiding these conditions. Irrigation, growing potatoes in rotation the year before lime is applied, and application of humus-forming materials all help to reduce scab damage. Some varieties are less susceptible than others – Maris Peer and Pentland Crown are fairly resistant; Maris Piper and Desiree are fairly susceptible.

A potato tuber infected by the potato scab fungus

Virus diseases

Viruses are responsible for many plant diseases incuding mosaic (so-called because of colour patterns on the leaves), virus yellows (a common disease of sugar beet), black ring top (a disease of Brassicas) and potato leaf-roll which is described in detail below.

Unlike bacteria, viruses are not able to multiply outside living tissue. They are carried from plant to plant by a wide variety of sucking and biting organisms, the most important of which are aphids. An organism that carries a virus disease from one plant to another is called a *vector* – control of vectors and production of healthy plant stock are man's only methods of combating virus diseases in his crop plants.

Potato leaf roll

Damage to a potato plant caused by the potato leaf roll virus

The potato leaf roll virus causes the lower leaves of a potato plant to thicken and curl upwards from the mid-rib. A badly diseased plant will make a rustling sound if shaken, and the yield of tubers is reduced by up to 90%. All tubers from a diseased plant will be infected with the virus and, if planted, will produce diseased shoots.

The main vector of potato leaf roll is the peach-potato aphid (*Myzus persicae*). This aphid overwinters as an egg on peach trees, but in mild winters, it can be found on Brassicas throughout the year.

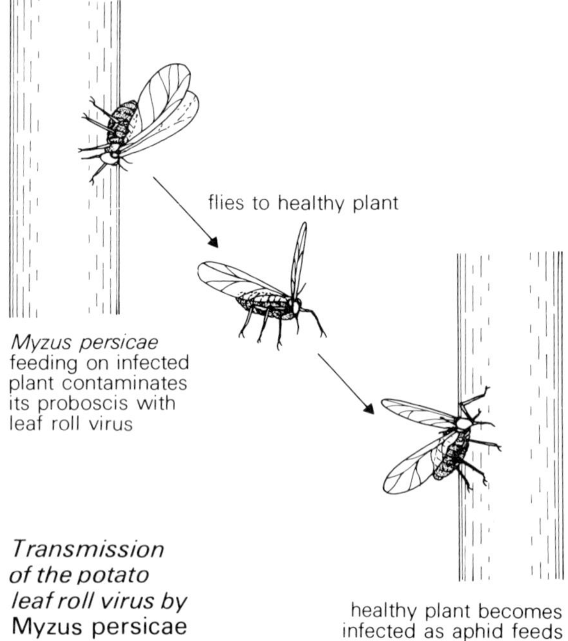

Transmission of the potato leaf roll virus by Myzus persicae

Aphids are common throughout many parts of the U.K., and most healthy potatoes become infected during their first season of growth. This initial infection has little or no effect upon yield, as the tubers are well formed before the virus takes effect. If the tubers are used for 'seed' the following year, very low-yielding diseased plants will result. The only way to prevent losses from leaf roll is to plant only healthy tubers.

Production of healthy 'seed' potatoes

Aphids do not fly when wind speed exceeds 6 km/h, the temperature is below 18° or the relative humidity is more than 75%. In certain areas of Scotland and Ireland these conditions are never satisfied, so aphids cannot fly, and potato leaf roll will not spread. In these areas 'seed' potatoes are grown for the rest of the country. The production of 'seed' potatoes is strictly controlled by law and all 'seeds' offered for sale must have a certificate from the Agricultural Department of the Government. Growers purchase AA (first quality commercial) or CC (healthy commercial) seeds. The stock from which 'seeds' are produced are VTSC (virus-tested stem cuttings). VTSC 'seed' are produced as follows:

1. Healthy potatoes are grown in pots in aphid-free greenhouses, and cuttings are taken.

2. The base of the cutting is removed and sent to the laboratory to test for virus. As virus moves up the growing stem from an infected tuber, if the stem below the cutting is virus free, the cutting will also be virus free.

3. If the laboratory test is negative, the cuttings are rooted and grown on to produce virus-free tubers. These tubers are the foundation stocks from which commercial 'seed' will be grown.

Questions: Pests and diseases of plants

1. Write single sentences to answer the following questions.
   (a) How can a male cabbage white butterfly be distinguished from a female?
   (b) What is the common name of a crane fly larva?
   (c) When did Colorado beetles first appear in Europe?
   (d) Upon which kind of tree does the black bean aphid prefer to lay its eggs?
   (e) What type of organism causes club root?
   (f) Where does the Ichneumon fly lay her eggs?
   (g) Why are ladybirds not very effective at controlling black fly on broad beans?
   (h) Is 'Pentland Javelin' an early or late variety of potato?
   (i) Which disease caused the Irish famine in 1846?
   (j) What is a systemic insecticide?

2. Describe the life cycle of a sucking insect pest of plants. How does knowledge of the life cycle assist you in control measures?

3. (a) Describe the complete life cycle of a named insect.
   (b) State *two* ways by which an adult insect can be recognised as an insect.
   (c) Name a beneficial insect, giving reasons.
   (d) Name a harmful insect, giving reasons.
   (*W.M.E.B.*)

4. In summer, you noticed that greyish patches were appearing on the leaves of your potato crop. On examining some of the exposed tubers underneath, soft patches were evident.
   (a) Name the disease involved.
   (b) How is the disease transmitted?
   (c) How does the disease gain entry to the leaves?
   (d) How could you have minimised the direct effect of the disease on the tubers?
   (e) What weather condition should warn the gardener of a likely attack?
   (f) Outline any preventative measures you could take in the future to reduce the risk of attack. (*W.M.E.B.*)

5. (a) Name *one* pest and *one* disease which may cause damage to horticultural crops
   Either (i) above the ground;
   Or (ii) below ground level.
   (b) Choosing either the pest or disease you have named in (a) above, answer the following:
      (i) Describe all the ways it can spread through the crop.
      (ii) What are the symptoms of attack?
      (iii) List in the correct order and explain what steps you would take to control the pest or disease.

   (S.E.R.E.B.)

6. Outline the life cycle of potato root eelworm and describe the damage caused by this pest. Discuss methods of control available.

7. By reference to the life cycle of the Colorado beetle, explain why a law has been made preventing farmers from dealing with this pest themselves.

8. Indiscriminate use of insecticides has given rise to resistant strains of cabbage root fly. Describe *two* methods of reducing root fly damage to garden Brassica crops, that do not involve the use of chemicals.

9. Describe a plant disease caused by a soil-inhabiting fungus, using the following headings:
   (i) Life cycle
   (ii) Crops infected
   (iii) Symptoms of the disease
   (iv) Control methods.

10. (a) What do the letters VTSC stand for?
    (b) Why are VTSC necessary?
    (c) What are the tubers grown from VTSC used for?
    (d) What is the connection between aphids and potato leaf roll?

4 Further plant science

Plant names

Throughout this book, two words have appeared in brackets after the name of each plant – these two words are the botanical name of the plant. Common names of plants often vary in different parts of the country, for example 'goosegrass', 'cleavers' and 'herrif' all refer to the same plant; this can be very confusing. In 1600 the idea was floated that plants, like people, could be given two names – a forename and a surname. The Swedish naturalist Linnaeus (1707–1778) took up this idea and gave two names to thousands of plants and animals, using words from several different languages. He put the 'surname' first (*generic name*) with a capital letter and the *specific name* last, with no capital letter, e.g., the common daisy is called *Bellis perennis*: *Bellis* is derived from *bellus*, the Latin word for pretty, and *perennis* is the Latin word for perennial. *Bellis silvestris* is a woodland daisy (*silva* is the Latin word which means a wood).

This system has been universally accepted and is used by botanists, naturalists, horticulturists and many others the world over. *Bellis perennis* means exactly the same plant in Russia, America, Africa or any other part of the world.

Plant breeders have produced many varieties from a single species and, with many garden plants, it has become necessary to add a third name – the *varietal name*, e.g., the many varieties of *Brassica oleracea* are named as follows (the meaning of the last word is in brackets):

Cabbage:	*Brassica oleracea capitata* (having a head)
Sprouting broccoli:	*Brassica oleracea acephala* (without a head)
Cauliflower:	*Brassica oleracea botrytis* (like a bunch of grapes)
Brussels sprouts:	*Brassica oleracea bullata* (studded)
Savoy:	*Brassica oleracea major* (larger)
Kohlrabi:	*Brassica oleracea caulo-rapa* (turnip-stemmed)

Brassica is Latin for cabbage, and *oleracea* is Latin for 'kitchen-garden'.

The first part of the name (the *generic* part) was usually chosen in a haphazard way, often using the Latin or Greek word for that plant or the name of a botanist; it tells nothing about the botany of the plant. The second part of the name (the *specific* part) often refers to a special characteristic of the plant, e.g.:

elegans	=	elegant
variegatum	=	variegated
media	=	medium (sized)
minutum	=	small
alba	=	white
ovata	=	egg shaped
bicolor	=	two coloured
aureus	=	golden
grandiflora	=	large flowered
japonica	=	from Japan

As many English words were derived from the Latin language it may have been possible to guess the meanings of some of the above.

What could you deduce about plants that have the following specific names: *fragrans, bulbosa, maritima, trifoliata?* **. . . Q.1**

The botanical names of common vegetables

Vegetable	*First word*	*Language*	*Meaning*	*Second word*	*Language*	*Meaning*
Potato	*Solanum*	Latin	Latin name for the plant – night shade	*tuberosum*	Latin	tuber bearing
Jerusalem artichoke	*Helianthus*	Greek '*helios*'	the sun (sunflowers are included in this group)	*tuberosum*	Latin	tuber bearing
Onion	*Allium*	Latin	garlic	*cepa*	Latin	onion
Pea	*Pisum*	Latin	pea	*sativum*	Latin	cultivated
Carrot	*Daucus*	Greek	vegetable of carrot or parsnip family	*carota*	Greek	carrot
Lettuce	*Lactuca*	Latin '*lac*'	milk – refers to the white sap (*lactuca* is also Latin for lettuce)	*satica*	Latin	cultivated
Beetroot	*Beta*	Latin	beetroot	*vulgaris*	Latin	common
Radish	*Raphanus*	Greek '*ra phaino*'	'Quickly I appear' refers to the rapid germination	*sativus*	Latin	cultivated
Cress	*Lepidium*	Greek '*lepis*'	a scale – refers to the shape of the seed pods	*sativum*	Latin	cultivated
Marrow	*Cucurbita*	Latin '*cucurbita*'	a gourd	*pepo*	Latin	large melon

Classification of plants

Some plants are closely related, e.g., peas and beans have similar flowers and the seeds are carried in pods. Wheat is similar to barley but very different to peas and beans.

The binomial names of plants refer to the species of plant (a species can be interbred); the first of the two names is the *genus* to which that plant belongs – there are different *genera* (plural of *genus*) with very similar flower structures, e.g.:

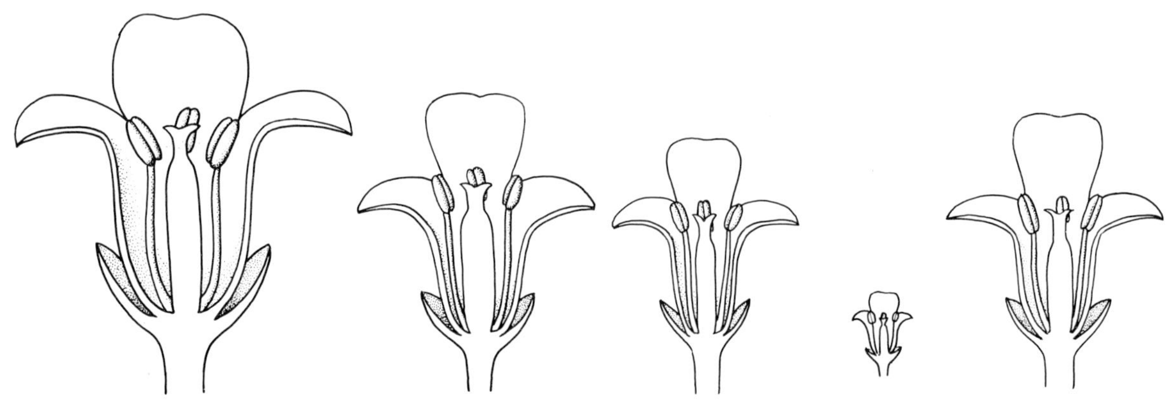

The five flowers illustrated on page 78 all have four petals arranged like a cross, four sepals, six stamens and one stigma; they all belong to the plant family *Cruciferae*.

Genera with similar flower structures are called families. There are over 200 families of flowering plants in the world, 120 of which grow in the U.K. The most important family of food plants is Graminae, the grass family which includes the cereal crop plants (the structure of these flowers was described in Book 1).

Umbelliferae

Investigation 4.1

Collect a single flower of three of the plants on the following list: pea, lupin, clover, vetch, broom, laburnum, bean, gorse, trefoil. Carefully take each flower to pieces, noting the numbers and arrangements of each part. The plants listed above all belong to the same family – *Leguminosae*.

Solanaceae

The half flowers of common families:

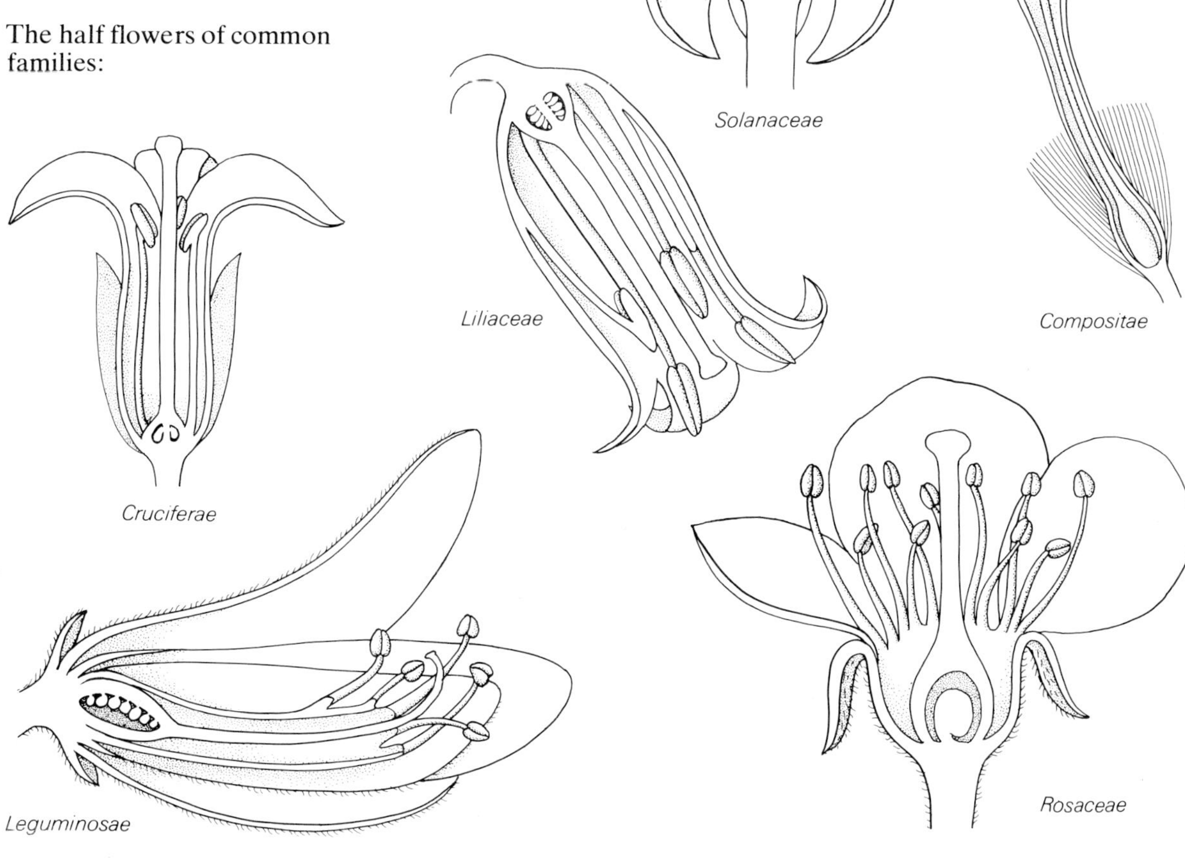

A

B

The families of plants are grouped into two different classes: monocotyledons and dicotyledons. There are important differences between the two classes:

	Monocotyledons	*Dicotyledons*
Food stores in seed	one	two
Seed leaves	one	two
Leaf veins	parallel	branched
Flowers	parts in 3's or multiples of three	parts in 4's, 5's and 7's or multiples

The internal structure of the stem of the two classes is also different (see Book 3).

Examine the two groups of plants in the photographs opposite; one is a group of monocotyledons and the other is a group of dicotyledons. Which is which? . . . Q.2

Examine the photograph of the flower below – is it dicotyledon or monocotyledon? . . . Q.3

Task 4.1

Draw two columns and head one dicotyledon and the other monocotyledon. Using your knowledge of the leaf shapes, place the following food plants in the correct columns (answers at the end of the book): potatoes, tomatoes, cucumber, barley, onion, lettuce, wheat, maize, carrot, cabbage, apple, mustard, leeks and oats.

Monocotyledons and dicotyledons are all flowering plants, and are placed in one division separating them from the non-flowering plants which form another division.

Name a group of non-flowering plants. . . . Q.4

All plants grouped together form the plant kingdom and the 'family tree' of peas, beans, wheat and barley look like this:

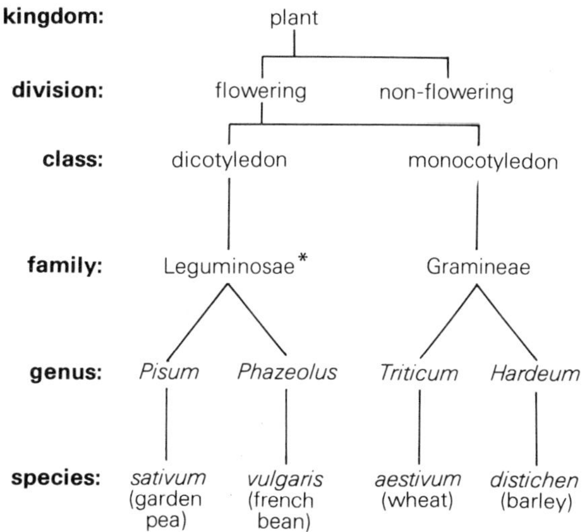

* (some botanists divide this family into two groups – Leguminosae and Papilionaceae)

Task 4.2

Draw a family tree of (a) cabbage and (b) onion (family *Alliaceae*)

Fertilisation in flowers

Fertilisation is a process that follows pollination (see Book 1) – you will remember that pollination leaves a flower with pollen stuck upon its stigma.

Experiment 4.1

1. Prepare a little sugar solution by dissolving 4 g of sugar in 100 ml of distilled water (if several experiments are done the sugar concentration can be increased for some and decreased for others).
2. Place a small amount of wet shredded filter paper in the centre of a microscope slide and surround it with a glass ring 15 mm diameter and 8 mm deep.
3. Tap a little pollen from a hyacinth or a sweet pea into the sugar solution.
4. Hold a cover slip and, using a teat pipette put one drop of the sugar solution containing pollen onto the underside of the slip.
5. Place the cover on the glass ring taking care not to dislodge the hanging drop. Examine the pollen grains in the drop through a microscope.
6. Leave for 24 hours.
7. Examine the pollen grains again, looking for any signs of change.

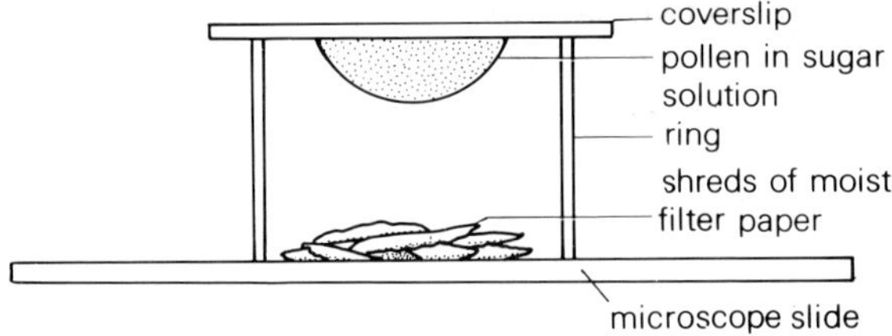

The pollen grains should have germinated and each one should have a 'hair' growing from it. This structure is not a hair but a *pollen tube*:

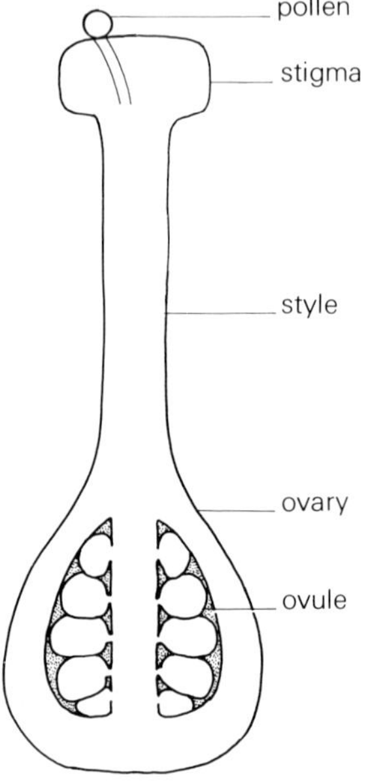

1 pollen grain grows a tube which enters the stigma

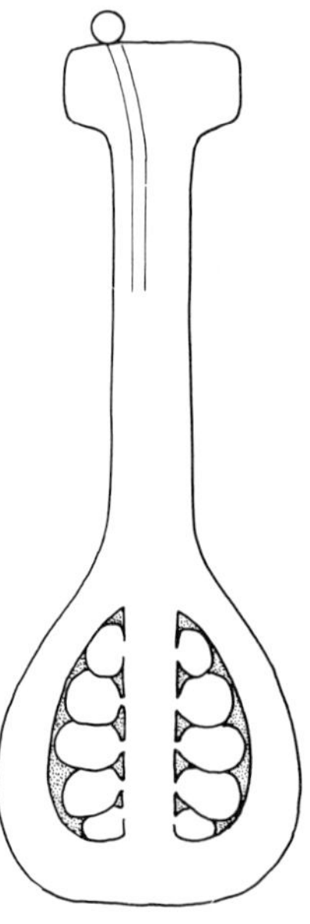

2 pollen tube grows down the style

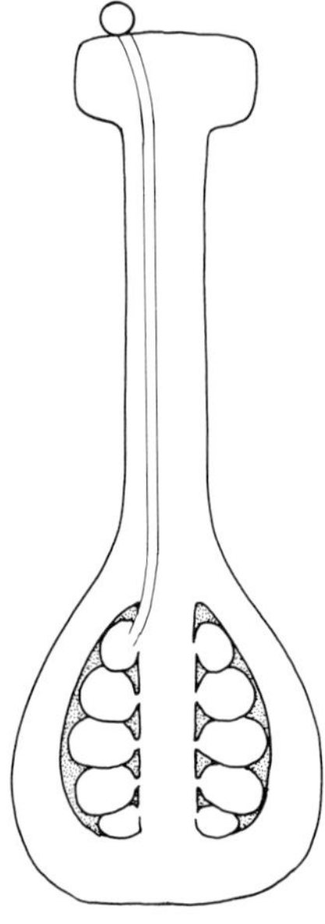

3 the pollen tube enters an ovule, the contents of the pollen fuse with the contents of the ovule

In the flower, the pollen grain absorbs nutrients from the stigma and grows a tube, which passes down the style and penetrates the ovary. Inside the ovary, the tube continues to grow until an ovule is reached. The pollen tube pierces the ovule and the contents of the pollen grain fuse with the contents of the ovule. The ovule, which now contains material from two flowers, develops into a seed. A seed cannot develop from an ovule until it has fused with the contents of a pollen grain.

What is the connection between fertilisation and the micropyle on a seed? . . . Q.5

Sexual reproduction

The principle of sexual reproduction is the same in animals and plants. An animal has two parents and inherits its characteristics from both, in exactly the same way as a plant, grown from seed, has two parents and inherits its characteristics from both.

How many 'parents' has a plant which is grown from a cutting? . . . Q.6
How many 'parents' has a potato tuber? . . . Q.7
How many 'parents' has a potato seed? . . . Q.8

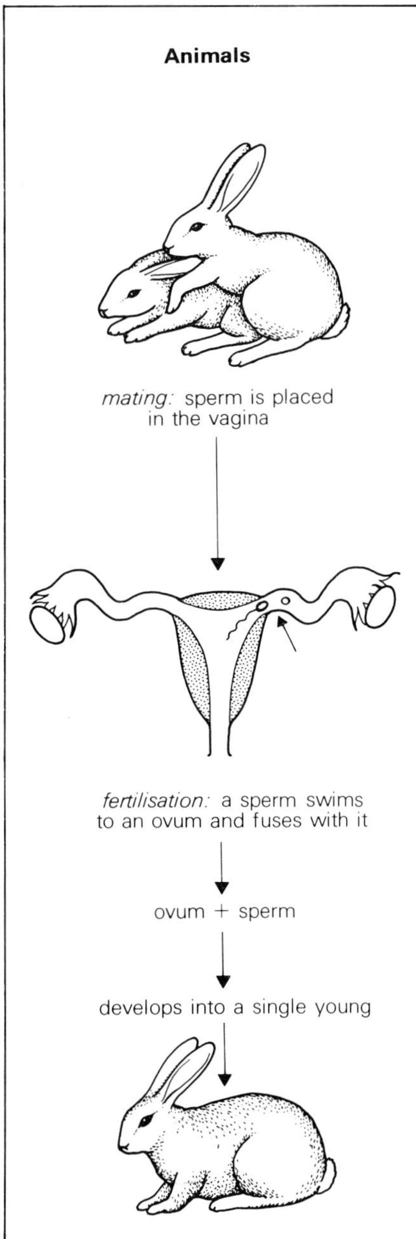

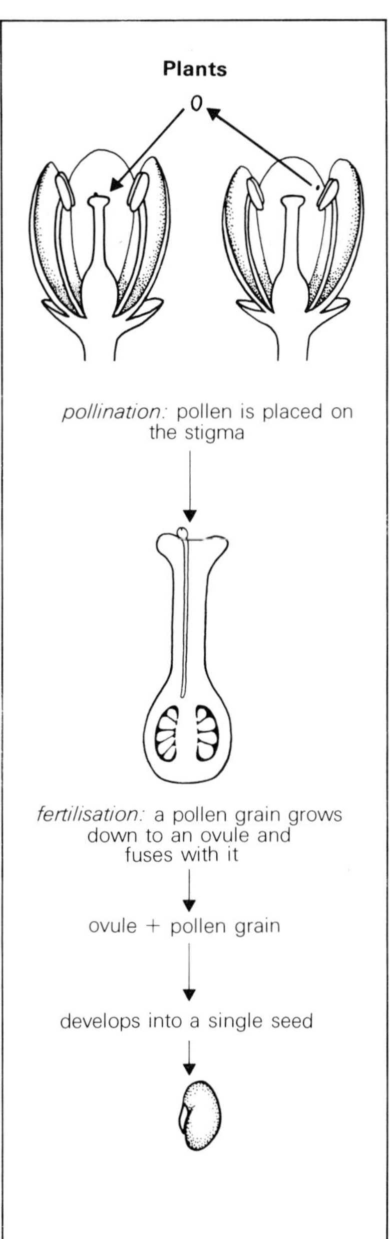

Plant breeding

In order to improve their stock animal breeders select the best males and mate them to the best unrelated females; plant breeders do exactly the same, but they have to prevent unwanted pollen from reaching the stigmas of the flowers of their choice. In order to achieve this plant breeders:

1. Remove the stamens from the selected flowers to prevent self-pollination.
2. Protect the flowers from pollinating insects which may be carrying unwanted pollen.
3. Transfer pollen by hand from the selected flower; a soft brush is sometimes used for this purpose or the male flower is picked and its anthers are tapped on the stigma of the other flower.

The seeds saved from the hand-pollinated flowers are usually grown the following year. Large organisations engaged in plant breeding often fly such seeds to another part of the world and sow them immediately, enabling two generations to be grown in one year, thus halving the time of the breeding programme.

Many plant breeders develop two pure strains of one plant species, cross them, and sell the seeds as F_1 hybrids:

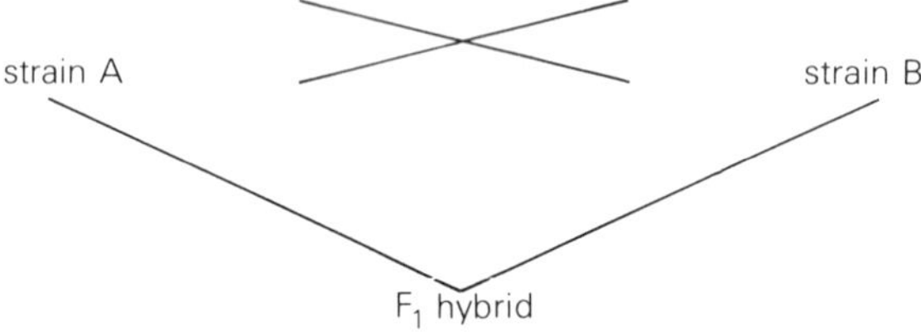

The F_1 hybrid plants are often better than either of the parent strains as they have the 'hybrid vigour' associated with first crosses.

Seeds saved from purchased F_1 hybrids often give very disappointing results. Why is this?

. . . Q.9

In addition to sexual reproduction, many plants reproduce *asexually* (non-sexual) e.g., from cuttings, tubers, runners, and other forms of *vegetative* reproduction. A plant that is grown by vegetative reproduction has only one parent and can only have the characteristics of that parent, i.e., the shape of its leaves, the colour of its flowers and so on. Such plants will be identical to the parent plant.

Investigation 4.2

(This is a long-term investigation but is easily completed in one school year if begun in the autumn.)

1. Select a large *Coleus:*

These Coleus *plants have been grown from seed and are all different*

2. Remove all shoots except the leader, cutting them through a node with a very sharp knife, to a length of about 60 mm.

These three Coleus *plants have been grown from cuttings from the same plant and are therefore all similar*

3. Fill a 225 mm pan with wet, coarse sand. Insert the cuttings in the sand, to a depth of 30 mm and spaced 70 mm apart; water and cover with a ploche.
4. When the cuttings have rooted, plant them individually in 80 mm pots containing John Innes compost.
5. Allow the parent plant to flower, and collect the seed.
6. Sow the seeds, in a pot of John Innes seed compost, as thinly as possible and no more than 2 mm deep. Cover the pot with a piece of glass and a sheet of paper.
7. Examine the pot each day and as soon as the seeds germinate, remove the covers.
8. When the seedlings are large enough to handle, plant them individually in 80 mm pots.
9. Grow the seedlings on and compare them with the plants grown from cuttings.

The plants grown from cuttings will have very similar colours and patterns on their leaves. The plants grown from seeds will have a variety of colours and patterns on their leaves.

Many new varieties of plants are produced by *cross-pollinating* (see below) and growing the resulting seeds. If a plant with special qualities results, it is propagated by vegetative means to retain these qualities. It was by this method that, during the last century, a country vicar grew Cox's Orange Pippin apples:

Rev. Cox sows many apple pips.

Several years later, he selects a tree, from the many that grew from his pips, that has a very good dessert fruit.

Cuttings and buds are taken from the original Cox's Orange Pippin, to grow other trees with the same characteristics.

Today thousands of Cox's Orange Pippin trees are grown, all propagated from the original tree (or rather from trees that were themselves propagated in this way). The Rev. Cox was lucky – one of his pips happened to have excellent qualities. Today, plant breeders understand how inheritance works and their breeding is based upon scientific principles discovered by an

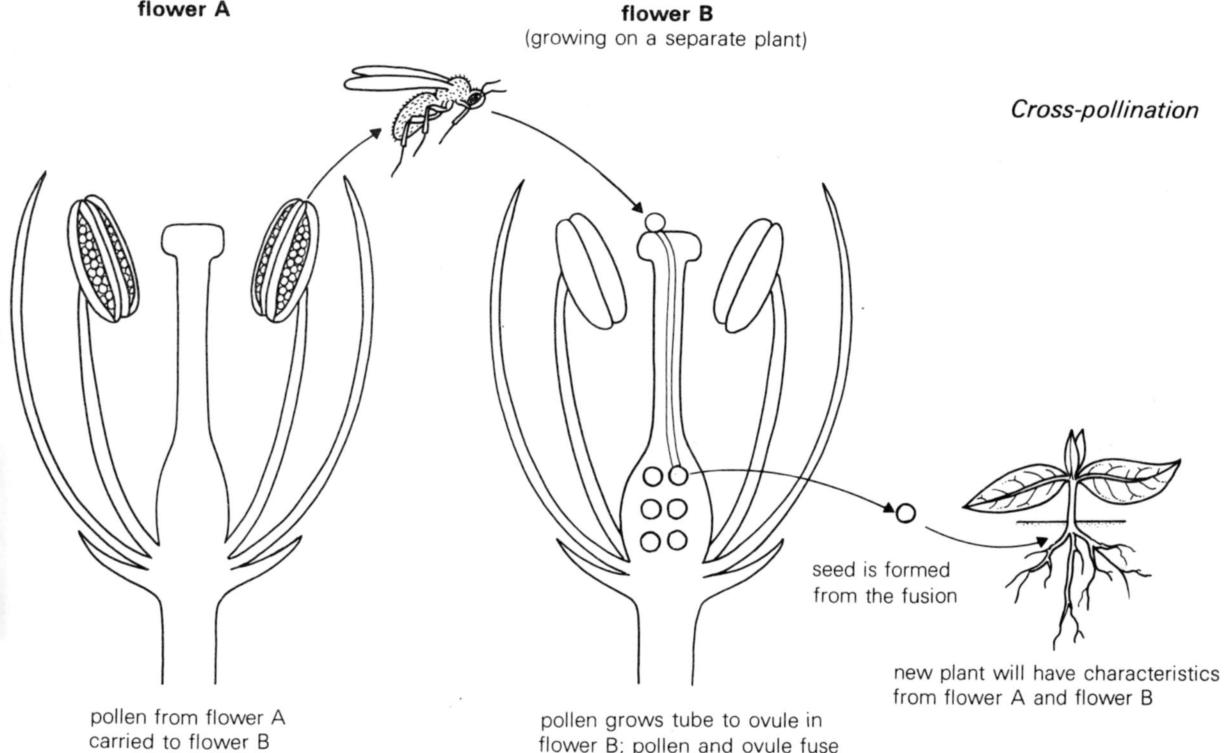

Cross-pollination

An orchard of Cox's Orange Pippins

Austrian monk, Gregor Mendel (1822–1884). Working with garden peas Mendel discovered:

1. An ovule carries a set of chemical 'messages' that determines the characteristics of the next generation.
2. A pollen grain carries a similar set of messages; Mendel called these 'messages' *genes*.
3. One gene governs one characteristic (e.g., there is a gene for plant height, one for leaf shape, one for flower colour and so on).
4. Some genes are more powerful than others. Mendel called the powerful genes *dominant* and the weaker genes *recessive*.
5. Each plant contains *two* genes for each characteristic – one from the pollen grain and one from the ovule, i.e., one from each parent.
6. A plant has two sets of genes: each pollen grain will carry only one set; each ovule will carry only one set. Thus pollen grains and ovules from the same plant will carry different sets of genes.
7. When a pollen grain and an ovule fuse during fertilisation, each contributes a set of genes, giving the seed (and hence the new plant) two sets of genes.

Example

(considering only one characteristic – *tallness*)

1. Crossing: two tall pure-bred plants. Gene for tall = T (capital T because tallness is dominant):

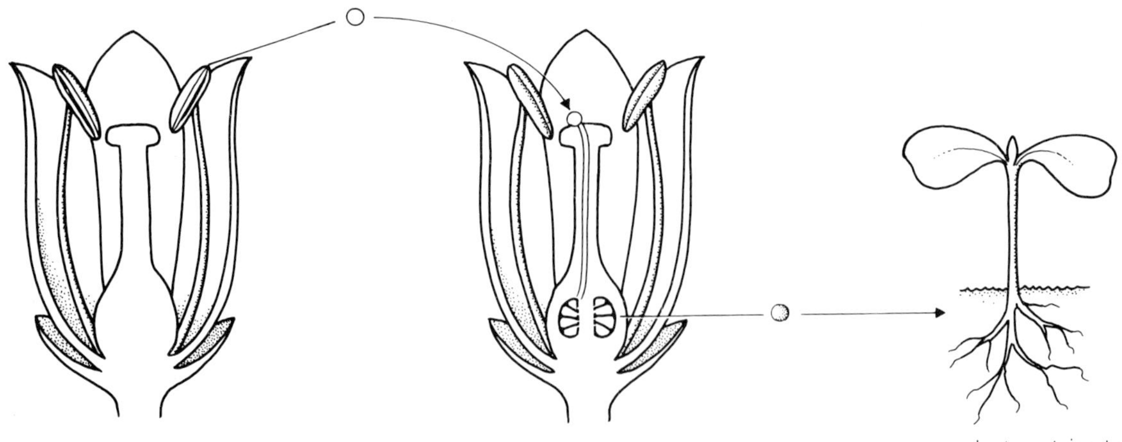

2. Crossing: two dwarf pure-bred plants. Gene for dwarf = t (lower case t because dwarf is recessive):

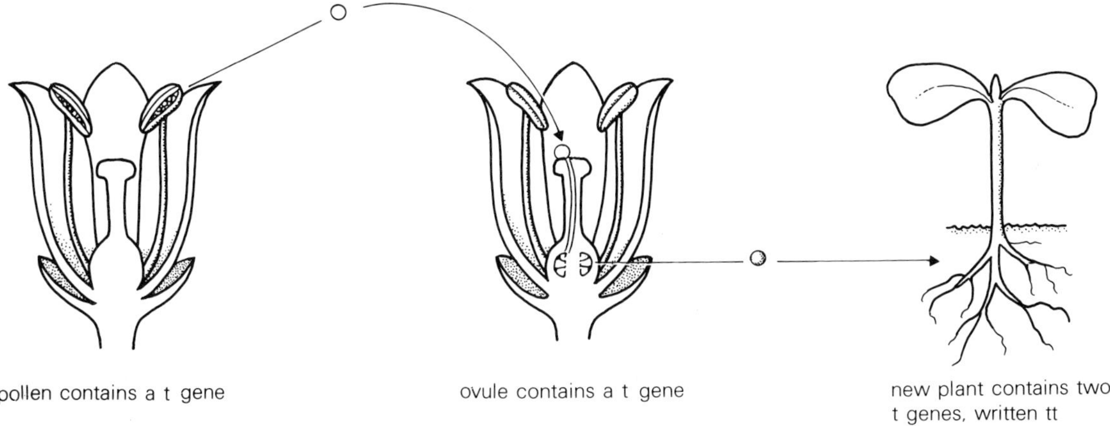

3. Crossing: a tall pure-bred plant with a dwarf pure-bred plant:

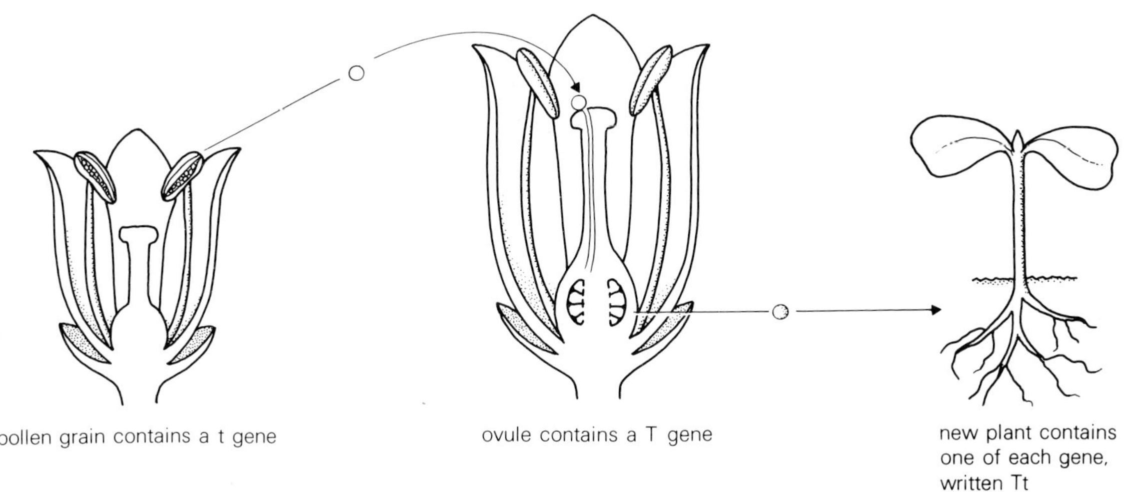

The new plant, in (3) above, contains two different genes, one to make the plant tall and the other to do just the opposite, which make the plant dwarf. In this situation the new plant will *not* be medium sized, it will be tall. The new plant is tall because the T gene is dominant.

What is the first cross between two pure breeds called? . . . Q.10

In peas, the gene that gives rise to red-coloured flowers is dominant, and the gene that gives rise to white-coloured flowers is recessive.

What colour flowers will result from crossing two pure white-flowered plants? . . . Q.11
What coloured flowers will result from crossing a pure white pea with a pure red-flowered pea? . . . Q.12

During this experiment, Mendel cross-bred the F_1 hybrids to produce an F_2 generation:

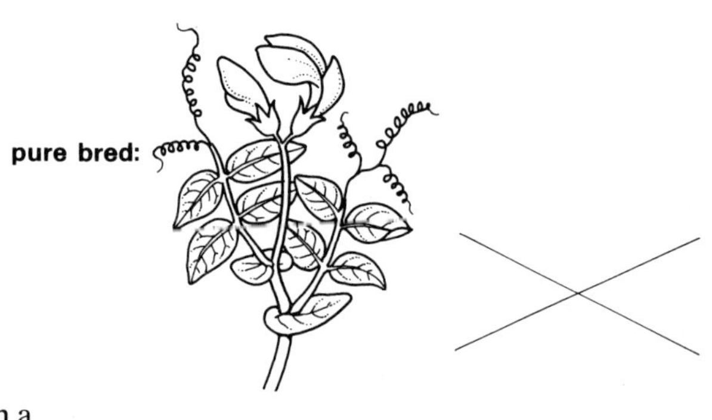

The F_1 hybrids contain a mixture of genes, and half the pollen will contain T genes and the other half will contain t genes. Similarly, in the ovary, half the ovules will contain T genes and the other half will contain t genes. Crossing two F_1 hybrids:

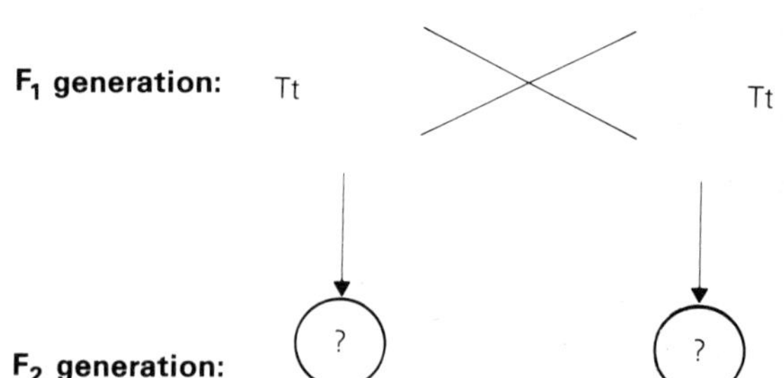

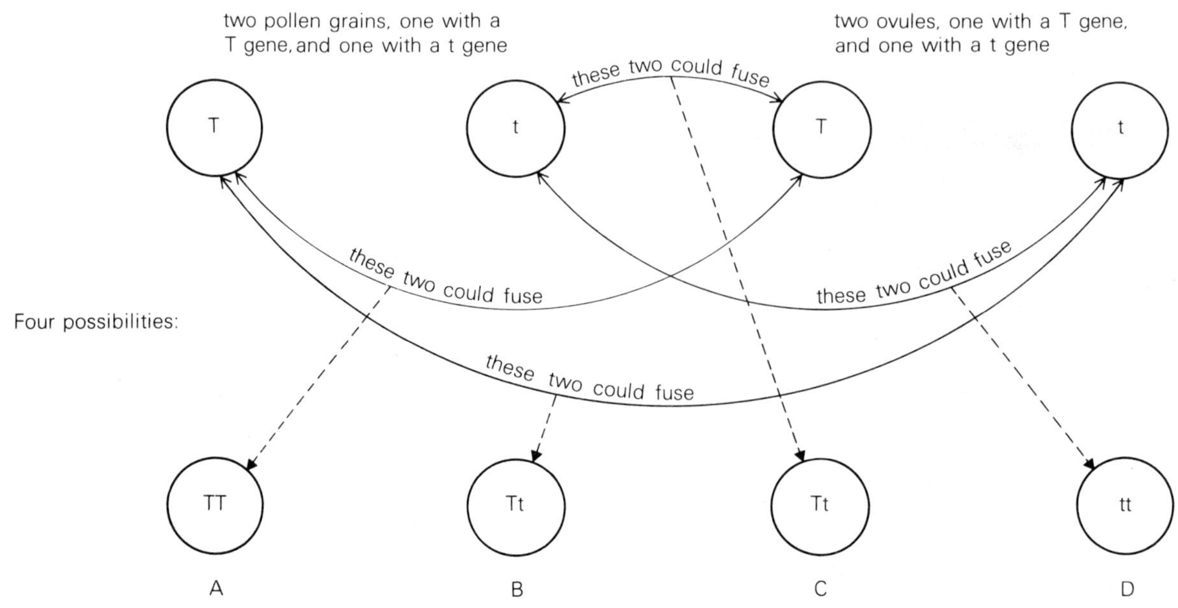

Plant A will be tall; plant B will be tall; plant C will be tall; and plant D will be dwarf (although both parent plants are tall). In the F_2 generation there are three tall plants for every one dwarf plant.

If 800 F_2 generation plants were grown, how many would be tall? . . . Q.13

A few years ago the deep freeze trade wanted a variety of pea with the following characteristics:

1. Dwarf plants.
2. Resistant to disease.
3. Wrinkled seeds.
4. Bearing two pods on each stalk.

There were several varieties of peas with one or two of these characteristics, but none with all four. The four characteristics were found in four different varieties of peas, including a wild pea from Afghanistan. Using Mendel's principles, cross-pollination and very careful recording, the plant breeders bred the four required characteristics into a single variety of pea. The garden pea is a good subject for this type of work as the flowers are self-fertile and usually self-pollinate.

In animal breeding, the ova and sperm carry genes in exactly the same way – Mendel's laws and the principles of breeding apply equally to animals and plants.

The cattle in the photograph below are cross breeds of several different breeds of cows; in every case the sire was a Hereford.

What dominant characteristics does a Hereford bull carry? . . . Q.14

Questions: Further plant science

1. Write single sentences to answer the following questions:
   (a) To which *family* does the onion belong?
   (b) What does the Latin word, *vulgaris* mean?
   (c) How do the contents of a pollen grain reach the ovule?
   (d) What is an F_1 hybrid?
   (c) Which plant did Gregor Mendel use in his experiments?
   (f) Are the cereal crop plants monocotyledons or dicotyledons?
   (g) What is meant by self-pollination?

2. A species of garden flower has both red and white varieties. If a pure white is pollinated with pollen from a pure red, all F_1 generation plants have red flowers.
   (a) What colour will the flowers be in the F_2 generation?
   (b) What colour will flowers be, if they are grown from seed that was saved from a white flower, that was pollinated from an F_1 hybrid?

3. With words and diagrams show that you understand the difference between pollination and fertilisation in flowers.

4. (a) By reference to either the Cruciferae or the Leguminosae, briefly explain the meaning of the terms *genus*, *species* and *variety*.
   (b) State the chief characteristics of the family you select.

5. The diagram opposite shows a vertical section of a flower.
   (a) Write down each of the following words on a separate line: POLLINATION, FERTILISATION, PROTECTION OF THE FLOWER. and opposite write the numbers that correspond to the parts of flower involved.
   (b) How do you think pollination is achieved in this flower? Give a reason for your answer.
   (c) Name the structures numbered 1 to 4.
   (d) What happens to parts 2, 3, 5, after fertilisation has been completed? (*W.M.E.B.*)

6. In pigs, the genetic character, smallness, is dominant over that of largeness (recessive character).

   A farmer has a small-sized sow which he wants to mate with a large boar, in an attempt to improve the general size of his herd.
   (a) What sized pigs would be produced from the first litter?
   (b) If he continued to mate the large-sized boar with some of the gilts from the first litter, would he produce any small- or large-sized pigs?
   (c) What problems might arise when using the same boar in two successive generations?
   (d) From this example, do you think it is easy or hard for a pig farmer to improve the size of his pigs? Give your reasons. (*W.M.E.B.*)

7. (a) Describe how you can recognize monocotyledon and dicotyledon plants by an examination of the leaves, flowers and seeds.
   (b) Classify the following plants as either dicotyledon or monocotyledon: meadow grass, dandelion, onion, snowdrop, primrose, cabbage, daffodil, buttercup. (*W.M.E.B.*)

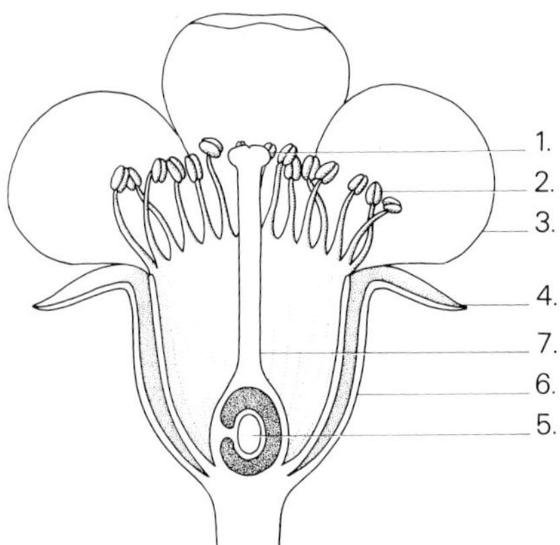

5 Pigs

One-third of all the meat consumed in this country is from the pig. U.K. farmers send 15 000 000 pigs for slaughter each year, providing almost all the pork and half the bacon we eat (pork is fresh pig meat, and bacon is pig meat that has been preserved by either salting or smoking).

Other products include pork pies, sausages, black pudding, bacon burgers, luncheon meat, bacon and leather. Not all of the pig is good to eat (see chart on page 92).

By referring to the chart on page 92, say what is the total weight of food in a 100 kg pig? . . Q.1

The pig was domesticated thousands of years ago by the cave dwellers of the late Stone Age (Neolithic man). These pigs were bred from the local wild pig (*Sus scrofa*), and were the ancestors of the pigs kept in large herds in the oak forests by the Anglo-Saxons. The forest pig would obtain much of its own food by digging up the earth with its strong snout in the search for grubs and roots, and to supplement, acorns, beech mast and other seeds which fell from the trees.

As the forests were felled, the large herds of pigs disappeared. Instead, most farmers kept a few pigs to utilise waste products, which included: skim milk from butter making, whey from cheese making, unsaleable corn from cereal growers and, later, small and damaged potatoes

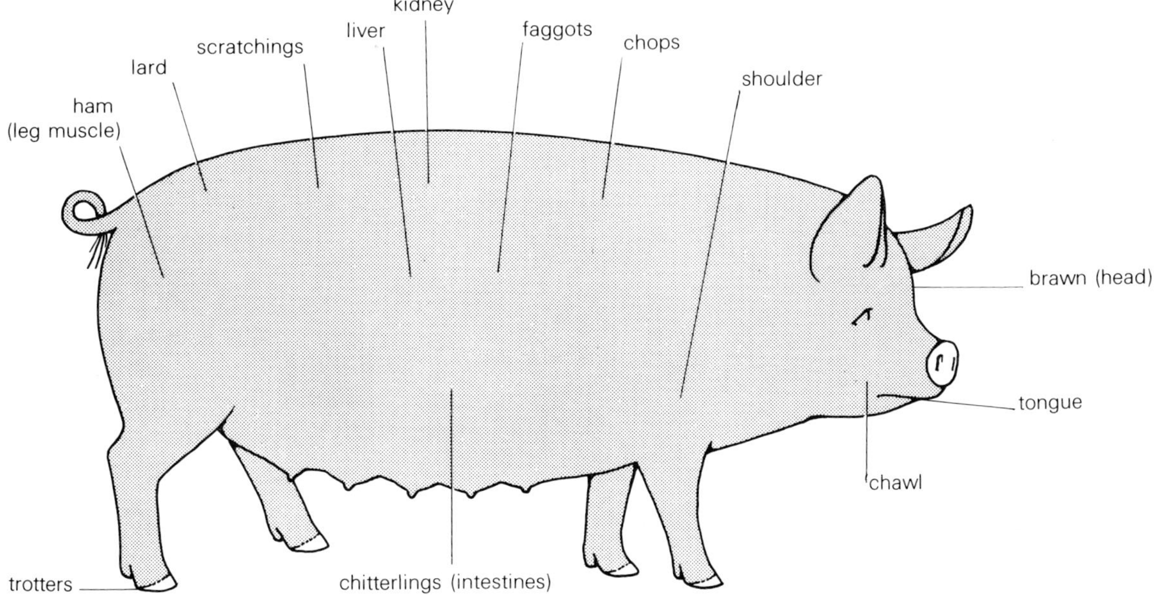

Pig products

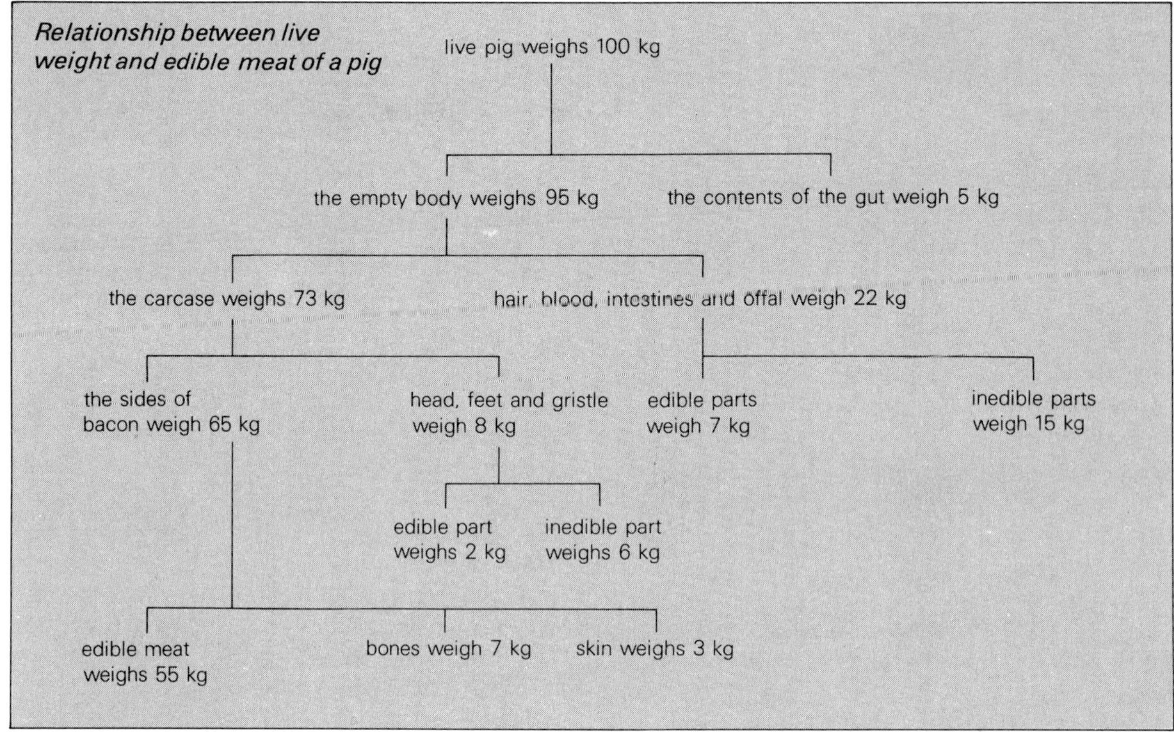

from potato growers. The diet of these pigs was supplemented with peas and beans grown for the purpose, and husks from the milling of wheat.

The practice of keeping a few pigs on every farm continued until the 1960s after which time the pig gradually disappeared from the mixed farms and the industry became more specialised. By 1980 most pig herds had over 100 breeding sows, and during this time the number of pig breeders had fallen from 80 000 to 20 000:

Herd size	*Percentage of total sows and in-pig gilts*			
sows and in-pig gilts	*1963*	*1968*	*1975*	*1980*
1–19	53	34	13	10
20–49	26	28	18	11
50–99	12	20	24	27
Over 100	9	18	45	52
Number of farms	80 000	52 000	25 000	20 000

Pig keeping is now an industry based upon scientific principles and pig farmers have many thousands of pounds invested in both stock and equipment.

The breeds

Large white

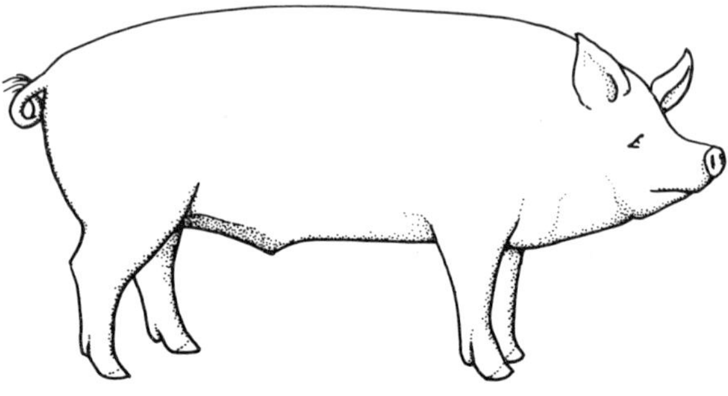

Large white pig

Developed in Yorkshire this breed makes a good bacon pig by the age of seven months, it is a prolific breeder (litters of over 10 are common). Mature boars weigh half a tonne when fattened.

Middle white

Bred by crossing the large white with pigs imported from China (*Sus indicus*). Matures rapidly and makes a good pork pig.

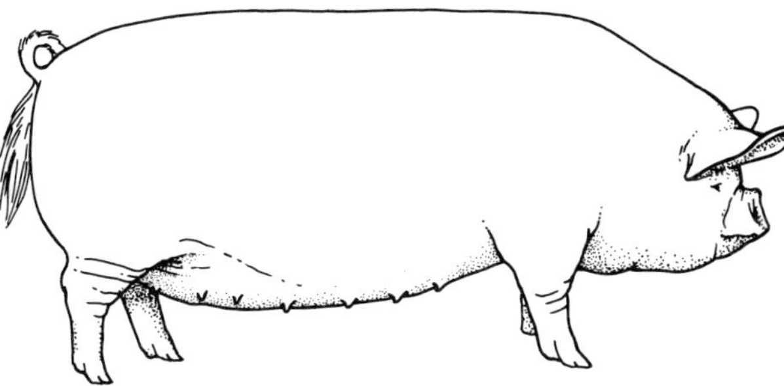

Middle white sow

Large black

Large black boar

An old breed from Devon and Cornwall; except for colour, similar in many ways to the Large white, although they have the disadvantage of smaller litters and less smooth flesh. A docile breed with good mothering qualities.

British saddleback

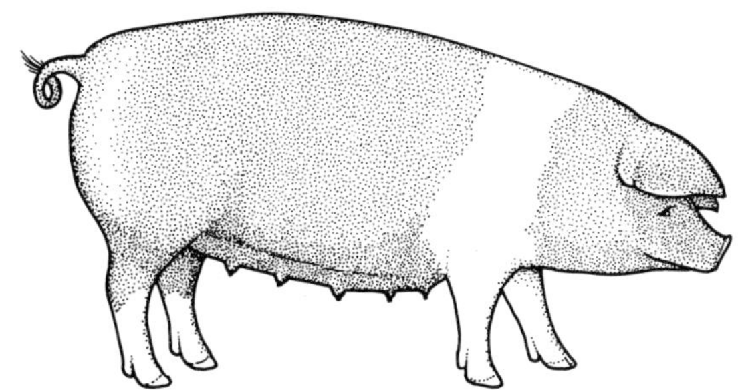

British saddleback sow

Formed from two once popular breeds (Wessex saddleback and Essex saddleback) with very good mothering qualities. The carcase has a greater proportion of fat than the Large white. In common with other black breeds, it is less likely to suffer from sun stroke.

Landrace

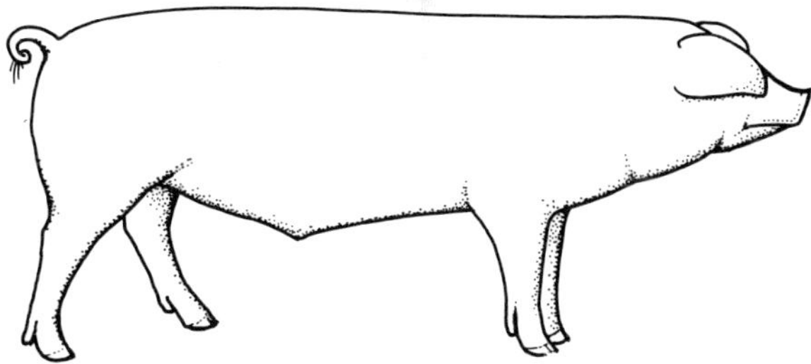

Landrace boar

In 1949 the Swedish Landrace was imported. This long lean bacon pig was quickly accepted by British farmers as the chart shows:

	Number of boars in England and Wales	
Breed	*1954*	*1960*
Large white	19 051	12 703
Wessex saddleback	1371	715
Essex saddleback	1031	351
Large black	620	253
Welsh	985	342
Landrace	251	5356

Other pig breeds have been imported but have failed to compare well with existing breeds; these include the Pietrain from Belgium, the Lacombe from Canada, the Duroc and the Hampshire from America.

Although the most important breeds are the Large white and the Landrace, many farmers use cross-bred sows with pure-bred boars. Cross-breds have hybrid vigour and the litters are 10% heavier than pure-bred litters at the age of six weeks.

Housing for pigs

The majority of pigs in the U.K. are kept indoors throughout their lives. Pigs being fattened for market make better use of the food they eat if they are housed in dry, warm and draught-free houses.

Pregnant sows are often housed in the type of stall shown overleaf, here there can be no fighting and each animal will receive its fair share of food.

Stall for pregnant sows

Farrowing crate: a mother suckling her young

Open-fronted pens

Close-up view of an open-fronted pen

The sows are moved to farrowing crates a week or so before their litters are due to be born. A farrowing crate is designed to prevent the sow from crushing her babies as she lies down as they can escape under the rail. An electric pig lamp provides warmth and the piglets lie underneath this when they are not feeding.

After two weeks or so in the farrowing crates, the sows and litters are moved to other types of housing. These open-fronted pens allow plenty of exercise and fresh air. At the rear are enclosed pens with small entrances, through which the piglets can pass but not the sow. These are called *creeps*; nutritious food is available *ad lib* in the creeps, which increases the growth rate of the piglets.

Task 5.1

Using the figures from the charts below, draw two line graphs, one showing how the piglet's food consumption increases with age, and the other showing the piglet's increase in weight (in both graphs put age, in weeks, along the horizontal axis).

Food consumption in creep by single piglet, food provided ad lib

Age of piglet (weeks)	1	2	3	4	5	6	7	8
Food eaten per day (g)	0	10	70	140	200	300	550	750

Weight of piglet

Age of piglet (weeks)	1	2	3	4	5	6	7	8
Weight (kg)	2	5	7	9	12	15	18	20

After the age of eight weeks, food is usually restricted, and supplied in two feeds each day. Many farmers do not use troughs, and the dry food is supplied on the floor; this is made possible by the clean habits of the pig as they lay their dung in only one corner of the pen. Water is always available from a nozzle which the pigs operate.

Food

Pigs are kept to convert animal food into food for human beings. The pig eats about 3 kg of food for each kg of weight increase (this is an average figure). Pigs kept under poor conditions will need more food than pigs kept under ideal conditions. The amount of food required to produce 1 kg of weight gain is called the *food conversion ratio.*

Food conversion ratio

$$= \frac{\text{weight of food eaten}}{\text{increase in weight of the pig}}$$

The food conversion ratio of a 100 kg pig that had eaten 300 kg of food during its life would be:

$$\frac{300}{100} = 3$$

A litter of pigs weighed 200 kg when weaned, and 1000 kg when slaughtered. If from weaning to slaughter they consumed 2800 kg of food, what was the food conversion ratio of the litter?

. . . Q.2

Pigs are not able to digest grass, hay or straw and must be fed on other types of food, including barley, wheat, oats, maize, fish meal, meat meal, soya beans and groundnuts. Many items of the pigs' diet are waste products from the food industry, e.g., the husks (bran) from wheat that is milled into flour. The pig food is ground into meal and pressed into pellets or nuts. The contents of each mix are analysed to make sure that the nutrients in the food are correctly balanced, to ensure a good rate of growth; minerals and vitamins are also added.

Analysis of pig food

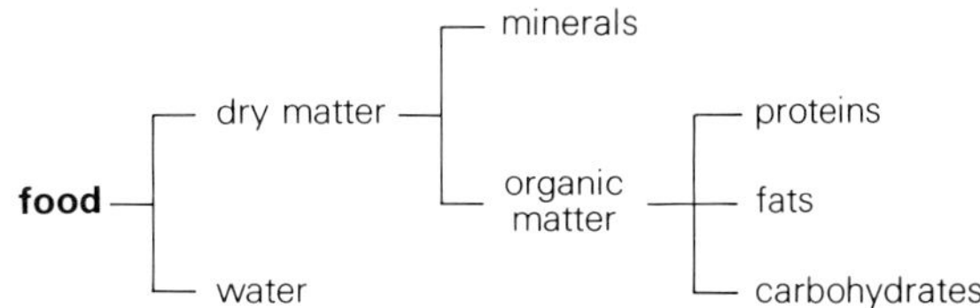

Minerals
Minerals, such as calcium, phosphorus and iron, are necessary in very small quantities for the body to function properly. Pigs living outside obtain many of the minerals they require from the soil,

Pig nuts and creep feed pellets

but pigs kept inside have to have all their minerals provided in their food. If a pig is short of the mineral iron, its blood loses its colour and the animal becomes anaemic. Sows' milk is deficient in iron, and pigs reared inside receive an injection of iron shortly after birth. This syringe injects a measured dose and holds enough to inject 25 piglets without refilling.

Piglets reared outside are not injected with iron. Why not? . . . Q.3

Proteins
The protein is the most expensive part of the food and it provides materials for growth of muscle (the lean meat of the pig).

Fats and carbohydrates
Starch and sugar provide the energy that keeps the pig active and warm.

Daily intake of food by a sow

The sow's food intake varies according to whether she is pregnant or nursing as shown in the graph:

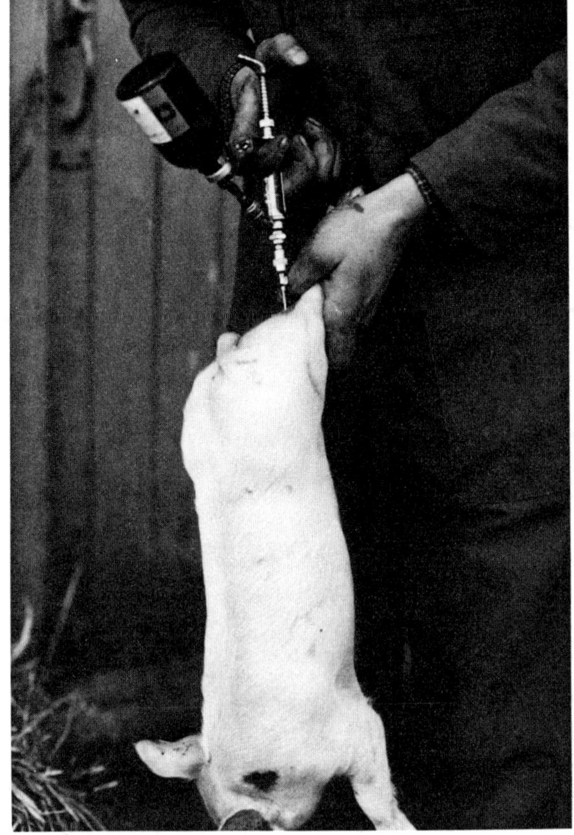

Injecting a piglet with iron

How much food per day does the sow receive during:
(a) the first part of her pregnancy;
(b) the second part of her pregnancy? . . . Q.4
What is the maximum amount of food the sow receives in any one day? . . . Q.5
What happens to the extra food given to the sow after farrowing? . . . Q.6

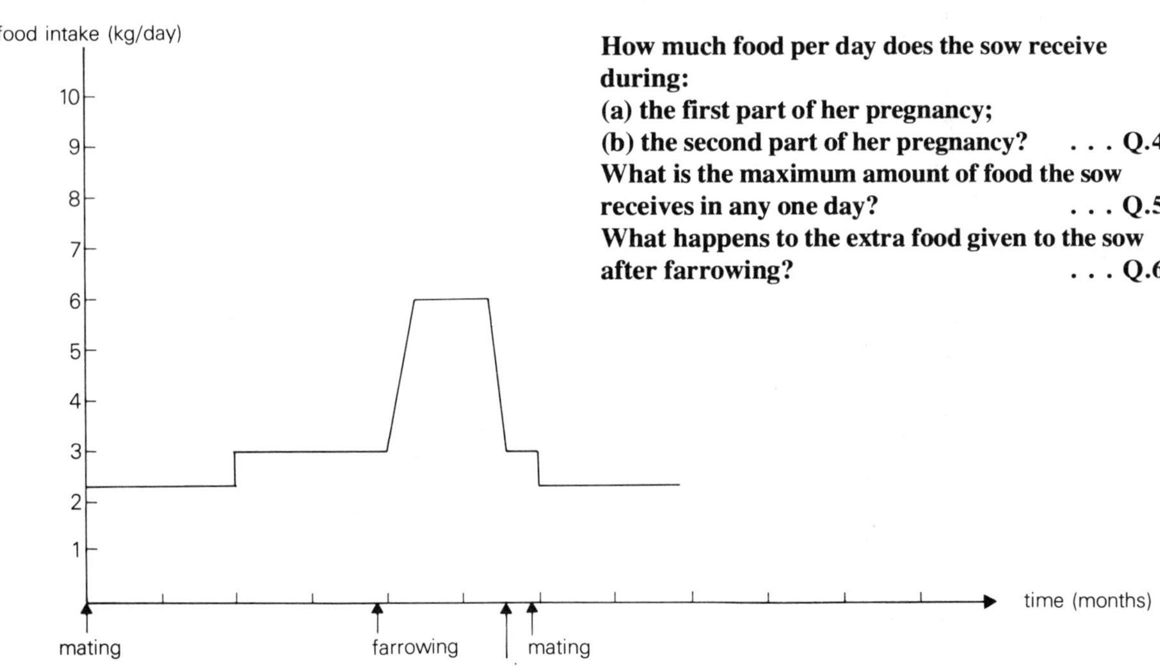

Food intake of a sow

The life of pigs

1. A pig kept for pork

The pork pig suckles its mother within an hour or so of birth; the liquid it receives is not milk but *colostrum* ('milk' produced only during the first few days after birth) which contains substances to protect the young from disease. The piglet always feeds from the same teat – any unoccupied teat the sow has soon ceases to function. Most of the piglet's time is spent lying under a warm pig lamp with its brothers and sisters. After a day or so mother's secretions change to milk, which is creamy and rich in protein. The amount of milk mother produces increases daily for the first three weeks of the piglet's life, after which it begins to reduce. However, the piglet does not go hungry, as there is a constant supply of very nutritious meal in the creep where the piglets can go but mother cannot. The piglet soon learns to operate the nipple on the water bowl and obtains drinks of clean, cold water.

As soon as the piglet is six weeks old, the mother is taken away (a process known as *weaning*), and the piglet has to be content with twice-daily feeds of pig nuts, which are dropped upon the floor. There is plenty of food, and after each feed the piglet spends a good deal of time resting with the other pigs.

After the age of four months the pig is weighed each week, and as soon as it 'tips the scales' at 50 kg, it is sent to the slaughter house.

2. The bacon pig

The life of the bacon pig is similar to that of the pork pig except that it is kept for some two months longer to reach 70 kg (the weight required by the bacon curers). Some pigs are kept until they weigh 100 kg – these are used partly for bacon and partly for other products.

3. The mother pig

The mother pig lives for about four years – she is known as a *gilt*, until she has reared her first litter, and afterwards as a *sow*. Breeding gilts are selected from the best mothers. The stock man making the selection considers the following points:

1. The number of teats – a breeding gilt must have at least 14 well-placed teats.
2. Length of body – this is an inherited characteristic. A pig with a long body will produce long-bodied piglets, if mated to the correct boar (a long pig will produce more slices of bacon than a short pig).
3. Rate of growth – the breeding gilt must have grown a little more rapidly than her brothers and sisters.
4. Temperament – a quiet and docile pig makes a much better mother than an excitable one.
5. The gilt should have sound feet and legs and a good health record.

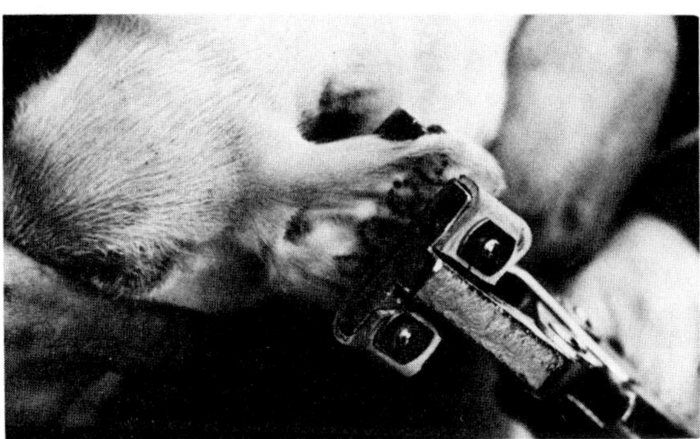

Pedigree pigs have their own numbers tatooed in an ear

After selection, the gilt is kept outside, in well-fenced fields, where she will get plenty of exercise and access to grass. Feed is restricted to maintain a good growth rate without making the animal too fat.

When the gilt is large enough, usually at eight months of age, she is put with the boar. Mating will only take place when the gilt is on heat – this happens once every three weeks during the oestrous cycle. At this time the vulva becomes large and red, and the gilt will stand still and allow the boar to mount her. If mating is successful, there will be no further heat period until after the young are born and weaned.

During the gestation period, which lasts for about 115 days, the gilt is housed with other pregnant animals, the rations are restricted to prevent over fatness and, if no grass is available, these rations are fortified with vitamins and minerals.

A week or so before *farrowing* (giving birth) the gilt is moved to her farrowing quarters. To make the birth as easy as possible some wet bran, or other laxative is fed to the gilt for a day or two before birth. The actual birth process is not usually difficult, as piglets are very small compared with the size of the mother. As the piglets arrive they are removed and put under a pig lamp. The *placenta* (afterbirth) is then discharged, usually with the last piglet, which may be smothered by the placenta if the pig man is not there to remove it. When birth is complete, the piglets are put on the mother for their first feed of colostrum.

A litter of pigs being weighed as they are weaned – the best sows produce the heaviest litters

Six weeks later, when the piglets are weaned, the mother (now called a *sow*) is taken to the boar and mated during the following week. The sow is therefore either pregnant or nursing for the rest of her life. After she has raised six litters (about sixty young in all), the sow is too large and clumsy to be a reliable mother, and is fattened and sold. The meat from a sow is low quality and is used to make sausages and pork pies.

How many piglets will a sow rear in one year if the average number is ten per litter? . . . Q.7

4. The boar

One boar is kept for every 30–40 sows, and, as he may father over 5000 pigs during his lifetime, the boar must be selected with very great care. The boar is reared in the same way as a bacon pig until he becomes fertile at the age of six months – after this time he is usually housed on his own. The boar house should be warm and comfortable, with a good area of concrete for exercise – this will keep the animal fit and its feet in good condition. The boar receives the same type of food as the sows and is allowed 3 kg each day whilst working (if this is increased he tends to become fat). The canine teeth grow into tusks as the boar gets older – these can be dangerous to man as well as to the sows, and are usually removed by a veterinary surgeon. The Meat and Livestock Commission (a government body) operates a number of boar-testing schemes, in an attempt to improve the national stock. The young produced by certain boars are tested for the following points.:

1. The size of the litters.
2. The rate of growth.
3. The food conversion rate.
4. The quality of the carcase.
5. The percentage of lean meat compared with the percentage of fat (the depth of fat is measured on the live animal with an echo-sounding instrument).
6. The killing-out percentage (the weight of the carcase compared with the weight of the live animal: the killing out percentage of a pork pig is about 75%).

Each boar being tested is given a mark for his offsprings' performance, the average mark is 100 and any boar scoring less than 90 is slaughtered. The boars that score the highest marks are used in nucleus herds which provide the breeding stock for commercial farmers.

The biology of the pig

A healthy pig at rest has:

(a) A temperature of 39°C
(b) A respiration rate of 10–12 per min.
(c) A pulse rate of 70–80 per min (the pulse is felt inside the thigh if the pig is not too fat).
(d) A gestation period of 3 months 3 weeks 3 days.
(e) An oestrous cycle (female sex cycle) of 21 days, and heat period lasts for 2–3 days.

Teeth

The pig's tooth has an internal structure similar to that of other mammals:

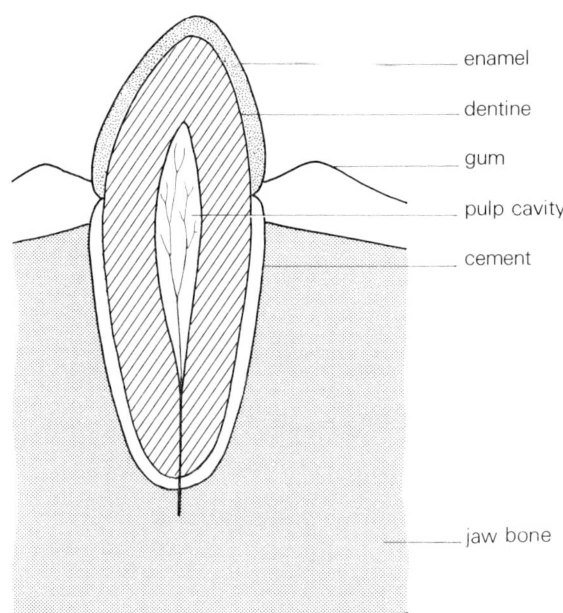

The cement holds the tooth firmly in the jaw.
The enamel is a hard, white material which wears away very slowly.
The dentine is similar in structure to bone; it forms the skeleton of the tooth and, if exposed, wears away much more quickly than enamel.
The pulp contains the blood supply and the nerves of the tooth.

Although similar in structure, the arrangement of teeth in the mouth varies considerably in different species, to suit their particular diet. Teeth are named according to their position in the mouth:

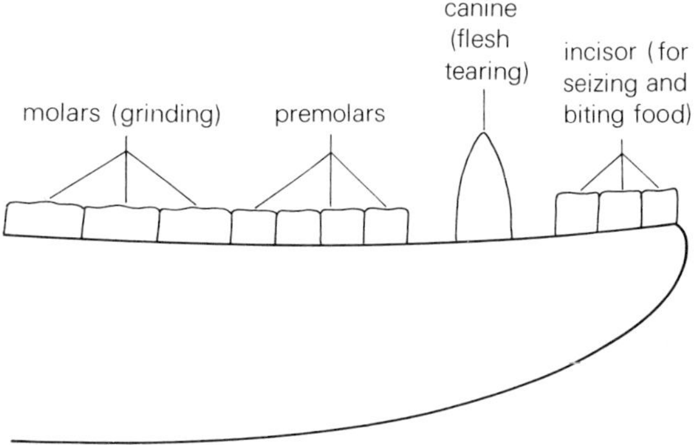

By the time a pig is 18 months old it has the following teeth:

	Incisor	*Canine*	*Premolar*	*Molar*
Upper Jaw	6	2	8	6
Lower Jaw	6	2	8	6

This can be written as a *dental formula*. A dental formula indicates, for a given species of mammal, the number of each kind of its teeth. The number in the upper jaw of one side is written above that in the lower jaw of one side; and the categories are given in the order: incisors, canines, premolars, molars. The dental formula of a typical pig is:

$$i\,\frac{3\text{–}3}{3\text{–}3}\qquad c\,\frac{1\text{–}1}{1\text{–}1}\qquad p\,\frac{4\text{–}4}{4\text{–}4}\qquad m\,\frac{3\text{–}3}{3\text{–}3}$$

The digestive system

(The digestion of the pig is very similar to that of man.)

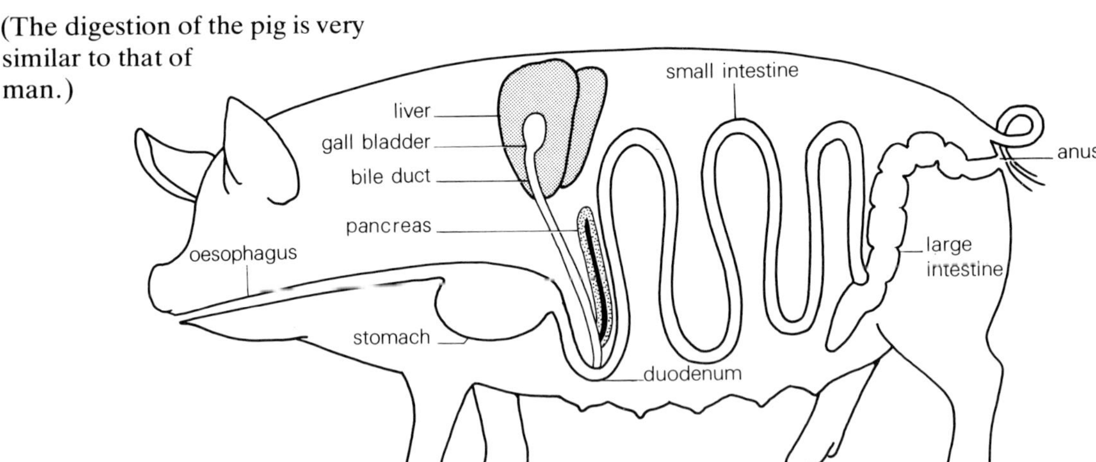

Mouth
Food is *masticated* (chewed) and mixed with saliva.

Oesophagus
Small boluses (lumps of food) are swallowed and the oesophagus pushes these down into the stomach.

Stomach
Gastric juice *secreted* (produced) from the stomach wall is mixed with the food. The gastric juice contains hydrochloric acid and *enzymes* (substances which cause chemical reactions, or speed them up). The exit from the stomach opens to allow soft food through, and closes when hard food is in that area of the stomach.

Duodenum
As the food passes along the duodenum it is neutralised by alkaline juices which flow from the gall bladder and the pancreas. The bile (from the gall bladder) causes fats to break into very small drops. The enzymes from the pancreas break large molecules in the food into much smaller ones.

Small intestine
The lining of the small intestine produce enzymes which complete the breakdown of the large molecules into smaller ones. Blood flows in vessels just under the inside wall of the intestine, and the small molecules produced by digestion pass through the wall into the blood; this process is known as *absorption*. The area of the intestinal wall through which absorption takes place is increased by hair-like projections known as *villi* (plural of villus):

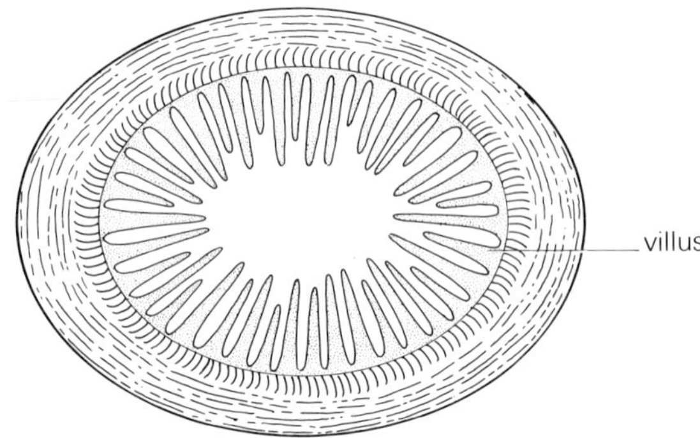

Cross section through the small intestine of a pig to show the villi

Which would give the greatest area for absorption, a long intestine or a short intestine?

. . . Q.8

Note: digested proteins and carbohydrates are carried in the blood stream to parts of the body where they will be used either for body building or for providing energy; digested fats are distributed around the body by a different system – the lymph system.

Large intestine
The large intestine is a much wider and shorter tube than the small intestine. The first part is called the *caecum*, in which some cellulose (hard plant material) is digested by bacteria; the second part is called the *colon*, in which water is removed from the fluid contents, and faeces are formed which are semi-solid.

Rectum
Faeces are stored in the rectum until they are voided through the *anus*.

Task 5.2

Compare the digestive system of the pig with that of the chicken described in Book 1. Say in what ways they are similar and in what ways they are different.

The respiratory system

Air breathed in through the mouth or nostrils enters the *trachea*, which is a flexible tube kept open by rings of cartilage; this tube divides into two smaller tubes each of which enters a lung. In the lungs, the tubes branch into hundreds of much smaller tubes, each of which ends in a very small sac. Small blood vessels (*capillaries*) carry blood around the sacs and it is here that oxygen passes through the sac wall to enter the blood stream; at the same time carbon dioxide leaves the blood, passes through the sac wall and enters the air in the lungs. Movements of the ribs and diaphragm (a sheet of muscle that separates the thorax from the abdomen) alternately increases and decreases the volume of the thorax causing air to be drawn into or exhaled from the lungs:

	Composition of air breathed in %	*Composition of air breathed out %*
Nitrogen	78.09	78.09
Oxygen	20.93	16.02
Carbon dioxide	0.03	4.38

The kidneys

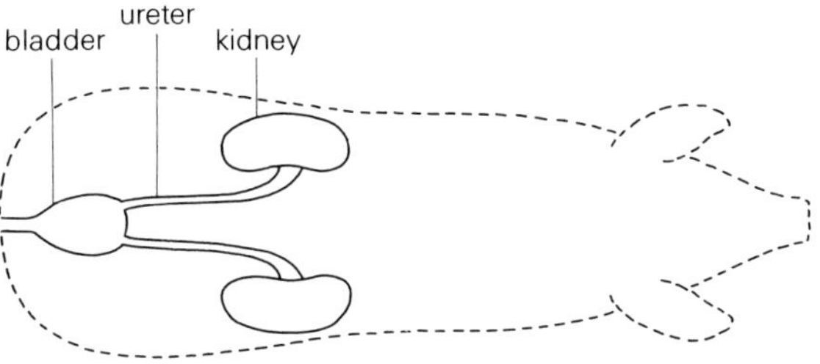

The excretory system of the pig (dorsal view)

The respiratory system of the pig (lateral view)

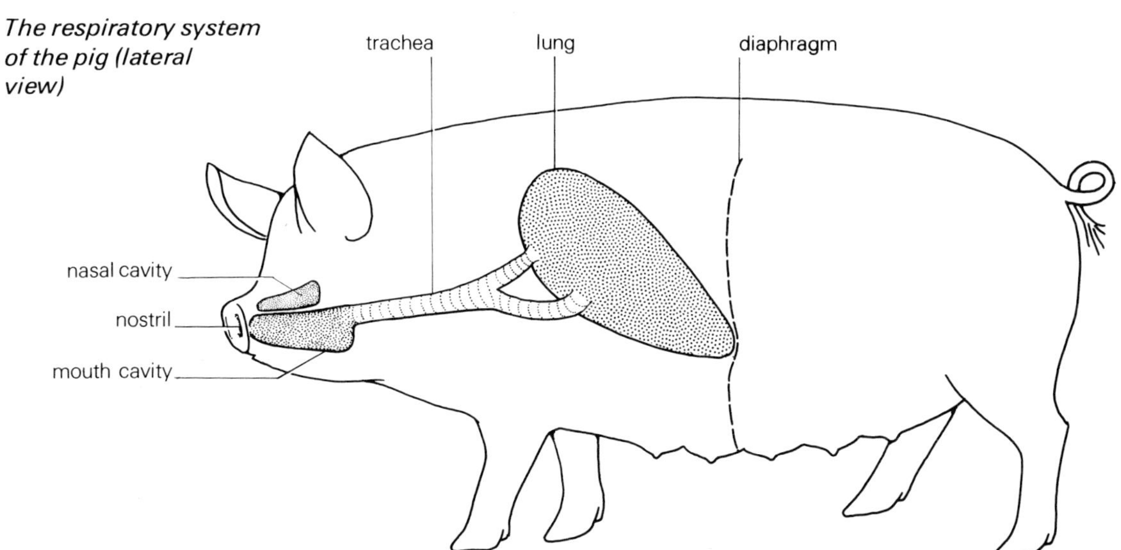

The two kidneys are held in a bed of fat, just beneath and on either side of the backbone. The function of the kidneys is to filter waste substances from the blood – these substances are formed from proteins and contain the element nitrogen. The *urine* (waste substances in water), formed in the kidneys, passes down the *ureter* to the *bladder*, where it is stored. When the bladder becomes full the animal urinates and the waste leaves the body.

The circulatory system

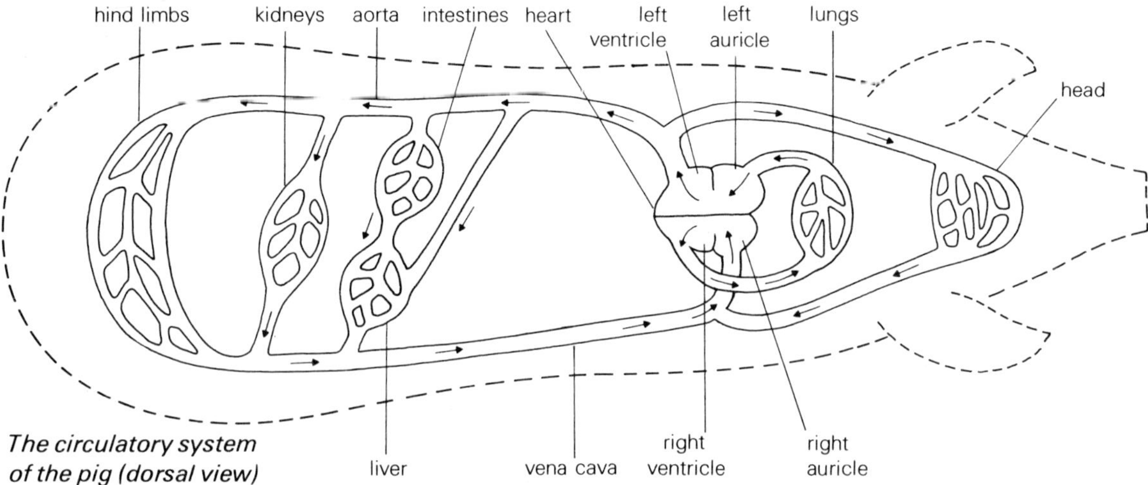

The circulatory system of the pig (dorsal view)

The blood is the main transport system within the body, it carries substances to and from the various organs. There are three types of ducts which carry blood to the body:

1. Arteries
These are thick-walled vessels which carry blood from the heart to the organs.

2. Veins
These are thin-walled vessels which carry blood from the organs back to the heart.

3. Capillaries
These are very fine ducts. It is whilst the blood is in the capillaries that substances are collected or deposited.

What substance is collected in the lungs? . . . Q.9
What substances are collected in the intestines? . . . Q.10
What substance is deposited in the lungs? . . . Q.11
Is the *vena cava* an artery or a vein? . . . Q.12
Is the *aorta* an artery or a vein? . . . Q.13

Valves through the system ensure that blood can only flow in the directions as indicated by the arrows in the diagram.

Task 5.3

Using a pencil, and taking care not to mark the book:
(a) Follow the flow of blood from the hind limbs, through the heart and back again.
(b) Follow the flow of blood from the head, through the heart, to the kidneys and back again to the head.
Note that the blood always flows through the lungs, where it picks up oxygen, before it reaches an organ where the oxygen is used up.

Task 5.4

Copy the diagram above, and colour the vessels that are carrying blood with little oxygen in blue, and colour the vessels which are carrying blood which is rich in oxygen in red.

The reproductive system

1. *Male*

During sexual excitement, the flow of blood to the penis increases, whilst the flow away from the penis is restricted. This results in the penis filling with blood, it becomes rigid, and the sigmoid flexure straightens, pushing the penis from its sheath. In this condition the penis is able to enter the vagina of the female. Sperms produced in the testes travel up the deferent duct and mix with the semen (fluid) from the seminal vesicle. The semen travels along the penis and is forcefully ejected into the vagina.

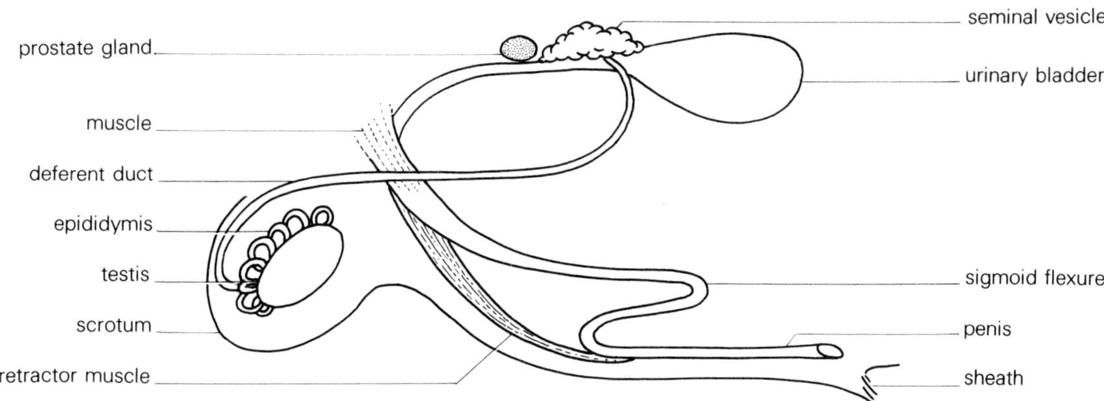

2. *Female*

Eggs released by the ovaries pass slowly down the Fallopian tubes where, if the animal has been mated, there are sperms swimming up. Each egg will fuse with a single sperm and divide in half, the halves sticking together. The division process is repeated several times and the tiny ball of cells enters the uterus where it becomes embedded, and develops into a single piglet.

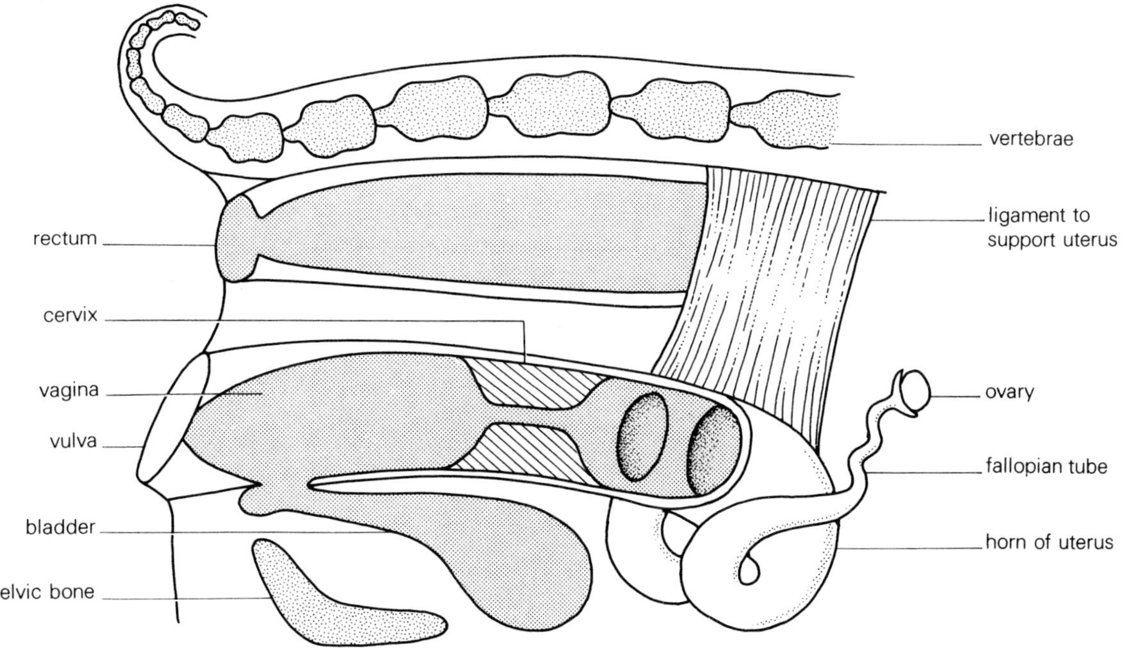

Pig health

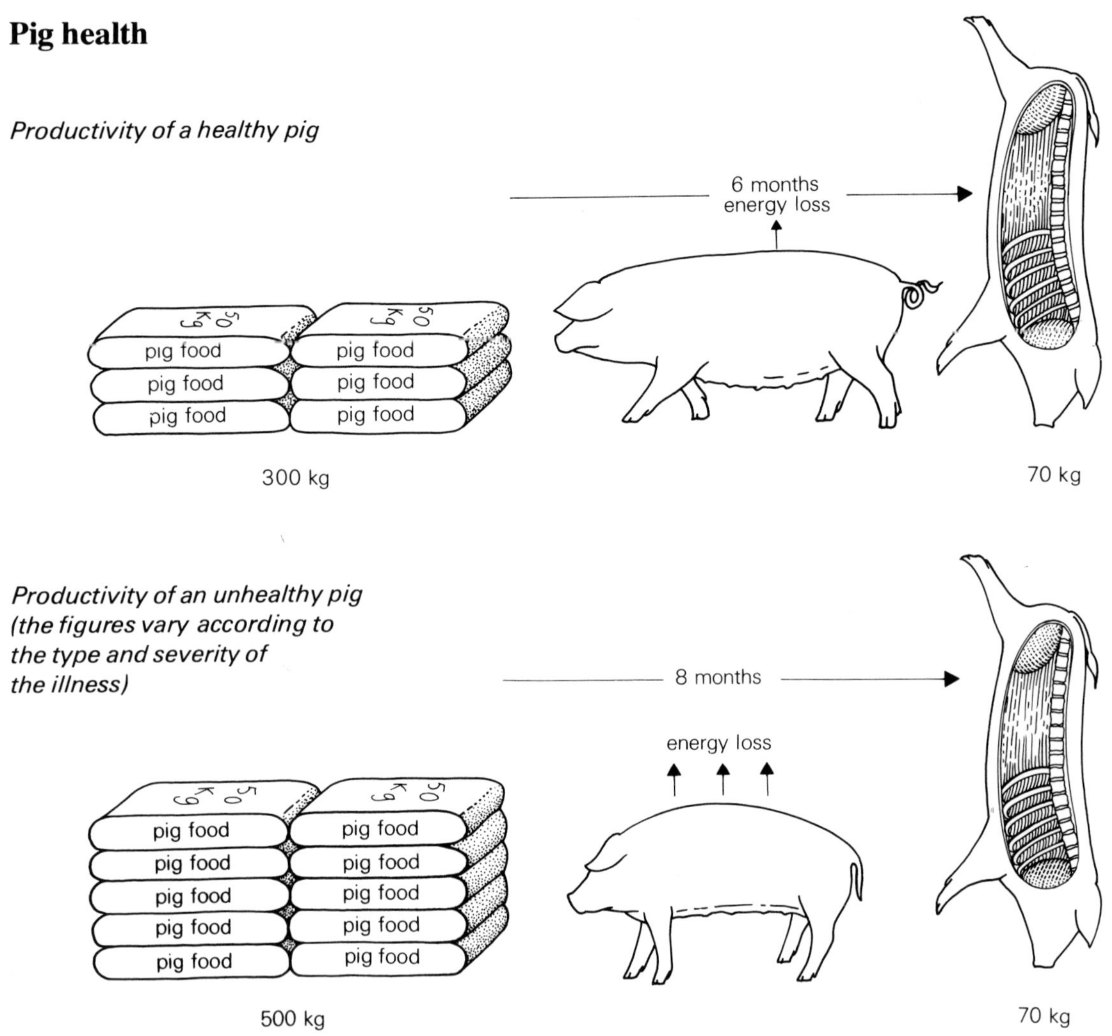

In order to produce the maximum amount of human food, from the animal food he buys, the pig farmer must keep his pigs in good health. There are many different diseases and parasites which affect pigs, the most important of which are described below.

1. Enzootic pneumonia

Fifty per cent of all pigs slaughtered in the U.K. are affected by this disease – their lungs having lesions (damage) caused by the disease. The disease is caused by a virus, which results in coughing and a high temperature; all pigs suffer from loss of appetite and some die quickly. The majority of sufferers recover, however, but their lungs will have suffered permanent damage. Unlike many virus diseases, animals which have had the disease once have built up no immunity to the disease, and are likely to become infected a second and third time. As there is no immunity it is not possible to inoculate with a vaccine to control this virus.

Many farmers have established herds free from this disease (*virus tested herds*). These herds are isolated and no one is allowed to visit who has been in contact with other pigs.

People who do visit disease-free herds are given sterile overalls and have to dip their boots in disinfectant before entering the premises. Why is this? . . . Q.14

The virus-free foundation stock from which these herds have been established was obtained by the following method:

A very good, but old, pregnant sow is slaughtered at the end of her gestation period and her uterus, complete with piglets, is removed and placed in a sterile bath. Two men pick up the bath and make a 100 metre dash away from any possible sources of infection, and tip the contents onto a disinfected table in the open air. The piglets are removed from the uterus and taken by helicopter or fast car to a farm that has no pigs and therefore no pig viruses. The piglets are artificially reared and kept isolated for the remainder of their lives. It is from these pigs that the foundation stock of the commercial virus free herds are bred.

Every three months, the lungs of slaughtered bacon pigs from the virus tested herds, are examined by a veterinary officer to make sure that they are disease-free.

2. Foreign virus diseases

The United Kingdom is free from *swine fever, swine vesicular disease* and *foot and mouth disease,* but sometimes infected material is imported from abroad and an outbreak occurs. A common source of outbreak is unboiled *swill* (kitchen waste) fed to pigs (by law all swill must be boiled for one hour before being fed). Foreign virus diseases are notifiable diseases and outbreaks must be reported *at once* to the Police or the Ministry of Agriculture, who then take the following action:

1. All infected animals are slaughtered and burned.
2. All animals that may have been in contact (including cattle and sheep in the case of foot and mouth disease) are slaughtered and used for human consumption.
3. No animal may be moved (except under licence for immediate slaughter) within a radius of ten miles.
4. The premises are thoroughly disinfected and kept free from all animals, for at least 28 days after the slaughter of the last animal.
5. During this time no unauthorised person is allowed onto the premises.

3. An internal parasite – *Ascaris lumbricoides*

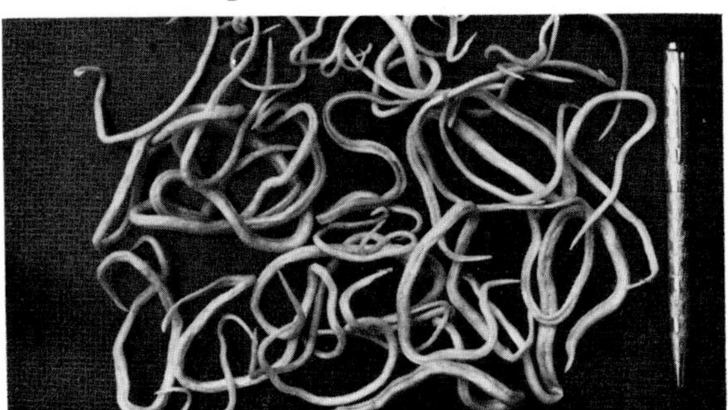

The worms in the photograph were taken from a small section of small intestine of a single pig. They are roundworms (Nematodes) – unseg-

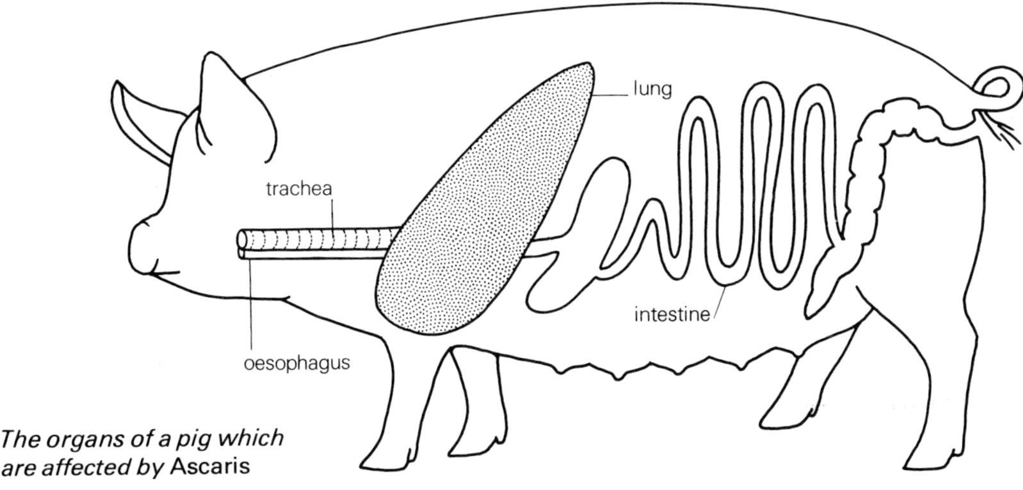

The organs of a pig which are affected by Ascaris

mented, long cylinder-shaped bodies, pointed at both ends. *Ascaris* grows to a length of 250 mm and is a very common parasite in the national pig herd. Although they live in the gut and use food which the pig would otherwise have, it is the damage they do to the lungs during their life cycle which has the greatest effect upon the health of the pig.

Life cycle of Ascaris lumbricoides
Tiny, round worm eggs are swallowed by the pig. In the intestines the eggs hatch, releasing worms less than ¼ mm long. The worms burrow through the wall of the small intestine into the blood stream, in which they are transported around the body and eventually reach the lungs. Here they leave the blood and spend time in the lungs growing to about 4 mm in length, and doing considerable damage to the lung tissue. They burrow into the air sacs and move up the trachea into the throat, where they are swallowed and enter the intestines for a second time. Inside the intestines the worms 'swim' against the flow of material through the gut and remain in more or less the same spot. They grow to full size and, after mating, the females produce many thousands of eggs which pass out with the faeces. If these are picked up by another pig the whole cycle begins again.

Control
Strict hygiene on the pig farm, isolation and dosing of bought-in pigs are good control measures against *Ascaris*. Worm powders are available, which are added to the pig's food (the dose varies according to the weight of the pig) – the worms are stunned and, being unable to swim, pass out with the faeces.

4. An external parasite – *Haematopinus suis*

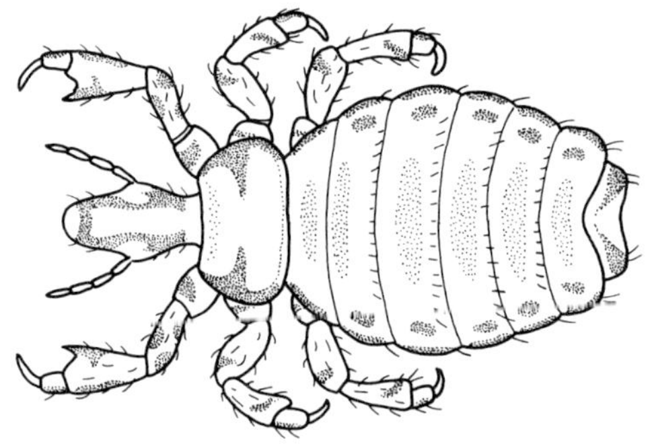

Dark spots can sometimes be seen on the back of a pig, especially close to the ears. On closer examination the 'spots' can be seen to be moving – they are lice. Lice are insects which have become adapted to biting or sucking. The pig louse (*Haematopinus suis*) is a large sucking insect, which grows to a diameter of about 5 mm. The lice cause intense itching and seriously reduce the pig's growth rate. In severe cases, young pigs die from loss of blood. Lice attach their eggs to hairs and the young which hatch from these are identical to the adult except for size.

Treatment
Gammexane powder or derris dust applied to the infected areas kills the adults but not the eggs – treatment must therefore be repeated seven days later. Rubbing posts, around which oil-soaked sacks have been wound give a good measure of control against lice – the oil enters the insects' breathing tubes, effectively blocking them.

Why is a second application of derris dust applied to pigs with lice seven days after the first?

. . . Q.15

Questions: Pigs

1. Write single sentences to answer the following questions:
   (a) From which part of the pig is brawn made?
   (b) From which country was the Landrace pig imported?
   (c) What is a creep?
   (d) How long is a pig's gestation period?
   (e) Which mineral is deficient in a sow's milk?
   (f) At which period of her life does the sow receive most food?
   (g) In which part of the female pig does fertilisation take place?
   (h) What is a notifiable disease?
   (i) Which organ is damaged by *Ascaris lumbricoides*?
   (j) What is the temperature of a healthy pig?

2. Describe an internal parasite of the pig under the following headings:
   (a) Life cycle.
   (b) Effect upon host.
   (c) Control methods.

3. (a) What do you understand by food conversion rate?
   (b) Calculate the food conversion rate of a pen of pigs which weighed 200 kg when purchased as weaners, and 500 kg when sold as pork, if they had consumed 975 kg of food.

4. (a) What is meant by a notifiable disease?
   (b) Describe with labelled diagrams the life cycle of *one* parasite of farm livestock.
   (c) State, with reference to this parasite,
      (i) what harm is done to the farm animal,
      (ii) how the parasite is passed on,
      (iii) how the parasite can be controlled or destroyed. (*N.W.R.E.B; part qn.*)

5. Write an account of the management of a sow from the time her last litter of piglets has been weaned up to and including farrowing of her next litter. You should include details of service, feeding, maintenance of health and housing. (*S.E.R.E.B.*)

6. (a) Name and describe *two* commercial breeds of pig.
   (b) List all the factors you would be looking for in deciding which young female pigs should be kept for breeding.
   (c) Give all the reasons which would help you to decide that a breeding pig is no longer worth keeping in the herd. (*S.E.R.E.B.*)

7. Give an account of *one* animal disease. Use the following headings in your answer:
   (a) Name of animal;
   (b) Signs and symptoms;
   (c) Causes;
   (d) Treatment;
   (e) Precautions. (*W.J.E.C.*)

8. (a) Describe the daily feeding routine for an animal in your care.
   (b) Explain the purpose of the foods which make up the ration.
   (c) Why is it necessary for the animal to have a balanced ration? (*W.M.E.B.*)

6 Commercial rabbits

The flesh of the domestic rabbit is rich in protein and minerals and low in fat:

Comparative qualities of edible meats

	Protein %	*Fat* %	*Minerals* %
Lamb	17.5	20	1.0
Beef	19	17	0.9
Pork	16	25	0.9
Chicken	21	2.5	1.1
Rabbit	21	3.5	1.5

100 000 tonnes of rabbit meat was consumed annually in the U.K. until the incidence of myxomatosis in the 1950s, which caused consumption to fall by 95%. Since that time, consumption has increased steadily to the present 20 000 tonnes per annum. British rabbit keepers supply some of the demand; the rest is imported, mostly from China.

Relationship between live weight and edible meat of a rabbit

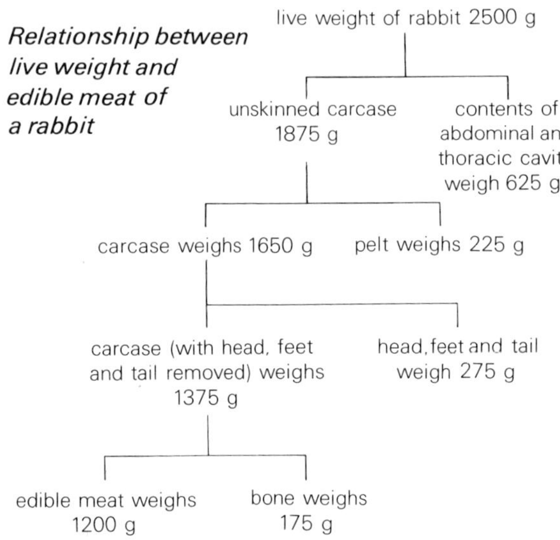

Breeds

There are over thirty breeds of rabbit in the U.K., which are kept mainly for show purposes. Almost half of these breeds have some value for meat production, and of these two are outstanding – the New Zealand white and the Californian – both of which were bred in America.

The New Zealand white

A pure white breed. The adults average 4 kg, although individual does (♀) weigh up to 5½ kg and bucks (♂) 5 kg. The fat-free carcase is well fleshed with white meat. A doe will rear 50 young a year, which grow to 2 kg in 65 days.

The Californian

This breed has a white body with black on nose, ears, feet and tail. The hind quarters carry more flesh than the New Zealand white, and the meat/bone ratio is slightly better. Colour of the flesh is white and it is almost fat-free. A doe will rear 48 young per year, which will grown to 2 kg in 68 days.

The Californian

In addition to these two breeds, hybrids are available from most of the large breeders. Hybrids are usually superior to the pure breeds, giving larger litters, better food conversion rates and quicker maturity.

What is a food conversion rate? . . . Q.1

The young of hybrids do not themselves make good breeding stock and rabbit farmers have to replace their parent stock by purchasing more hybrids from the breeders.

Housing for rabbits

Rabbits are housed in low buildings which must have good, draught-free ventilation and be vermin proof. Inside these buildings, the rabbits are housed in wire cages with wire floors through which the droppings pass. Each breeding animal has its own cage, the does, of course, sharing with their litters.

What information would you expect to find on the record card if the cage held a doe? . . . Q.2

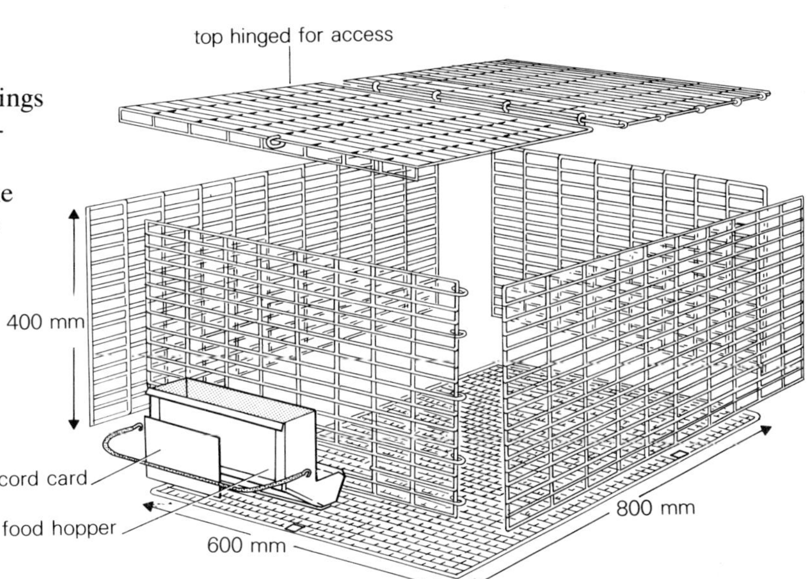

A typical rabbit cage

This cage is large enough to house a doe, and her litter up to eight weeks old. Cages are usually suspended from the roof to allow free access underneath for cleaning. Each cage is fitted with a food hopper, which can be filled without opening the cage, and a rabbit-operated water valve gives a constant supply of clean water.

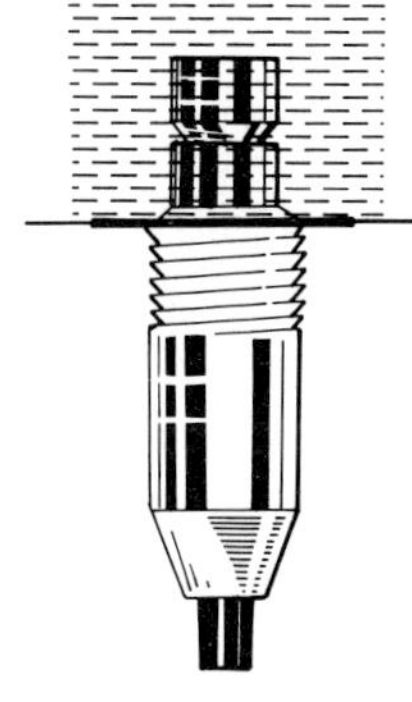

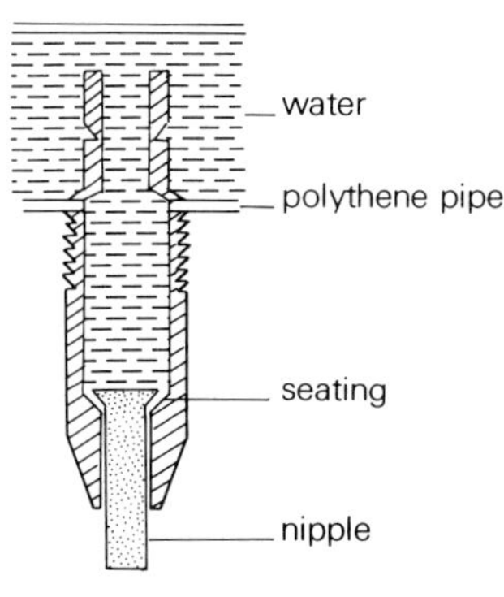

Drinking valve (left), and cross section (right); when the nipple is raised, water flows out, and when the nipple rests in its seating, water stops

Young rabbits drinking from a nipple

What breed are the young rabbits in the photograph? . . . Q.3

Two days before a litter is due a wooden nest box is put into the doe's cage:

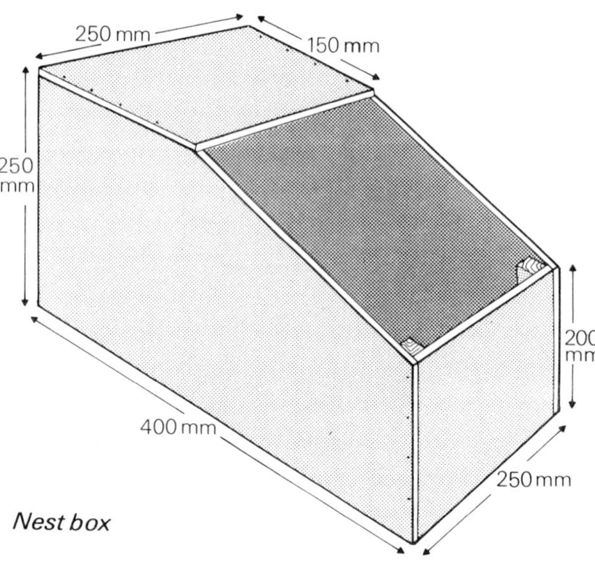

Nest box

Rabbit houses are best provided with natural light from windows. Breeding begins to decline in autumn as the days become shorter – it can be stimulated by lengthening the day artificially with electric lights.

Food

Rabbits are fed on pellets which are specially compounded by the large animal feeding stuffs manufacturers. Measured quantities are fed to bucks, and does in the first part of their pregnancy, to keep them healthy but not fat. Does in the late stages of pregnancy and nursing mothers are fed *ad lib.* A suitable food can be made by mixing:

ground barley	12 kg
ground oats	4 kg
ground maize	12 kg
soya bean meal	9 kg
meat and bone meal	3 kg

A vitamin and mineral supplement must be added according to manufacturers' instructions. Home mixes are cheaper, but are inclined to be dusty, and can cause respiratory disorders.

What is a 'respiratory disorder'? . . . Q.4

The life of a rabbit

Baby rabbits are born, blind and naked, in a nest of fur which the mother has plucked from her own body, in litters of about nine. The doe feeds her young once a day from her eight teats, and keeps them warm by spending a good deal of time alongside the nest. At three weeks old the babies, now covered with fur, begin to leave the nest and share mother's food and water. At four weeks old the young are removed to another cage and fed *ad lib* until they weigh about 2 kg, at eight or nine weeks old, when they are killed.

The life of a doe

Although the normal life span of a pet rabbit is nine years, the commerical doe lives for only two years. The doe is weaned at four weeks and fed *ad lib* for the next six weeks, after which time her rations are restricted (to prevent over fatness) to about 120 g per day.

At the age of twenty weeks, the doe is taken to the buck, who immediately mates with her. If the buck is taken to the doe, she will fight him and refuse to mate. The act of mating stimulates ovulation, and a number of eggs are shed into the Fallopian tubes to be fertilised by the buck's sperm. Ten days or so later, the owner gently lifts her from the cage, and puts his hand under her body between her back legs and pelvis. By moving his hand sideways he can feel the developing marble-shaped embryos between his finger and thumb. This pregnancy test is known as *palpation*, and if it proves negative the doe will be returned to the buck.

During the latter part of pregnancy the doe is fed *ad lib*, and the nest box is introduced. After a gestation period of 31 days the young are born. After three weeks, whilst still nursing, the doe is mated once more, and the young are removed a week or so later giving the doe two or three weeks before her next litter is born. This pattern is continued until the number of rabbits per litter begins to decline and the doe is then culled. During her short life, she produces some one hundred young at the rate of seven litters a year.

The life of a buck

Stock bucks are very carefully selected, by consulting records, handling and visual appearance. The young buck must have grown at a rate faster than the other rabbits in the same litter; his mother must be quiet and a proven rearer of large, heavy litters with a good health record. The young buck's sire must have proved his ability to father large litters with good conformation, rapid growth rates and low food consumption. The buck takes longer to mature than a doe and will not be able to start work until he is six months old. He is given enough food to keep him healthy and well-fleshed, but he is not allowed to become fat. At first he should mate with two does each week, and his work load should be gradually increased to a maximum of two does each day. The does should be placed in the buck's pen and removed immediately after mating. During his five year working life a good buck will sire some 20 000 young.

By-products of rabbits

Rabbit pelts have some value for producing cony fur coats – the selling of dried skins to fur processors gives the trade additional income. White fur is preferred – coloured pelts do not make as good a price.

Rabbit droppings have good manurial properties and are increasing in value as the price of artificial fertilizers increases. Some rabbit farmers use the droppings to raise a certain species of red earthworm for sale as bait to fishermen. The worms convert the droppings to compost which is sold to market gardeners.

Biology of the rabbit

Teeth

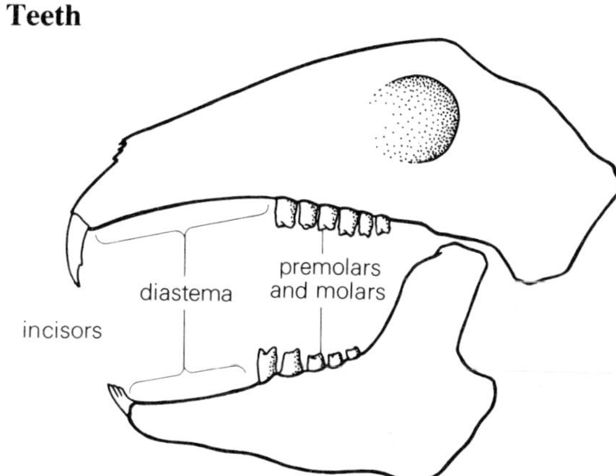

Skull and lower jaw, showing dentition of rabbits

The dental formula of a rabbit is:

$$i\,\frac{2\text{–}2}{1\text{–}1}\qquad c\,\frac{0\text{–}0}{0\text{–}0}\qquad p\,\frac{3\text{–}3}{2\text{–}2}\qquad m\,\frac{3\text{–}3}{3\text{–}3}$$

What is the total number of teeth in the rabbit? **. . . Q.5**

Which class of teeth, present in the pig, are missing in the rabbit? **. . . Q.6**

The digestive system of the rabbit

The digestive system of the rabbit has a number of important differences from that of the pig. Unlike the pig, the rabbit is able to digest the cellulose part of plants and can therefore make use of grass.

The rabbit has a very large organ – the *caecum* – which contains bacteria and enables the animal to digest grass. *Coprophagous pellets*, produced at night for reingestation, also assist in the digestion of grass. A rabbit on a wire floor does not lose the coprophagous pellets, as it takes them in its teeth directly from the anus, as they are produced.

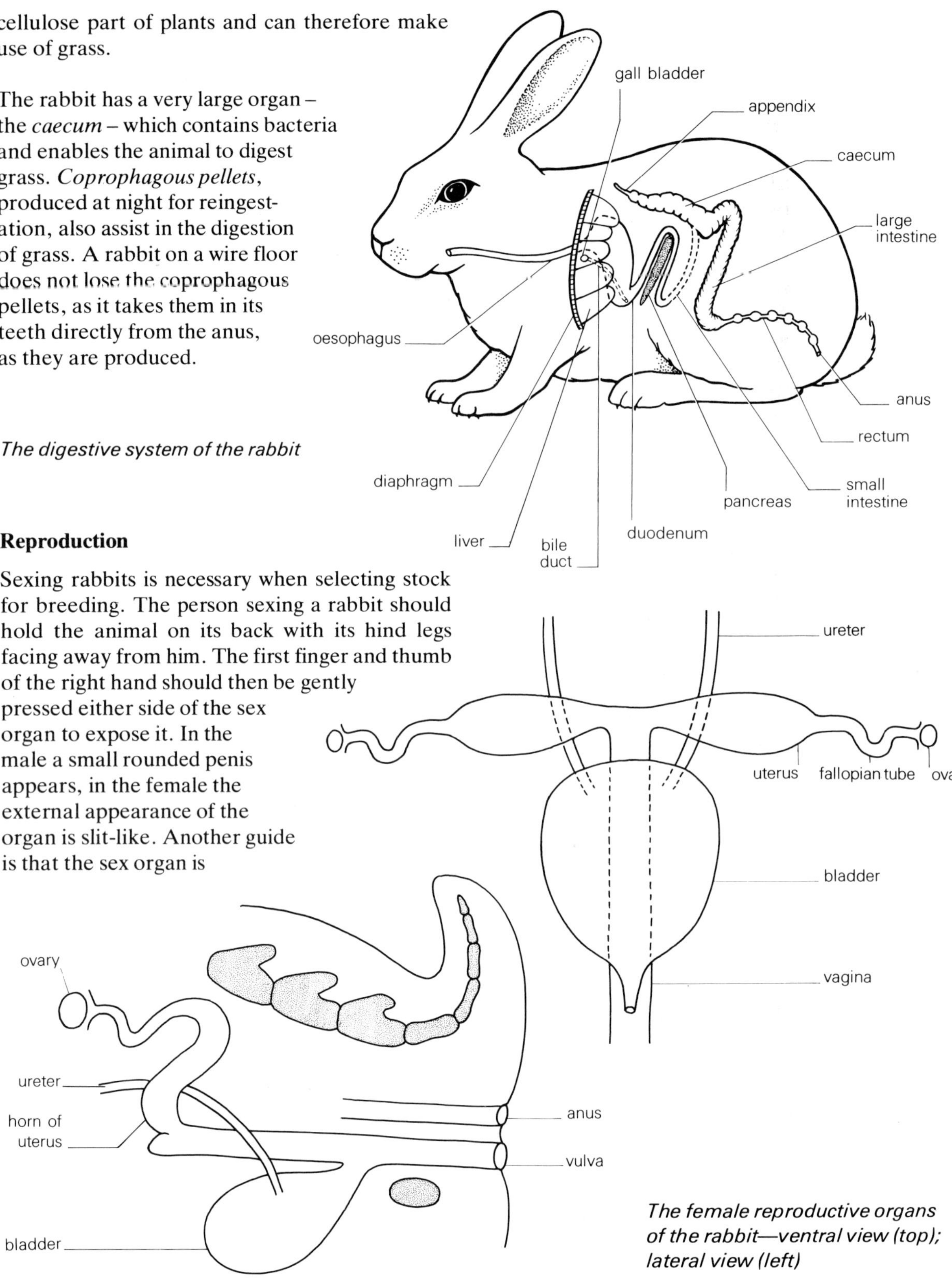

The digestive system of the rabbit

The female reproductive organs of the rabbit—ventral view (top); lateral view (left)

Reproduction

Sexing rabbits is necessary when selecting stock for breeding. The person sexing a rabbit should hold the animal on its back with its hind legs facing away from him. The first finger and thumb of the right hand should then be gently pressed either side of the sex organ to expose it. In the male a small rounded penis appears, in the female the external appearance of the organ is slit-like. Another guide is that the sex organ is nearer to the anus in a doe than it is in a buck. The older the rabbit is, the easier it is to sex – when sexing a very young rabbit, a hand lens can be useful.

developing embryos
blood supply
membranes
fallopian tube

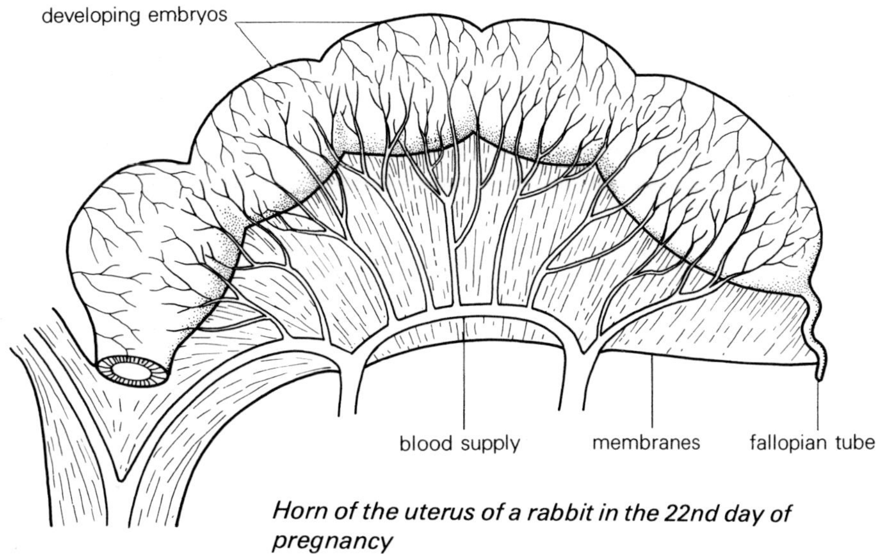

Horn of the uterus of a rabbit in the 22nd day of pregnancy

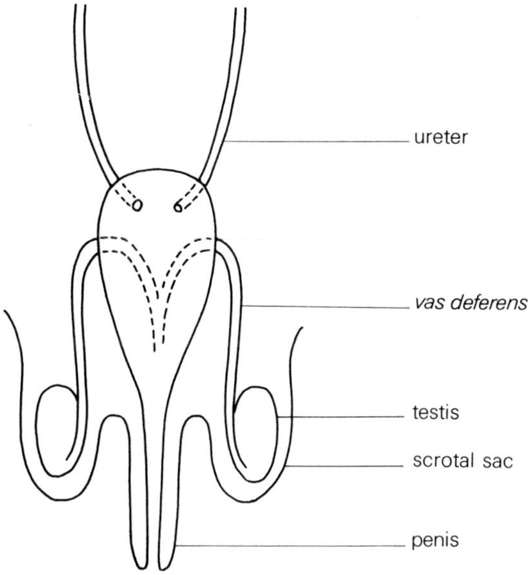

ureter
vas deferens
testis
scrotal sac
penis

The male reproductive organs of the rabbit—ventral view (left); lateral view (below)

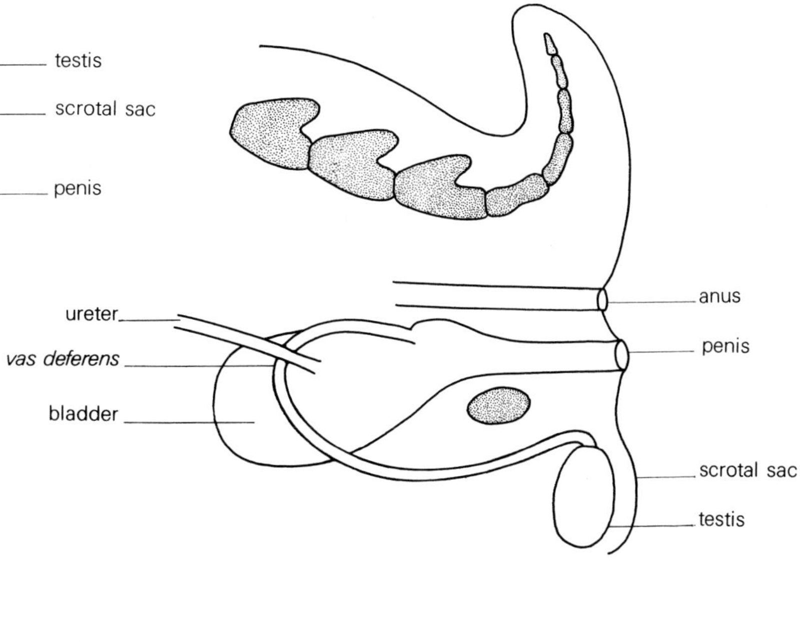

ureter
vas deferens
bladder
anus
penis
scrotal sac
testis

Pests and diseases of rabbits

Coccidiosis

This disease is very common, it is caused by extremely small protozoan parasites *Eimeria preforans*, which affects the intestines, and *Eimeria stiedae* which affects the liver.

Symptoms
Both forms of coccidiosis have similar symptoms and affect young rabbits more often than adults. Infected animals stop eating, become inactive and disinterested, and lose weight rapidly. The disease is always accompanied by severe *scouring* (diarrhoea), followed by death a few days later.

How coccidiosis is spread
Infected animals pass out thousands of egg-like structures (oocysts) with their faeces. These eggs have to go through a period of development in a wet, warm place before they can infect a second animal. For this reason, wire floors are much less likely to produce conditions favourable for spreading coccidiosis than solid ones. The disease is, however, very infectious and if one member of a litter becomes infected, the others will almost certainly catch it from him by ingesting oocysts that have developed from the 'eggs' in the infected rabbit's droppings.

Control
Prevention is the best way to combat this disease – avoidance of wet areas around drinking troughs, disinfection of equipment after use, and isolation of bought-in stock are helpful. In practice, most rabbit farmers add the antibiotic sulphamezathine to the drinking water of all their stock – this protects them from the disease. This type of blanket medication is not good husbandry, and there are reasons why it should be discouraged, e.g., the organism may become immune to the antibiotic.

Ear mange

Commonly called *canker,* ear mange is caused by the mite, *Otodectis cyanotis* which lives in the rabbit's ears.

Life cycle
Eggs hatch into a six-legged larvae, which feed inside the ear for two or three days before changing into eight-legged nymphs. The nymphs grow and reach adult size in about three days. Two days later, mating takes place, followed by egg laying. The whole life history of this mite

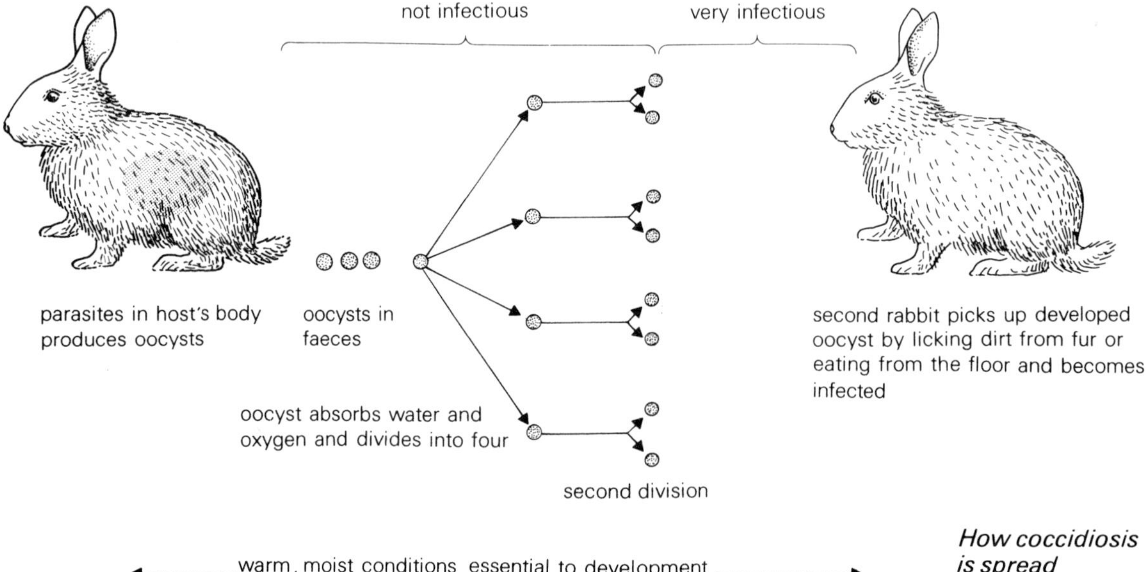

How coccidiosis is spread

takes less than two weeks – numbers therefore increase very rapidly.

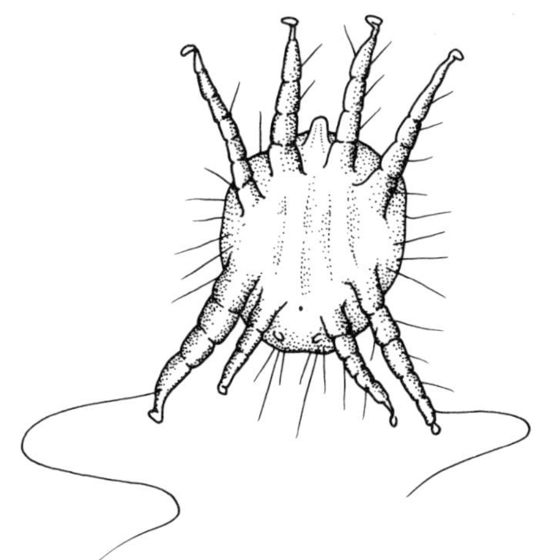

Ear mange mite (× 70)

Symptoms
Infected rabbits may shake their heads and attempt to scratch their ears. A greyish-brown, powdery material with a foul smell appears inside the ears and, if left untreated, secondary infection and death follows.

Control
Various powders are available for dusting into the ear, some of which kill the adult mites, but not the eggs or larvae. Treatment should therefore be repeated twice at three day intervals. The veterinary profession dislike powders being forced into animals' ears – they recommend cleansing with a solution of liquid soap in five parts of warm water, followed by an application of one per cent solution of Gammexane in medicinal liquid paraffin. If limited first aid treatment is not effective, the advice of a vet should be sought.

Questions: Commercial rabbits

1. Write single sentences to answer the following questions:
   (a) Why are white rabbits preferred to coloured ones for meat production?
   (b) What disease killed many wild rabbits in the 1950s?
   (c) From which country was the New Zealand white rabbit imported?
   (d) What is the advantage of using wire floors in rabbit cages?
   (e) How is water given to commercial rabbits?
   (f) How many young will the average doe produce during her working life?
   (g) What is the function of the caecum in rabbit?
   (h) What rabbit disease is caused by a mite?
   (i) What causes the female rabbit to ovulate?

2. Rabbits live well on green food, especially during the early summer. Suggest reasons why commercial rabbit keepers do not take advantage of this cheap food source for their stock.

3. In October a weaned litter of 12 rabbits was divided into two equal groups. One group (A) was reared in an insulated, well heated house; the other (B) in outside hutches.

   Both groups were reared for meat, being slaughtered at 4 kg live weight.
   Group A used a total of 60 kg of food.
   Group B used a total of 80 kg of food.
   Group A weighed 4 kg after 11 weeks.
   Group B weighed 4 kg after 14 weeks.
   5 kg of food costs 90p.
   (a) (i) What was the cost of feeding group A?
   (ii) What was the cost of feeding group B?
   (b) (i) Which group made the most 'profit'?
   (ii) How much more 'profit' did they make?
   (iii) Name two other factors that would affect the true profit.
   (c) *Either:*
   Draw a diagram of suitable housing for any mammal which you have studied; include all the necessary equipment and

explain in detail the management procedure.

or:

Draw a diagram of the alimentary canal of any mammal (other than man) which you have studied. Label the diagram and explain briefly what happens to the food during digestion. *(S.R.E.B.)*

4. Describe the digestive system of a mammal you have studied and say how it is related to its method of feeding. *(W.M.E.B.)*

5. Using words and diagrams, explain fully how the modern rabbit is housed.

6. Some commercial rabbit keepers leave the young with the doe until they are ready for slaughter at 8 weeks. Where this system is adopted, the doe is mated when the young are five weeks old.
   (a) What advantages has this method over the weaning at 4 weeks described in this chapter?
   (b) What disadvantages has this method compared with the 4 week weaning method?
   (c) What is the difference in young per doe per year between the 4 week and 8 week weaning method (assume 9 young born per litter)?

7. Design a record card suitable for attachment to the cage of a breeding doe.

8. Describe a common disease that affects rabbits, under the following headings:
   (i) Cause of disease;
   (ii) Life cycle of causative organism;
   (iii) Symptoms;
   (iv) Methods of control.

7 Power for crop production

In the U.K. almost all work connected with basic food production is performed by machines. Although the energy that drives the machines comes mostly from fossil fuels (oil, coal, gas) they are driven in a variety of ways:

1. The internal combustion engine – tractors, loaders, stationary engines.
2. Electricity – milking machines, grain driers, sheep shears, coolers, pumps, incubators and many more.
3. Hydraulic – lifting and manoeuvering (all tractors are fitted with a hydraulic system).
4. Wind (in certain areas) – pumping.
5. Gas – usually propane in large cylinders as few farms are connected to mains gas – brooders and other space heating

Which of the above does not involve the use of a fossil fuel? . . . Q.1

The internal combustion engine

In this type of engine, fuel is burned in cylinders which are fitted with pistons. The gases produced by the burning fuel force the pistons to the bottoms of the cylinders. Rods connect the pistons to a crankshaft in such a way that it is caused to rotate and push the pistons back up the cylinders for the cycle to be repeated. The end of the rotating crankshaft is geared to perform useful work.

Small engines have only one cylinder, the larger engines have three or four (sometimes more) cylinders, the pistons of which are connected to a common crankshaft.

Almost all internal combustion engines are driven by either petrol or diesel oil.

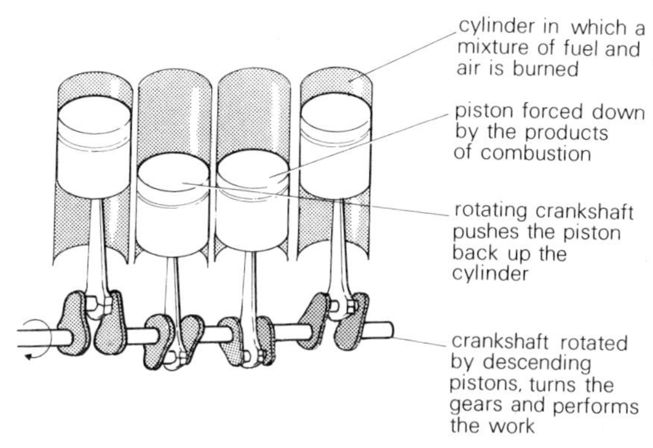

Function of the internal combustion engine

The four-stroke petrol engine

The four-stroke cycle of the petrol engine:

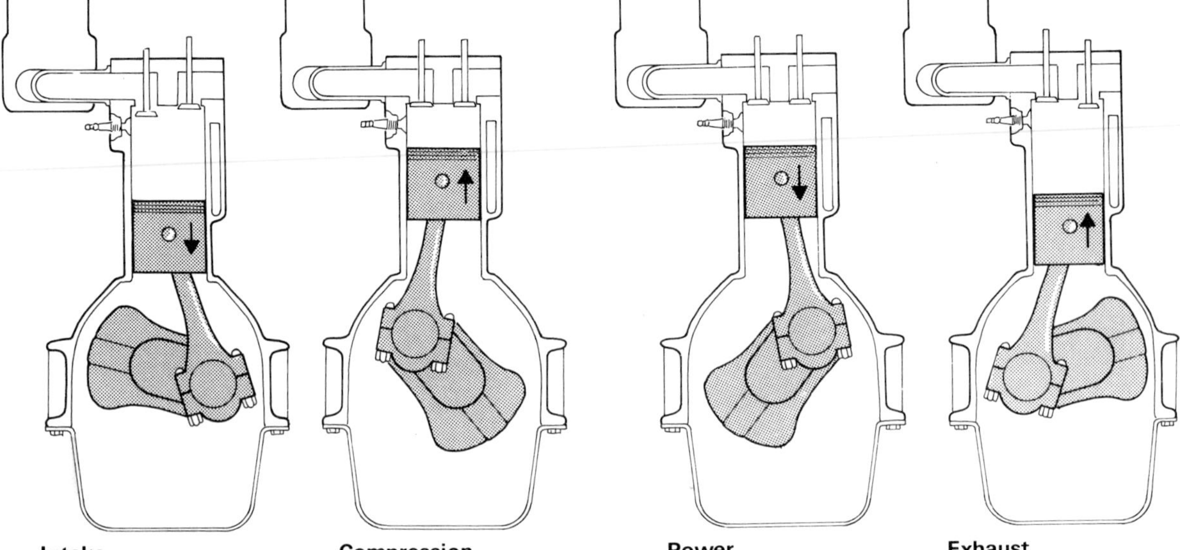

Intake
The piston descends, drawing fuel and air through the open intake valve.

Compression
Both valves are closed, sealing the cylinder; as the piston rises the gases are compressed.

Power
Both valves remain closed, the sparking plug ignites the mixture, which explodes, forcing the piston down.

Exhaust
The exhaust valve opens and the rising piston forces the spent gases out. The cycle is then repeated.

Carburettor

The petrol engine is fitted with a carburettor, which regulates the petrol-air mixture. A float-operated valve prevents too much fuel from entering the engine. A 'butterfly' (the throttle) which can partially block the mixture intake pipe, controls the flow of mixture and hence the speed of the engine.

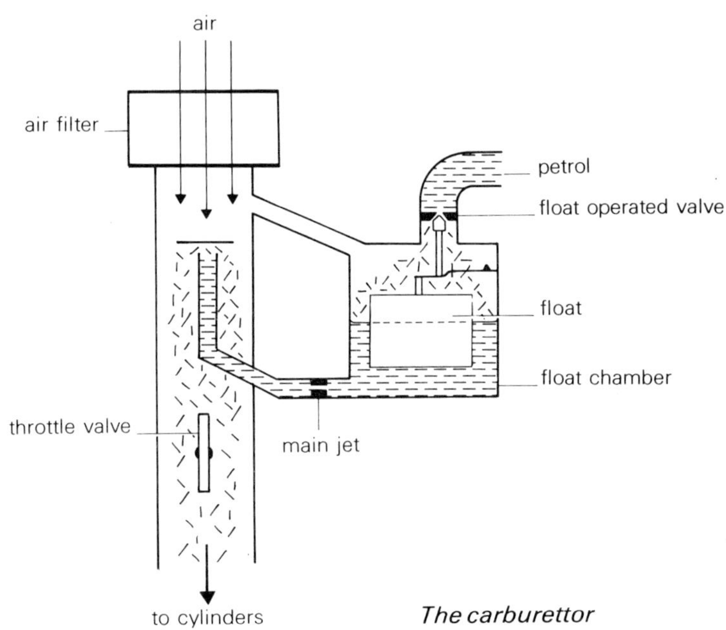

The carburettor

Sparking plug

The four-stroke engine has a dynamo or an alternator, which generates electricity as the engine turns, connected to a distributor. The sparking plug receives an impulse of electricity from the distributor whenever the piston reaches its highest point in the cylinder (top dead centre – *t.d.c.*) before the power stroke. If the plug is clean and properly adjusted, a spark will pass between the electrodes and ignite the mixture in the cylinder.

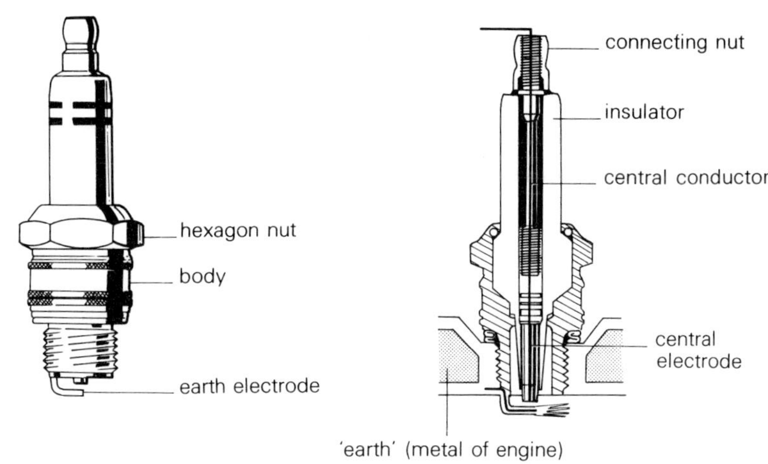

The sparking plug (left) and cross-section (right)

Lubrication

The lower part of the crankcase (sump) contains a reservoir of oil. As the engine runs, oil is pumped from this reservoir to the moving parts, and then drains back into the sump.

Before starting a four-stroke engine it is important to check that the oil level is correct – most engines are fitted with a dip stick for this purpose.

Why must the engine be level when the oil is checked? . . . Q.2

The two-stroke engine

Some small engines (usually single cylinder) work on a different principle and are called *two-stroke* engines. In this type of engine, the mixture explodes each time the piston reaches *t.d.c.* There is no pool

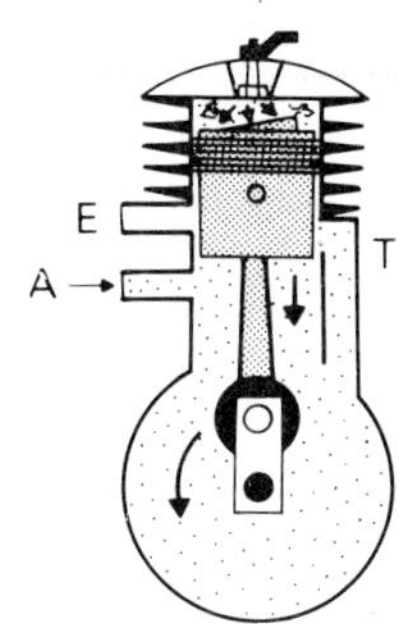

The air and fuel mixture enters the sealed crank-case through A. The mixture above the piston explodes, forcing the piston down.

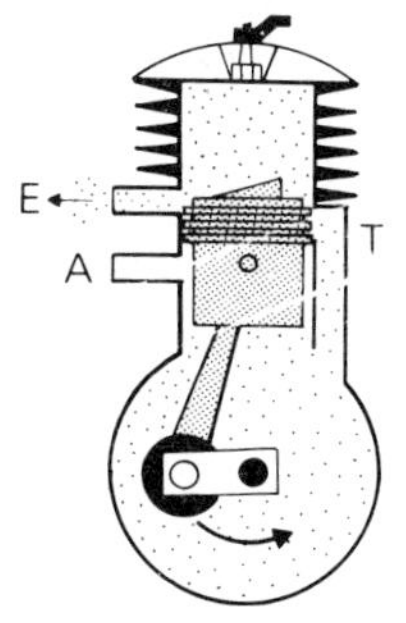

As the piston descends, E is opened, and exhaust gas escapes. Port A is covered, preventing entry or exit of gas. The gas in the crankcase is compressed.

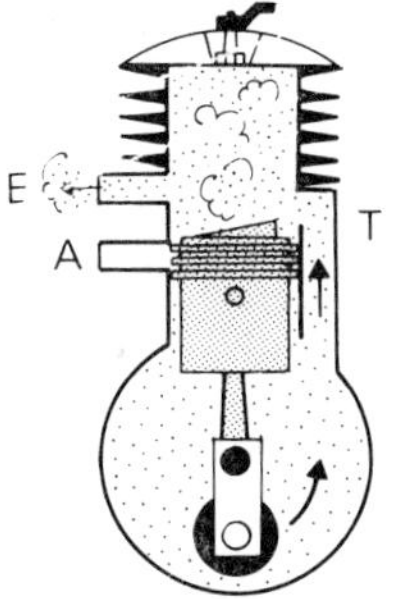

When the piston uncovers the transport port, T, compressed fuel mixture enters the cylinder.

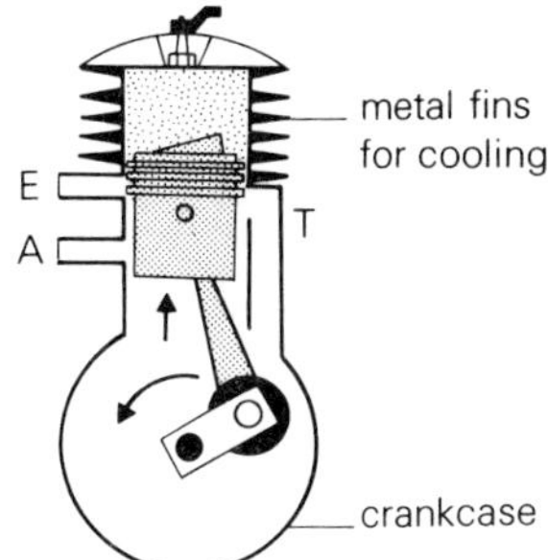

All parts are now closed, as gas in the cylinder is compressed. Suction is developed in the crankcase.

of lubricating oil in the sump, lubrication being provided by mixing a small amount of oil with the fuel – a common mixture is 25 parts of petrol to one of oil but the petrol/oil ratio varies with the make of engine.

Task 7.1

Study the diagrams and captions of the two-stroke engine and describe in your own words how the two-stroke engine works.

The diesel engine

The diesel engine works for very long periods, and uses less fuel, for the same amount of power, than any other type of engine. Almost all farm tractors are fitted with diesel engines. The ignition of a diesel engine depends upon the fact that when a gas is compressed it becomes hot:

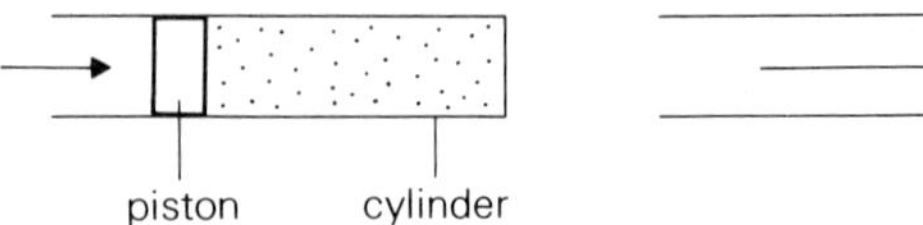

When a gas is compressed as in the diagram above, the heat contained in the gas is also compressed, resulting in a rise in temperature. The smaller the space the gas is forced into, the hotter it will become.

Which common piece of bicycle equipment demonstrates this principle? . . . Q.3

A diesel engine has a high compression ratio (i.e. the gas in the cylinder is compressed to about one twenty-fifth of its original volume), and the rise in temperature in the cylinder is so great that the gas ignites spontaneously – sparking plugs are therefore unnecessary in a diesel engine.

The fuel is introduced into the cylinder whilst the gases are under compression – considerable force is required for this and a fuel injection pump replaces the carburettor of the petrol engine. In theory, almost any type of fuel could be used in a diesel engine, but in practice a very light oil (*diesel oil* or *derv*) is used.

Task 7.2

Prepare a chart showing in what ways the four-stroke petrol engine is similar to the diesel engine and in what ways it is different.

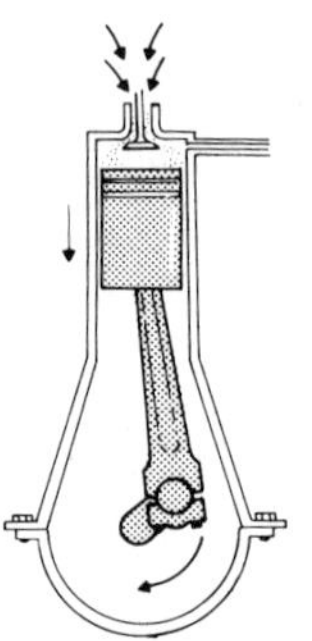

Intake
The valve opens, and the descending piston draws air into the cylinder until the piston reaches bottom dead centre (*b.d.c*); the valve then closes.

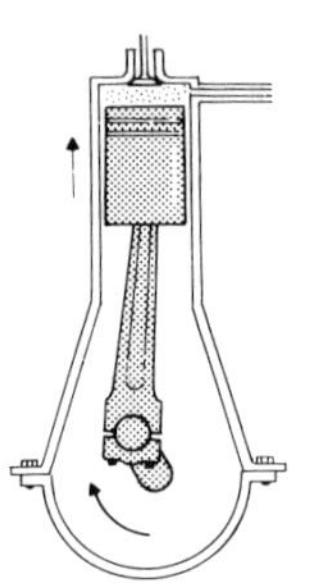

Compression
As the piston rises the air is compressed and becomes very hot (700°C–900°C).

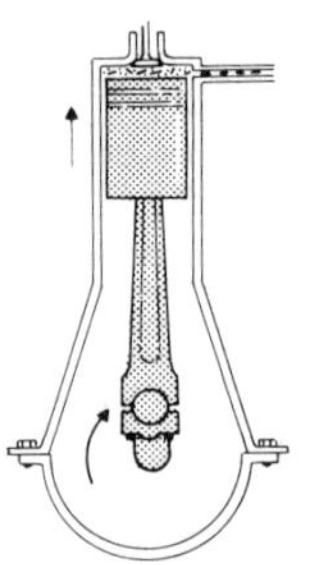

Fuel injection
Fuel is injected as a very fine spray into the hot air, and it immediately vaporises.

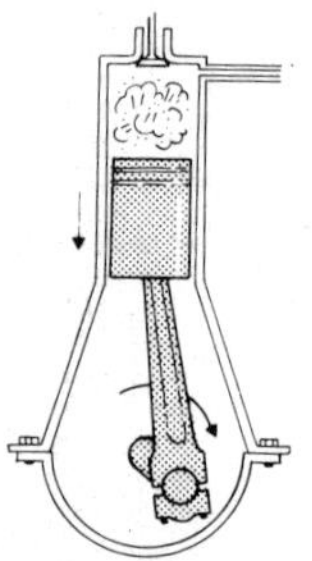

Combustion
The fuel/air mixture ignites and the gases produced force the piston down – this is the *power stroke*.

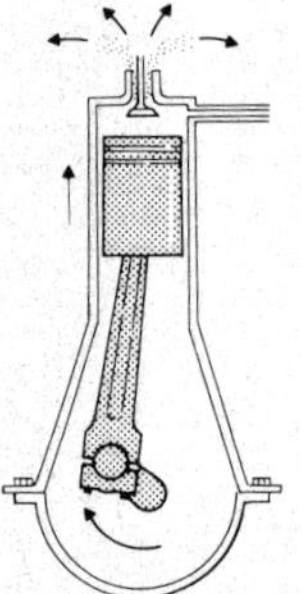

Exhaust
The valve opens and as the piston rises the burned gases are forced out of the cylinder.

Hydraulics

A sealed tank full of liquid has two cylinders attached: 'A', with a cross-sectional area of 1 cm^2, and 'B' with a cross-sectional area of 10 cm^2. The cylinders are fitted with pistons which, although free to move, do not allow any of the liquid to escape.

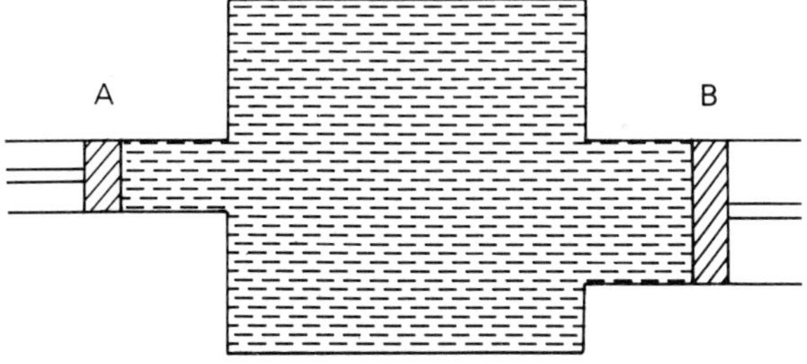

As it is not possible to compress a liquid, if 'A' is pushed in, 'B' will be pushed out. If a force of one newton is applied to 'A', it will be transmitted through the liquid and each square cm of 'B' will receive a force of one newton. As 'B' has an area of 10 cm^2 the total force on 'B' is 10 newtons. Thus a force of one newton on 'A' produces a force of 10 newtons on B.

In the terms of work done, however, the values at 'A' and 'B' are the same, as piston 'A' must be pushed along 10 mm to produce a one mm movement in 'B'.

What is the force on 'B' when a force of 3 N is applied to 'A'? . . . Q.4

If the area of piston 'A' were equal to the area of piston 'B', what force must be applied to 'A' to produce a force of 5 N at 'B'? . . . Q.5

In practice the liquid used in hydraulic machines is not water but a thin oil.

Name two advantages of using oil instead of water in hydraulic machines. . . . Q.6

The farm tractor

The basic power unit of the modern tractor is a diesel engine which provides power for:

1. Either two or four wheels for traction.
2. A pump which keeps oil under pressure for hydraulic work.
3. A rotating spline, which is used to power other machines (e.g., pick-up baler, mowing machine, etc.); this is called the *power take off* and abbreviated to p.t.o.

The majority of machines are attached to the tractor in three places (three-point linkage) – this enables the machine to be raised or lowered with the hydraulic system, and carried rather than pulled:

The power take off spline on the back of a tractor

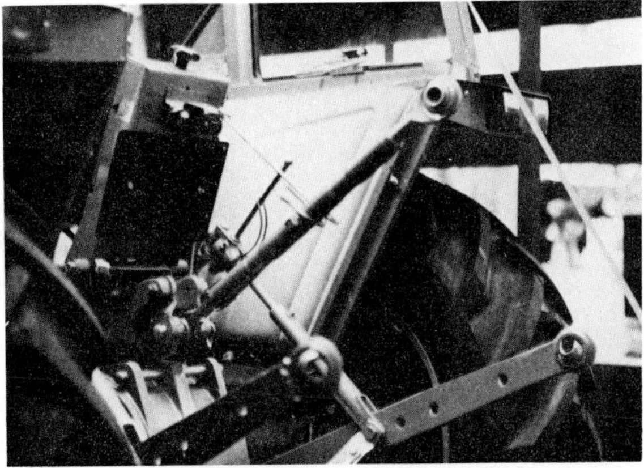

The three points on a tractor to which implements are attached

A tractor with a 72 kW, 4 cylinder diesel engine (16 forward gears and 4 reverse gears)

The tractor and machine becomes a complete unit, easy to control, very manoeuvrable and the additional weight on the tyres gives extra grip.

This tractor has a mounted disc harrow attached. The cab (or a roll bar) has to be fitted by law as many tractor drivers have been killed when their machines have overturned. The double wheels at the rear are fitted to reduce damage to the soil structure, and provide additional grip.

What is the purpose of the large weights on the front of the tractor? . . . Q.7

A track-laying tractor

The weight of a track-laying tractor is spread over a large area and does less damage to the soil structure than a wheeled tractor of similar power. The driver has reached the end of the furrow and has lifted the five furrow reversible plough from the soil before turning round. One set of ploughs turns the soil to the left and the other set turns the soil to the right. At the end of each furrow the driver has to rotate the plough in order that the soil is turned in the correct direction.

Has this driver rotated his plough at the end of this furrow? . . . Q.8

Flails rotating at high speed – these are cutting the hedge

The tractor p.t.o. drives a pump, which forces oil along a pipe to the top left-hand side of the cutting head. The small box which the pipe enters is an hydraulic motor; this hydraulic motor provides the traction which turns the cutting flails. The large tank on the right-hand side holds a reservoir of oil; it also prevents the tractor from tipping to the left by balancing the weight of the cutting head.

This tractor has a very narrow wheel base to allow passage between the rows of trees. The width between the wheels of most tractors can be adjusted.

Is this a two or a four wheel drive tractor?

. . . Q.9

Four wheel drive provides extra grip for the 135 kW tractor (illustrated below) to cultivate unploughed stubble to a depth of 250 mm. A small tractor would be unable to pull this implement.

A 33 kW tractor, with 4 forward and one reverse gear (Courtesy of Massey Ferguson)

A 135 kW tractor (Courtesy of Massey Ferguson)

An increasing number of farmers are using specialised lifting and loading trucks for handling materials as shown in the photograph opposite.

The 50 kg bags of fertiliser on the left of the photograph are stacked on pallets, ready for the fork lift truck to load onto the farm trailer. In the field each bag will have to be man-handled into the spreader. This latter chore is unnecessary with the large sacks on the right. Each of these large sacks contains one tonne of fertiliser, it is suspended above the hopper on the spreader and the contents discharged by pulling a ripcord on the bottom or cutting with a knife. If the whole contents are not required, the flow may be stopped by inserting a board to cover the cut.

A fertiliser spreader

Loading a cultivator into a trailer

A fork lift truck being used to carry hay to beef cattle (Courtesy of Lansing Bagnall)

Above: A telescopic handler being used to load sugar beet (Courtesy of J. C. Bamford)

Left: Lifting a 1 tonne bag of fertiliser

This machine has a 52 kW 4 cylinder diesel engine, and lifts loads of almost one tonne with its beam fully extended (4 m), and over 2 tonnes with its beam retracted.

The root crop bucket is one of a large range of attachments which includes grain buckets, forks for manure and silage, round bale forks, log grapples, concrete skips, and slurry blades.

A fore loader (Courtesy of Massey Ferguson)

In addition to driving a piston from a cylinder, oil under pressure can be used to power a hydraulic motor:

This small garden tractor uses hydraulic power throughout. An 8 kW engine operates a pump and the pressurised oil is used to drive the hydraulic motor which turns the wheels. The high pressure oil also operates the lift and a range of tillage and other implements.

A small garden tractor

Operation of an oil pressured hydraulic motor

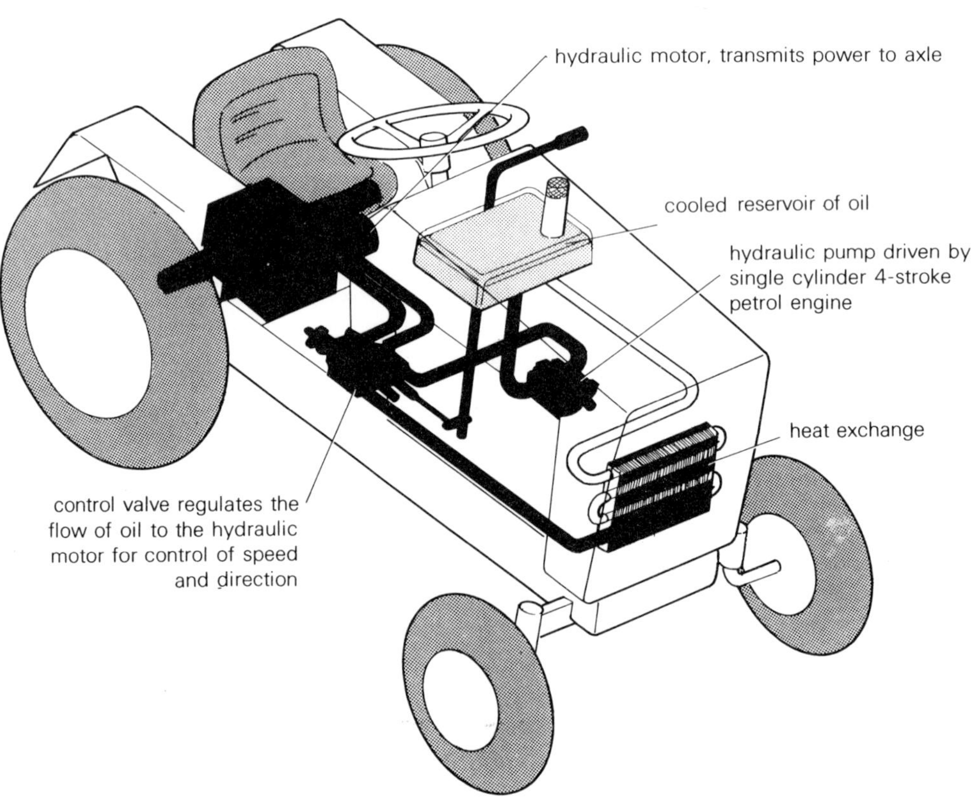

Questions: Power for crop production

1. Write single sentences to answer the following questions:
   (a) What is an internal combustion engine?
   (b) Where, in the cylinder, is the piston when the sparking plug sparks?
   (c) Why is a four-stroke engine fitted with a dynamo or alternator to generate electricity?
   (d) What fuel is used in a two-stroke engine?
   (e) What happens to the temperature of a gas as it is compressed?
   (f) What type of engine is fitted to most tractors?
   (g) What is the purpose of a carburettor?

2. Draw diagrams to show why a wet sparking plug will not work.

3. Write an essay entitled: 'The use of hydraulic power on the farm'.

4. (a) Describe the function of the four strokes of a compression ignition engine.
   (b) What is the approximate compression ratio in the cylinder of this type of engine?
   (c) What type of fuel does this engine use?

5. (a) What is the purpose of a carburettor?
   (b) Use a labelled diagram and notes to describe the function of a simple carburettor.

6. A number of horticultural machines are powered by a two-stroke engine.
   (a) Draw and label a simple diagram of the inside of a two-stroke engine and explain how it works.
   (b) If you could not start a two-stroke engine one morning,
      (i) what would you check as the possible reason for failure to start?
      (ii) how would you correct the faults you have listed in order to improve the chances of the engine starting?

   (*S.E.R.E.B.*)

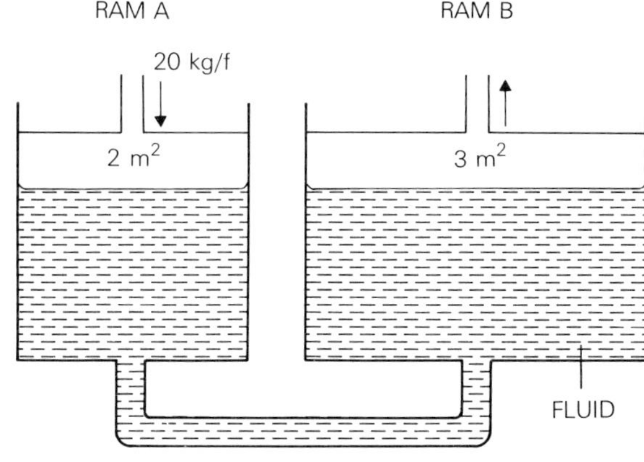

7. Study the diagram above.
   (a) What pressure will be exerted by ram A if pushed down?
   (b) What weight will ram B therefore lift up?
   (c) What is the name given to this method of transfer of energy?
   (d) We can use this transfer of energy to good effect e.g., on tractors. State *two* ways in which this is used on tractors.
   (e) What is the fluid used in the system?
   (f) How has the introduction of this method of using energy improved the working conditions of farm workers? (*W.M.E.B.*)

8. (a) In what ways do the principles of the operation of a four-stroke engine differ from a two-stroke engine?
   (b) Choose *either* the four-stroke *or* the two-stroke engine and use labelled diagrams to answer the following.
      (i) How is the air cleaned before it enters the cylinder?
      (ii) How is the flow of fuel to the cylinder controlled?
      (iii) How is the engine kept cool when running? (*S.E.R.E.B.*)

8 Farm crops

The total area of agricultural land in the U.K. is 18 553 000 hectares which is utilised as follows:

Crop	*Hectares*
Wheat	1 200 000
Barley	2 400 000
Oats	200 000
Mixed corn	15 000
Rye	9000
Maize	1000
Potatoes	212 000
Sugar beet	210 000
Oilseed rape	65 000
Hops	6000
Beans for stock feeding	39 000
Turnips, swedes and fodder beet	105 000
Mangels	7000
Rape (for grazing)	24 000
Kale	60 000
Grass	7 100 000
Rough grazing	6 000 000
Horticultural crops	400 000
Other (roads, buildings, etc.)	500 000

These are average figures, the actual areas vary from year to year.

Which cereal crop is most extensively grown? . . . Q.1

Which crop occupies the largest area? . . . Q.2

What is the total area of cereals in the U.K.? . . . Q.3

Which two of the areas listed above are never ploughed? . . . Q.4

Although the U.K. is a small area, the climate and soil type varies widely and farmers select crops that suit their particular area. Rainfall, temperature, amount of sunshine, soil type, altitude and market demands are all important factors in deciding which crops to grow.

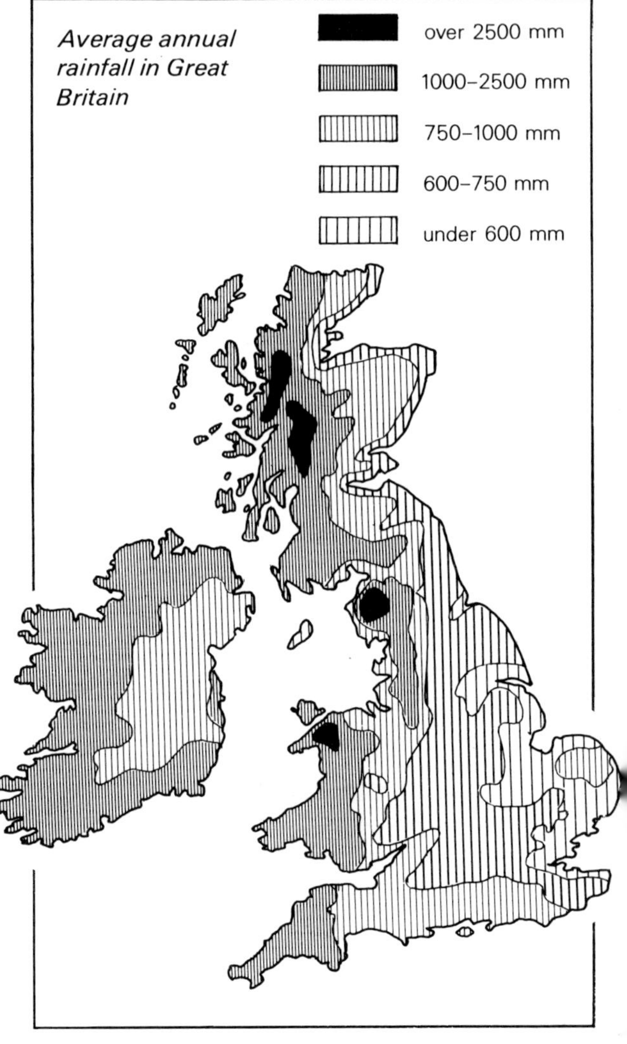

Grass

Grass requires a high rainfall, particularly in summer, to produce high yields. The rainfall map shows that the western side of the country is much wetter than the eastern half and it is for this reason that a much larger area is devoted to grassland in the West than the East.

Like other crops, grass must be tended, supplied with nutrients and kept weed-free if it is to produce a worthwhile crop. Unlike other crops grassland does not have to be resown each year.

On arable farms leys are grown to give the land a 'break' from growing cereals, the leys are left for one, two or three years. Unless grown for seed production, mixed species of grasses are nearly always sown. The following seed mixtures are suitable for sowing for a two year ley (units are the weight in kilograms of seed required for each hectare):

Italian ryegrass	3
Perennial ryegrass	9
Cocksfoot	9
Red clover	4
White clover	1
Total kg/ha	26

Timothy	7
Meadow fescue	9
Red clover	7
Total kg/ha	23

The choice of mixture depends upon the needs of the farmer – the first mixture would provide early spring and late summer grazing, the second mixture would provide a good silage or hay crop. The following mixtures are suitable for long duration leys:

Perennial ryegrass	15
Cocksfoot	6
Red clover	3
White clover	2
Total kg/ha	26

Meadow fescue	13
Timothy	6
Cocksfoot	3
Red clover	2
White clover	2
Total kg/ha	26

Temporary leys are usually sown at the same time as a spring cereal crop and in the same seed bed. Grass seeds are much smaller than cereal seeds and are therefore sown on the surface and harrowed in with a chain harrow. The two crops grow together, the larger quick-growing cereals shelter the grass acting as a 'nurse' crop. After the cereals are harvested the grass grows quickly and is soon ready for grazing:

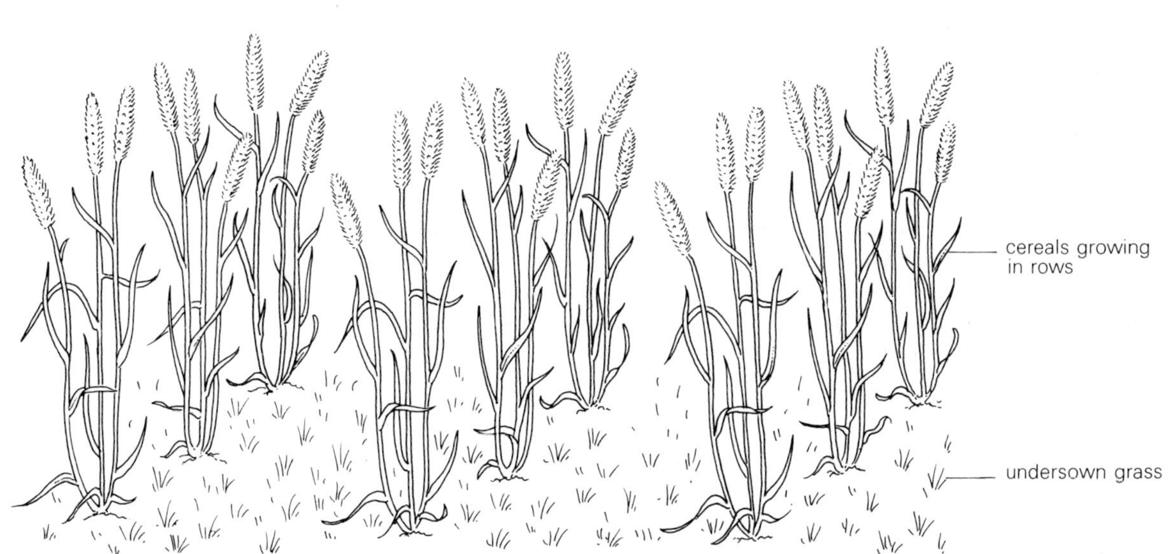

Permanent pasture is sown without a nurse crop in April or July/August directly into a well prepared seed bed, with a fine tilth which is then rolled firm. When weather conditions are good, the crop is ready for grazing about six weeks after sowing. It is important that this first grazing is light and not carried out if conditions are wet and the soil is likely to become poached by the feet of the grazing cattle.

Grazing

Last century a French farmer conducted an experiment to find the amount of grass his cattle consumed during a three month grazing period. He constructed a number of one metre cube wire cages, and placed them at random in the field at the end of March when he turned his cows into it. With the exception of the areas under the cages the cattle kept the pasture very short during April, May and June. At the end of this period the cattle were moved and the farmer clipped and weighed the grass in the cages. When his calculations were complete he found that his cattle had each consumed 180 kg of fresh grass each day. He knew that this amount was far too much and the most one of his cows could possibly eat in a day was 60 kg. What was wrong with his experiment?

The farmer had assumed that the grass under the cages had grown at the same rate as the grass outside, this assumption was quite wrong.

Had the grass under cages grown more or less quickly than the grass outside? . . . Q.5

In order to obtain the maximum growth of the pastures he is grazing, the farmer needs to understand the growth of the grass plant:

There are three stages in the growth of the grass plant:

Stage A is a period of slow growth whilst the plant has little leaf to trap growth-promoting light.

Stage B is a period of very rapid growth as the much larger leaf area traps lots of light.

Stage C is a period of little growth as the plant produces flowers and seeds.

Investigation 8.1

(This investigation must be started at the beginning of the summer term.) Select a uniform area of grass that has been recently cut and mark out five square metres with pegs and string.

Clip one of the squares twice a week, the next once a week, the next clip fortnightly, the next monthly and the last clip only once at the end of the eight week investigation.

Dry the clippings in an oven at 105°C as they are collected; weigh and record. Calculate how much grass has been grown by each square metre and see if your investigation verifies the statements made above.

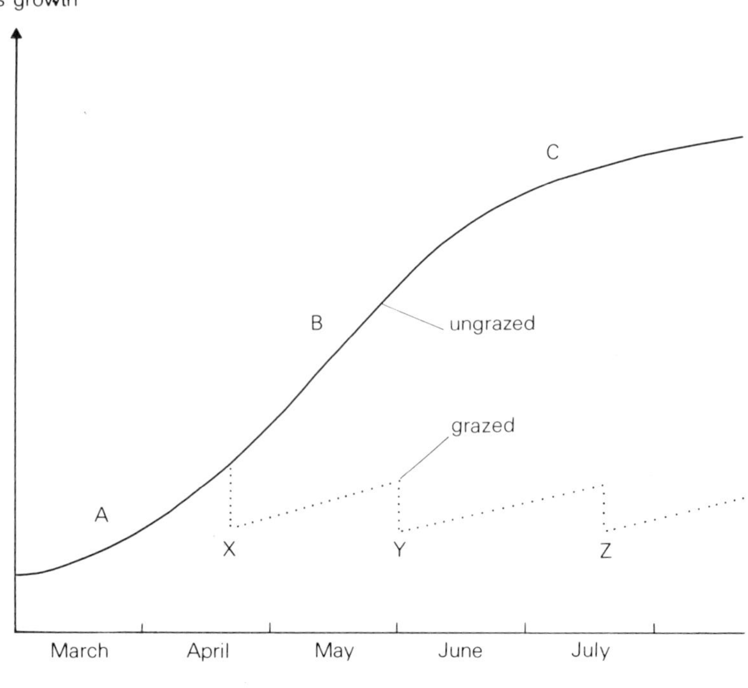

Rate of growth of grazed and ungrazed grass

Modern grazing techniques allow the grass to go through a period of rapid growth before the animals have access and prevent the animals from regrazing. Controlled grazing increases grass yields and gives the animals a more regular supply of nutrients.

Paddock grazing

The available grazing area is divided into paddocks small enough for the herd to graze in three days. If ten paddocks are in use, the first paddock will have 27 days' regrowth before the cattle return. In July, grass growth slows considerably and paddocks need longer rest periods in which to grow. This extra time is provided by introducing new paddocks which were used for silage or hay earlier in the season.

grazed April 1,2,3 May 1,2,3 June 1,2,3	April 4,5,6 May 4,5,6 June 4,5,6	April 7,8,9 May 7,8,9 June 7,8,9	April 10,11,12 May 10,11,12 June 10,11,12	April 13,14,15 May 13,14,15 June 13,14,15
April 16,17,18 May 16,17,18 June 16,17,18	April 19,20,21 May 19,20,21 June 19,20,21	April 22,23,24 May 22,23,24 June 22,23,24	April 25,26,27 May 25,26,27 June 25,26,27	April 28,29,30 May 28,29,30 31 June 28,29,30

Zero grazing

With this method the cattle are housed in yards throughout the year. Grass is cut by machine and dispensed into the cattle troughs. The advantages of this system are the reduction of treading and fouling the grass by excreta, badly fenced fields can be utilised and fields across busy roads can be 'grazed' without the need for cattle to cross. The disadvantages are increased costs due to the extra machinery required, and increased energy used in cutting and carting fodder which would otherwise be harvested by the grazing animals.

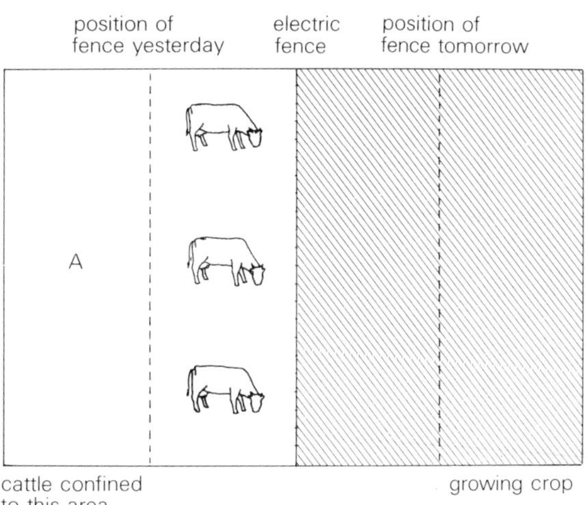

Use of the electric fence

Strip grazing

The grazing animals are contained in a portion of the field by means of an electric fence; each day the fence is moved a few metres to give additional grazing. The distance the fence is moved depends upon three factors:

(a) the length of the fence;
(b) the density and height of the sward;
(c) the number of grazing animals.

This method of controlled grazing has the disadvantage that it allows animals to graze grass in its first stages of regrowth at area A. This disadvantage is easily overcome by using a second electric fence to protect the grazed area.

Strip grazing

With all controlled grazing methods, availability of water is a problem – water tanks with drinking bowls attached are sometimes used, and also drinking bowls fixed to the end of a polythene pipe carrying mains water.

The electric fence

An electric fence is an electrified wire supported by insulating posts. It is very quickly erected and easily moved. The electric fence works from a 6 volt battery and has a transformer which produces an intermittant high voltage. The fence is connected to a wire which gives a mild shock to any animal that touches it. Animals soon learn not to touch an electrified wire.

If an electric fence wire becomes earthed by touching a tall crop, or by faulty insulation, the fence is ineffective. Why? . . . Q.6

For cattle and horses a single wire 600 mm high is sufficient. For pigs, two horizontal wires 300 mm and 450 mm high are necessary. Sheep and lambs require special electrified plastic netting.

Electric fences which work from the mains are becoming very popular. A control box connected to the mains, supplies impulses of safe low current, at a high voltage, to 25 km of fence.

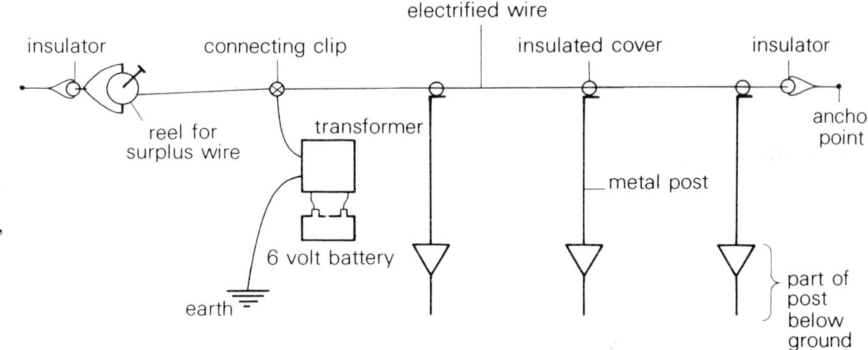

A battery operated electric fence

Sugar beet (*Beta vulgaris*)

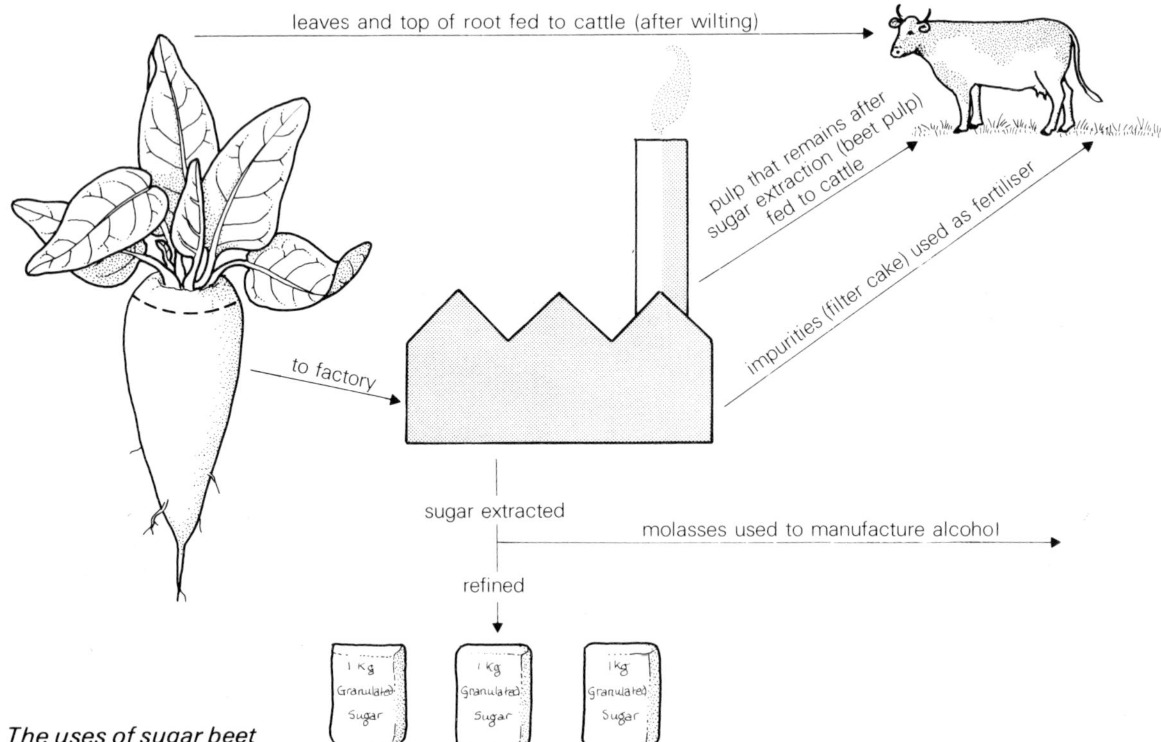

The uses of sugar beet

Wild beet grows on the shores of Europe and Africa, its slender tap-root contains as much as 14% sugar. The cultivated form of this species has a large tap-root (1 kg is a common weight) and a sugar content of up to 20% by weight. The sugar content is variable and may be as low as 10% by the end of the year. In the wild, the leaves tend to lie flat and shade each other, whilst the leaves of cultivated varieties stand in vertical array, trapping much more sunlight. Sugar is manufactured in the leaf and stored in the root.

In spite of the fact that the wild plant was known by the Romans, who used to chew the roots, sugar was not extracted until 1750 when a German chemist obtained over 6% sugar from wild roots. The gradual development of the crop was speeded up by Napoleon in an attempt to boycott sugar from the British Colonies, and a flourishing industry grew in Germany and France. Very little sugar beet was grown in the U.K. until 1920 when it was introduced to arable farms. Sugar beet processing factories were built in the areas most suited to this crop, and unlike grass production, sugar beet production is confined to certain areas of the country as the map shows:

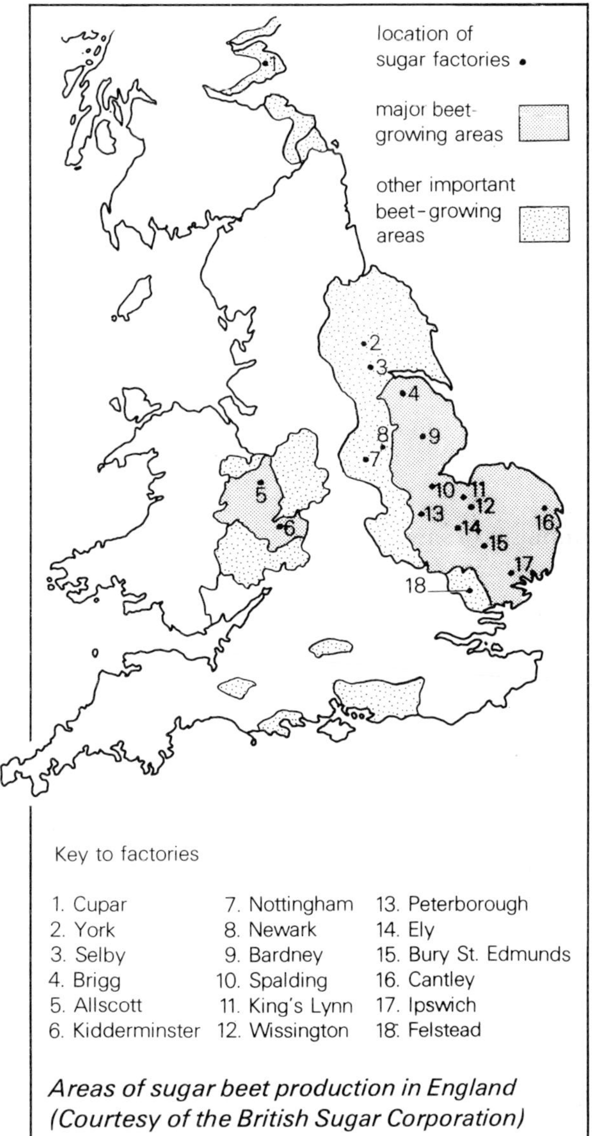

Areas of sugar beet production in England (Courtesy of the British Sugar Corporation)

Beta vulgaris is a biennial, grown from seed and harvested half way through its life cycle. The plant is subject to *vernalisation* (a change in plant behaviour induced by abnormal temperature) and will sometimes flower during the first year – growers refer to this as 'bolting'.

Any deep, stone-free soil with a good supply of lime (pH not less than 6.5) and well supplied with nutrients, will grow sugar beet. Light soils are preferred as lifting on heavy soils may be impossible in a wet autumn. The best crops are obtained by sowing early (March) in a very firm seed-bed with a good tilth, although early sowing can cause bolting. Spacing of rows and plants is adjusted to give a plant population of 65 000 per hectare: if the rows are 450 mm apart, the plant spacing should be 320 mm.

Like the closely related beetroot, sugar beet produces a *seed ball* (a cluster of two or more seeds). If sown, seed balls produce a clump of seedlings which have to be reduced by hand to a single plant.

Why is a single plant necessary? . . . **Q.7**

To avoid this labour-intensive task, the seed balls are rubbed by machine between a rubber pad and an emery wheel and the individual seeds separated into monogerm seeds, which produce only one seedling. The monogerm seeds are coated to form a pellet which can be sown by a special drill which individually places them the required distance apart (see over).

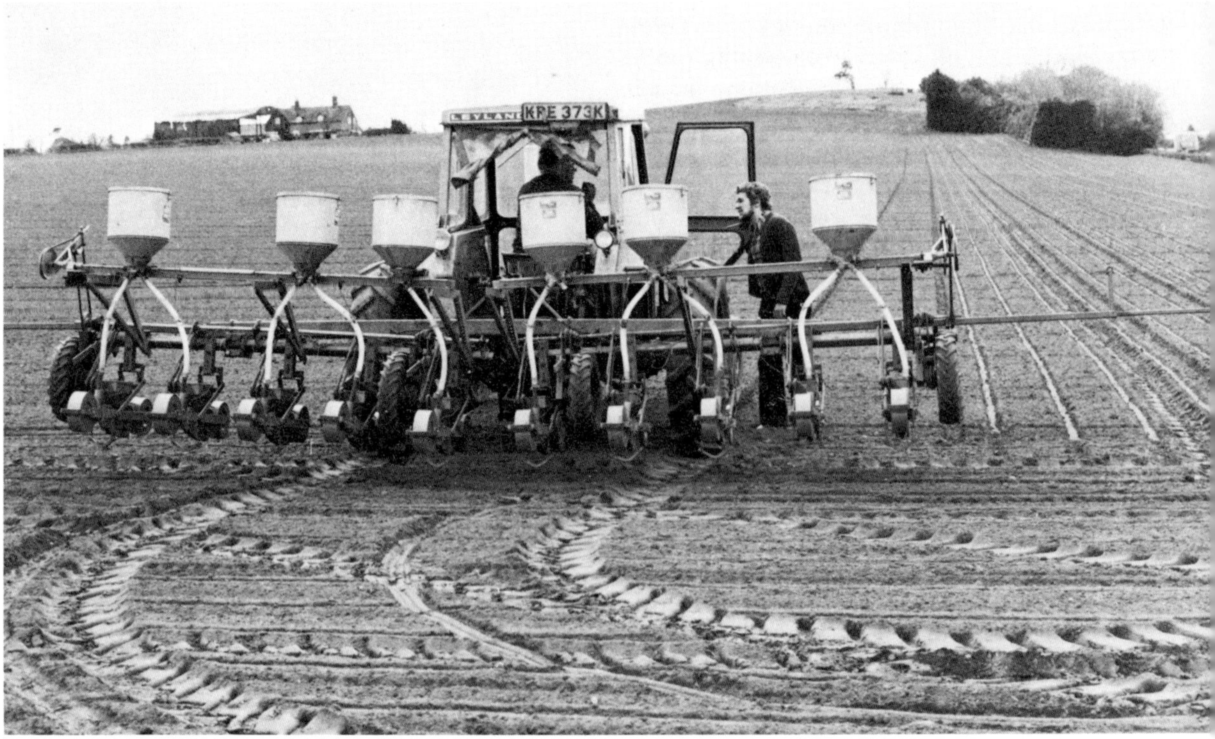
KRE 373K

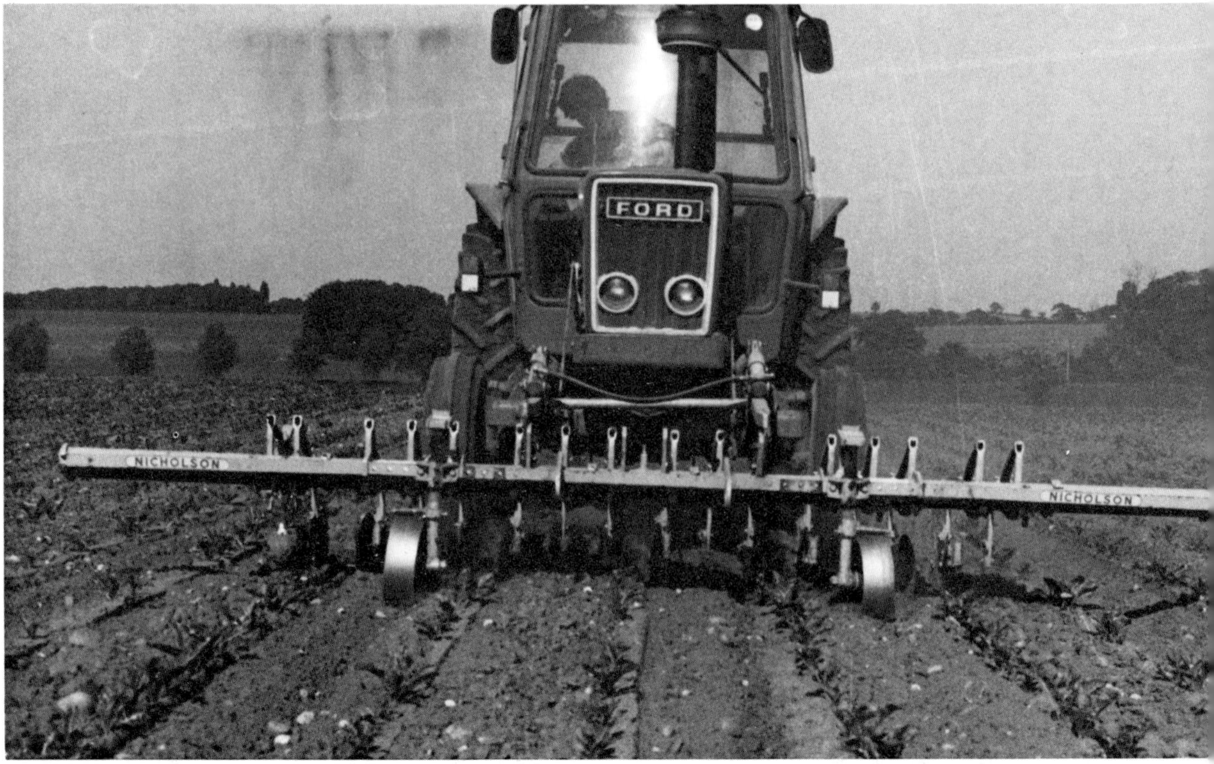
FORD
NICHOLSON
NICHOLSON

Weeds are controlled by inter-row cultivators and spraying with selective *herbicides* (chemicals which kill the weeds and not the crop). Lifting begins in September and continues until the end of the year. Growers are contracted with the British Sugar Corporation and supply the processing factories according to an agreed timetable. This enables non-stop processing from the time the factories open in September until they close down in January. The average yield of roots is 35 tonnes/ha, of which 16% is sugar.

What is the average weight of sugar produced by one hectare of sugar beet in the U.K.? . . . Q.8

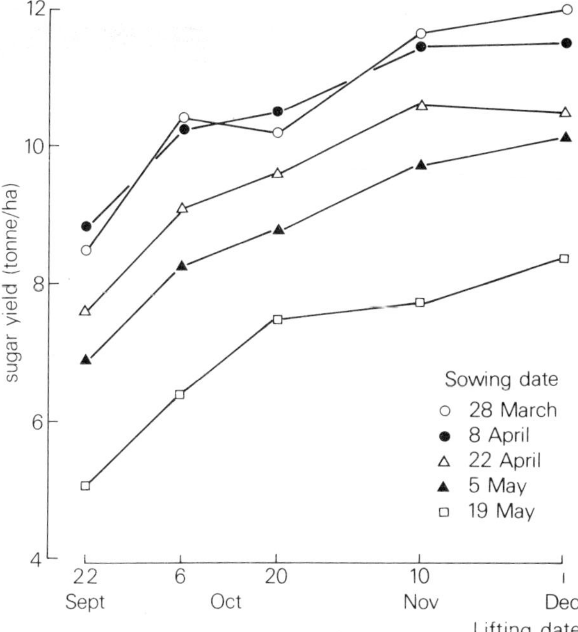

Effect of sowing and harvesting dates on the yield of sugar

What was the difference in yield on 10 November between a crop sown on 5 May and one sown on 19 May? . . . Q.9

Above left: Machine for sowing single seeds of sugar beet

Below left: Use of an inter-row cultivator to control weeds

Pests and diseases

An eelworm (*Heterodera schaohtii*), that affects both beet and mangels is present in some soils. The life cycle of this nematode is very similar to the potato root eelworm. In an effort to prevent the spread of this pest, strict regulations are in force: no farmer may grow sugar beet in the same soil more than once in three years; the growing of Brassicas is also controlled as they are susceptible to beet eelworm.

Virus diseases

In July the leaves of the crop may turn yellow due to one or two virus diseases, *mosaic* and *virus yellows*. Infected plants are incurable and only produce half their potential yield of sugar. Plant virus diseases are spread by aphids, and the only methods of control are to remove sources of infection and control the vector. Aphid control in sugar beet is implemented partly by spraying the aerial parts from above with a contact insecticide, and partly by adding a systemic insecticide to the soil during sowing.

Mineral deficiency diseases

Brown heart (in which the centre of the tap-root rots) and *speckled yellows* (in which the leaves become covered with small yellow areas) are two sugar beet diseases caused by shortage of certain soil minerals. Brown heart is the result of boron deficiency, which is corrected by applying 25 kg/ha of borax. Speckled yellows is the result of too little manganese and is treated by spraying 12 kg/ha of manganese sulphate on to the leaves.

Oilseed rape (*Brassica campestris*)

Whole fields covered with yellow flowers seen in spring and summer are most likely rape – a Brassica being grown for the oil contained in the seed. Each hectare of this crop yields over 2.5 tonnes of seed, containing one tonne of oil for margarine manufacture or industrial purposes, and one and a half tonnes of protein-rich rape meal for inclusion in livestock rations.

As oilseed rape is a Brassica, it should not be grown in the same rotation as kale, cabbage, swedes or cauliflower as club root-infested soils could result. The law prohibits the growing of oilseed rape during the two years preceding a sugar beet crop (see sugar beet).

Which pest is this law attempting to control? . . . Q.10

The law also prohibits the growing of oilseed rape in certain areas, where Brassicas are being grown for seed, for fear of cross-pollination.

Which crop is this law protecting – the Brassica seed crop or the oilseed rape crop? . . . Q.11

Sowing

Oilseed rape can be sown in late August, for harvest eleven months later, or it can be sown in spring for harvest in September. Winter-sown varieties yield ½ tonne/ha more seed with a 4% higher oil content than spring-sown varieties. As the seeds are very small (just like cabbage seed), a very good tilth must be produced to ensure even germination. The crop can be sown in close rows or it can be broadcast (scattered evenly over the surface) by mixing with fertiliser or sand and sown with a spinner or with a corn drill with the spouts removed. The seed should be harrowed to a depth of 10 mm and the seed bed rolled to conserve moisture. 8 kg/ha of seed will give a final plant population of 100 per m^2. All seed must be dressed with gamma BHC, or the flea beetle will destroy the crop by eating the cotyledons when they first appear.

Care of the growing crops

No cultivations are necessary during the growing period, as weeds are controlled by selective herbicides, sprayed during the early periods of growth. It is not possible to control charlock and mustard which are closely related to rape – fields containing these weeds are therefore unsuitable for oilseed rape production as their seeds would spoil the sample. Fertilisers are applied to the seed bed before sowing for spring crops; some of the fertiliser for winter crops is applied in spring – a process known as *top dressing*.

Winter-sown crops are at the mercy of pigeons and rabbits for a long period, and steps should be taken to control these pests. Spring-sown crops can suffer heavy losses from blossom beetle attack – if beetle populations exceed 15 per plant, an insecticide (malathion or gamma BHC) must be applied to the whole crop. On no account must this spraying take place after the flowers have begun to open, or the pollinating bees will be killed, in any case spraying should be carried out in late evening or early morning and local beekeepers informed.

Harvest

When the seed is black in the majority of pods the crop is ready for harvesting. A specially adjusted combine harvester is used to cut and thresh the crop, and the seed is taken to be dried. The plant remains that were left in the field after harvest have no value and are chopped and ploughed into the soil.

Transport

The small round seeds flow like fine dry sand, and considerable losses can occur through holes and cracks in trailers. When transporting by lorry, care must be taken that wind cannot get under the top sheet or seed will be blown over the tail gate – this kind of loss is not obvious as it stops when the lorry stops.

Task 8.1

As with other crops, plant breeders are continually attempting to improve the varieties. A good variety should have the following qualities:

(i) a high yield;
(ii) the seed should be rich in oil;
(iii) the plant must be short;
(iv) the stem must be strong to prevent lodging (falling to the ground);
(v) the crop must mature early;
(vi) the acid content of the seed must be low, as a high acid content spoils the flavour and keeping quality of margarine.

The following results were obtained from recent trials of six varieties – four established ones and two new ones. Study the figures and write an account of the qualities and faults of the two new varieties. Which of the six varieties do you consider to be the best (give reasons for your answer)?

Variety	*Seed yield, kg/ha*	*Oil content of seed %*	*Height 0 = tall 9 = short*	*Resistance to lodging 0 = poor 9 = good*	*Maturity 0 = late 9 = early*	*Acid content*
Englu	1800	43	7	6	5	low
Gaulle	2060	45	6	8	2	high
Maris	2100	42	8	6	5	low
Zephyr	1900	43	7	6	5	low
New Variety 'X'	2500	39	5	3	8	very low
New Variety 'Y'	1750	48	9	9	4	low

Root crops for stock feeding

(Grown in a similar way to sugar beet)

The Brassicas – turnip and swede and two plants derived from wild sugar beet – mangel and fodder beet, are widely grown for stock feeding.

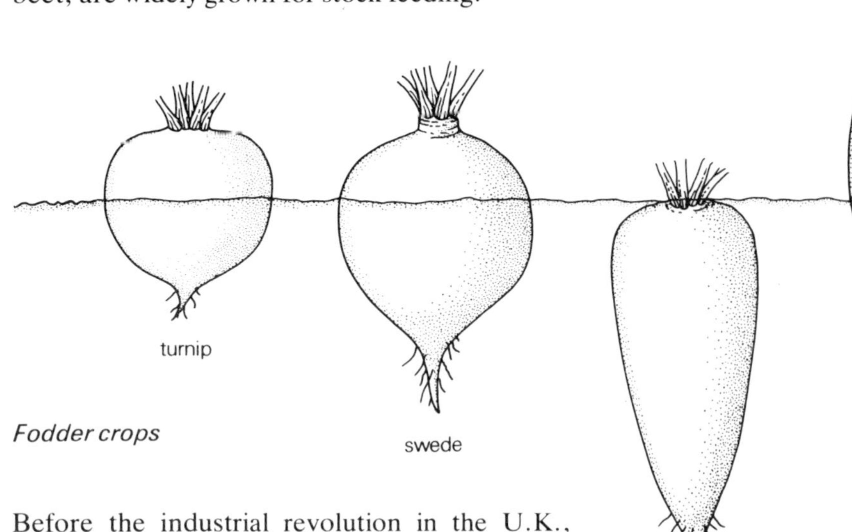

Fodder crops

Before the industrial revolution in the U.K., weed control, disease control and the maintenance of fertility were achieved by leaving one-third of the land fallow (without a crop) and cultivating it throughout the growing season to prevent weed growth:

	Area 1	*Area 2*	*Area 3*
Year 1	Wheat	Beans and barley	Fallow
Year 2	Beans and barley	Fallow	Wheat
Year 3	Fallow	Wheat	Beans and barley

This system kept the land in good heart, but was extremely wasteful of resources as only two crops were produced in three years. Lord Townshend (1674–1738) of Norfolk demonstrated that turnips could be grown in the rotation as a *cleaning crop* in place of the fallow, and fertility could be maintained by the introduction of clover. He also demonstrated how much easier weed control was if turnips were sown in straight parallel rows instead of being broadcast like the other crops. Sowing was carried out with a turnip drill invented by another famous agricultural reformer – Jethro Tull. Lord Townshend also established the *Norfolk four course rotation*.

(It is important to note that modern hushandry controls weeds with selective herbicides, and maintains fertility by application of fertilisers. Continuous cereal growing is possible on some soils but most soils require a break from cereals at various intervals.) Although turnips had been grown as a garden vegetable for centuries, this was the first time they had been grown as an agricultural crop. In addition to fitting in well with the principles of good husbandry, roots made excellent stock feed for the winter months. They provide a palatable, succulent food at a time when none other is available. Unlike potatoes, which are grown as a cash crop, roots are consumed on the farm where they were grown, thus conserving fertility.

Why does consumption on the farm conserve fertility? . . . Q.12

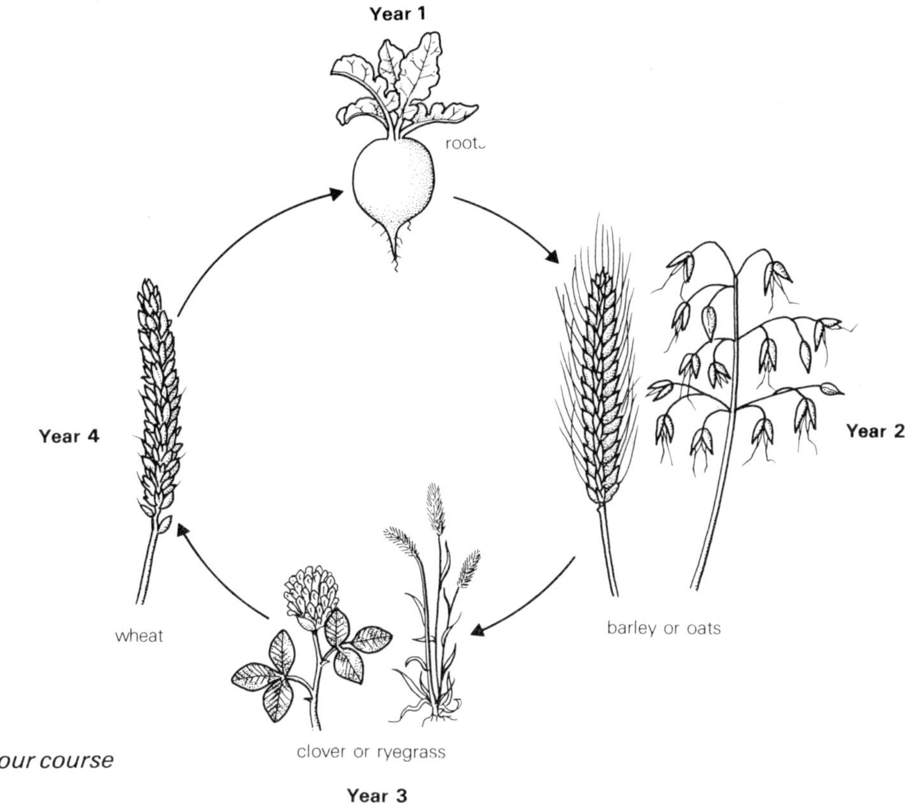

A Norfolk four course rotation

Swedes were introduced from the continent in about 1750, and were quickly accepted, as they had a higher proportion of dry matter (i.e., less water) than turnips. Although some swedes and turnips are harvested, they can be 'grazed' by sheep without lifting.

Turnips are sometimes sown directly into the stubble after a cereal crop has been harvested. 'Stubble turnips', as they are called, make a useful catch crop.

Mangels were bred in Germany from the wild beet plant and imported into this country as the value of root crops became recognised. Mangels are very high yielding but are not frost hardy and 'bleed' if damaged – they must therefore be lifted and carefully stored before any severe frost. Mangels continue to ripen in store and are ready for feeding after Christmas – if fed before that date, *serious* digestive disorders can result. Mangels keep better than any other root crop.

Fodder beet is similar in appearance and growth habit to sugar beet, it yields a lighter weight than mangels but has a higher dry matter content. The climate in Scotland, Wales and the North-West favours swede and turnips, and the climate in the South and East favours mangels and fodder beet. Although the chart shows mangels to be much higher yielding than turnips, if the two crops were grown side by side in the North, turnips would out yield mangels in most seasons.

	Turnip	*Swede*	*Mangel*	*Fodder beet*
Yield Tonnes/ha	50	40	90	60
% Dry Matter	8%	11%	12%	20%

The figures in the chart are averages. In practice, yields vary widely with soil type, manurial treatment, temperature, plant population, rainfall, weed control and sowing dates.

Kale (*Brassica oleracea*)

A kale plant is like a cabbage with long internodes – instead of forming a heart it grows to heights in excess of one metre. Kale is the most important of the Brassica forage crops, which include rape (for grazing), kohl-rabi and cabbage. The area devoted to Brassicas for stock feeding is three times the area grown for human consumption. Kale has the same soil and nutrient requirements as other Brassicas; it is also subject to the same pests and diseases. Kale is the most resistant of all Brassicas to club root, and can be grown successfully in soils where this fungus is present. There are several varieties of kale which fall into two groups (illustrated below).

In practice, farmers grow marrow-stem kale for use before Christmas and thousand-headed kale for use after Christmas. When kale is following a ley the field is usually grazed until May, ploughed and the seed sown in the back of the sod. Some farmers, in an effort to conserve soil moisture and reduce poaching, do not plough the grass, but kill it with chemicals and drill the kale seed directly into the soil containing the dead sward. The crop is sown thinly in drills during May and June; unlike cabbage and root crops the distance between the plants has little effect upon yield – thinning, or precision drilling is therefore unnecessary. Like other Brassicas, kale responds well to heavy dressings of manure and fertilisers.

Although kale can be made into silage, it is usually harvested by strip-grazing with dairy cattle. Kale has a strong smell which *taints* milk (causes it to smell) making it unsaleable. For this reason, kale is fed after morning milking and the cattle are removed from the field before lunchtime.

Feeding value

One hectare of kale (average crop) will feed 25 dairy cows for 10 weeks if the electric fence is moved to allow a daily ration of 25 kg per cow. The cow will require other food in addition to kale, as although kale is very digestible and rich in protein, it contains low levels of certain minerals essential to maintain the animal's fertility.

Marrow-stem kale, yielding up to 60 tonnes/ha, is tall with single thick stems, and is not very frost resistant

Thousand-headed kale, yielding up to 45 tonnes/ha, has a branching habit, and good frost resistance

Minerals in kale

Calcium	High
Phosphorus	Low
Copper	Low
Manganese	Low
Iodine	Low

The balance is restored by feeding 3 kg of mineralised barley and 5 kg of hay daily.

Cereal diseases

In cereal growing areas, field after field is filled with millions of plants of the same species. These unnatural conditions favour the spread of fungal diseases, of which there are more than twenty affecting cereals:

Disease	Barley	Wheat	Oats
Loose smut *(Ustilago nuda)*	✓	✓	✓
Yellow rust *(Puccinia striiformis)*	✓	✓	
Covered smut *(Tilletia caries)*	✓	✓	
Brown rust *(Puccinia recondita)*		✓	
Take-all *(Gaumannomyces graminis)*	✓	✓	✓
Eyespot *(Cercosporella herpotrichoides)*	✓	✓	
Powdery mildew *(Erysiphe gramminis)*	✓	✓	✓
Leaf stripe *(Pyrenophora graminea)*	✓		✓
Ergot *(Claviceps purpurea)*	✓	✓	
Leaf blotch *(Rhynchosporium scalis)*	✓		

Take-all

This fungus exists in the soil, and infests the roots and stem bases of all cereal crops. Affected plants ripen early and have white ears with little or no grain. The disease is starved out by growing non-cereal (or grass) crops for a year or two.

Leaf blotch

This disease became important in the early 1970s as the area of barley increased, and new varieties enabled barley to be grown in wetter areas.

The spores are carried over from year to year by infected crop debris and weed cereals. Spores blow onto the leaves, germinate and feed upon the leaf (in a similar way to potato blight), causing grey blotches. Loss of leaf reduces the plant's ability to form seeds, and yields are much reduced.

Control is by spraying a protective fungicide on the plant leaves early in the season.

Covered smut

Commonly called *bunt*, this disease is carried over from one season to the next by spores on the outside of seed grain. The fungus spore germinates at the same time as the grain and hyphae penetrate the young shoot. As the stem grows, the fungus also grows, maintaining its position in the tip of the plant, and enters the ovules as they form. Inside the ovule the fungus divides into millions of spores (*bunt balls*). When the crop is threshed, the bunt balls burst, releasing the spores, which stick to healthy grains. Control is by disinfecting seed before sowing with a Ministry of Agriculture approved seed disinfectant to kill any fungal spores.

Germinating spore of bunt

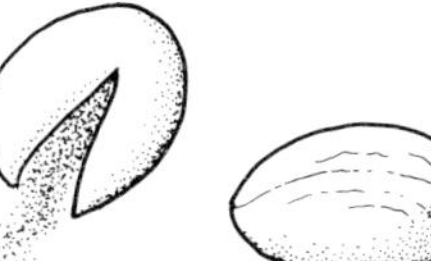

Bunt balls

Infected ear of wheat

Eyespot

This fungus grows on the lower part of the plant stems in a characteristic oval, or eye-shape with a dot in the middle. The fungal growth weakens the straw, and the plants fall in all directions. Spores produced in the spots fall to the ground and are spread to other plants by splashing rain.

Several varieties of wheat have been developed which are immune to this disease; otherwise control can be achieved by crop rotation avoiding wheat and barley for two years.

Questions: Farm crops

1. Write single sentences to answer the following questions:
   (a) What area of potatoes is grown in the U.K.?
   (b) What is a ley?
   (c) Name a dicotyledon that is included in a 'grass' seed mixture.
   (d) How do cattle damage a wet soil?
   (e) What is vernalisation?
   (f) Why are sugar beet seeds rubbed?
   (g) For what purpose is oilseed rape grown?
   (h) Why is it important to control aphids in the sugar beet crop?
   (i) Which root crop produces the highest yield?
   (j) How is kale harvested?

2. Describe a fungus disease of cereals, use the following headings:
   (i) Life cycle of fungus;
   (ii) Effect upon the crop;
   (iii) Methods of control.

3. The diagram shows the principle of the Norfolk Rotation.

A barley	B
C seeds or ley	D wheat

   (a) Name a suitable crop for field B.
   (b) Would you rotate the crops on the plan in a clockwise or anti-clockwise direction? Give a reason for your answer.
   (c) Give *three* reasons for growing crops in rotation. (*W.M.E.B.*)

4. Describe the growing of sugar beet using the following sub-headings:
   (a) Place in rotation, preparation of ground.
   (b) Method of drilling, type of seed and spacing.
   (c) Cultivations during growing season.
   (d) Pest and disease control.
   (e) Method of harvesting, probable yield, sugar content.

   (*W.M.E.B.*)

5. It is recommended that vegetable crops should be grown in a rotation. A four-course rotation could be divided into (i) Brassicas, (ii) legumes, (iii) roots and (iv) potatoes.
   (a) With the aid of diagrams, show the order in which the crops would rotate and why it is in that order.
   (b) State *two* reasons for having a rotation.
   (c) State the special requirements of each crop or plot giving reasons.
   (d) Give *three* examples of each of the following: (i) Brassicas; (ii) legumes; (iii) roots.
   (e) Which plot would include onions and leeks? State why you would put them in this plot. (*N.W.R.E.B.*)

6. What are the benefits derived from rotating crops in either gardens *or* farms?
   Describe in detail any well-established four-course rotation you have studied. In your answer, draw up a table to show the crops you would grow. Explain why these crops are included in your scheme. (*W.J.E.C.*)

7. Describe in detail how a farmer is able to get the maximum use of his pasture land by controlled grazing. (*W.J.E.C.*)

8. Name *one* arable crop grown on the farm you have studied and write short notes on it under the following headings:
   (a) preparation of the land,
   (b) manurial treatment,
   (c) method of sowing, time of sowing and seed rate,
   (d) cultivations and other treatments during the growing period,
   (e) method of harvesting and expected yields.
   (*S.E.R.E.B.*)

9. Write a paragraph on each of the following topics:
   (a) Zero grazing
   (b) Strip grazing
   (c) Paddock grazing
   In each case list *two* advantages or disadvantages of each system. (*W.Y. & L.R.E.B.*)

Answers to in-text questions

1. Soil Science

1. The largest particles form the lowest layer.
2. Sand particles are larger than clay particles.
3. Silt particles are of intermediate size, i.e., they are larger than clay and smaller than sand.
4. A soil consisting of 40% sand., 40% silt and 20% clay is called a *loam*.
5. As the third heating produced no further weight loss, the soil was taken to be completely dry.
6. A clay soil will hold more water than an equal volume of sandy soil (clay particles, being smaller, have a larger area of surface).
7. A sandy soil will hold more air than an equal volume of clay soil (large particles do not pack together as tightly as small particles).
8. The air content of a clay soil will increase if the clay particles join to form crumbs.
9. The four processes are physical.
10. Highest temperature was reaches at 1500 hours G.M.T.
11. The highest temperature was approximately 21.5 C.
12. In New Zealand and all the Southern Hemisphere, north facing slopes will be warmer than south facing slopes.
13. Most plants thrive at pH 6.5, i.e., between pH 6 and pH 7.

2. Soil Practice and Vegetable Culture

1. A spade would chop some of the tubers if used to harvest potatoes.
2. The weeds would die and be pulled into the soil by earthworms; they will eventually form part of the soil humus.
3. The blade of a spade carried on the shoulder could strike someone about the head or face.
4. A tool laid flat on the soil may be trodden on and damage a leg or foot.
5. Frost causes the water in the clay clod to expand – this expansion increases the distances between the clay particles and the clod crumbles.
6. No. Different varieties of lettuce grow to different sizes – some therefore require more space than others.
7. Sack 'D' contains bacteria, and the right conditions required for the bacteria to multiply – this sack will warm more quickly than the others.
8. Plant potatoes in one half of the section, and, three years later, when potatoes are again due to be grown in this section, plant them in the other half of the section.
9. The only method available to most gardeners for storing peas is to freeze them. Commercially, peas are dried, canned or frozen.
10. The turnip has food stored in the hypocotyl only; the swede also has part of the stem base swollen – this bears a number of ridges where the leaves were once attached.
11. An unharvested parship produces a flower.
12. Mustard.

3. Pests and Diseases of Plants

1. More losses of pupae occur during the long winter than during the short summer pupation period.
2. The eggs of crane flies quickly dehydrate. A weedy area will protect the eggs, and also the adult flies are much more likely to lay their eggs in grassy and weedy areas than on bare soil.

3. The new growth is soft and allows easy penetration of the proboscis; also there is a good supply of nutrients flowing to the area of growth.
4. Aphids prefer to feed on tender growing points – if these points are removed, flying aphids are less likely to settle, and newly arrived aphids and their young will be removed with the tops
5. The edible parts of the plant will also contain insecticide and should not be eaten.
6. Treading and watering makes conditions less favourable for egg laying by the carrot fly.
7. The eggs have not been seen. Search for eggs at the base of growing plants – they are very small, but can be seen with the naked eye.
8. *Predators:* rove beetle, hover fly, black-kneed capsid bug, green lacewing, ladybird. *Parasite:* icheumon fly.
9. Early potatoes may be lifted before the potato eelworm has completed its life cycle and no cysts have formed; maincrop potatoes are lifted after cysts are formed. Maincrop potatoes therefore leave much heavier infestations of cysts than 'earlies'.
10. The compost will become infected with spores, and when spread on the garden will transmit the disease to areas which may not have been infected.

4. Further Plant Science

1. *fragrans* – sweet smelling (fragrant); *bulbosa* – has a bulb; *maritima* – sea-side plants; *trifoliata* – leaf in three parts.
2. Group A – dicotyledon; group B – monocotyledon.
3. The flower is a monocotyledon – flower parts are in threes (six petals, six stamens).
4. Mosses, Ferns, Liverworts, Horsetails and Algae are all groups of non-flowering plants.
5. The micropyle is the point of entry of pollen tube.
6. One.
7. One.
8 A potato seed has two parents. A 'seed potato' is not a seed, but a tuber, and has only one parent.

Task 4.1

Dicotyledon	*Monocotyledon*
potatoes	barley
tomatoes	onion
cucumber	wheat
lettuce	maize
carrots	leeks
cabbage	oats
apples	
mustard	

9. Seeds saved from F_1 hybrids are not the first cross and have no hybrid vigour; they could also contain some undesirable recessive characteristics which show in the next generation.
10. F_1 hybrid.
11. White.
12. Red.
13. 600 tall plants, 200 dwarf plants.
14. The dominant characteristic of Hereford cattle is the white face.

5. Pigs

1. 64 kg.
2. 3.5.
3. The piglets obtain iron from the soil.
4. (a) 2.25 kg; (b) 3 kg.
5. 6 kg.
6. The extra food is converted into milk (the sow also loses body weight during her lactation – this too is converted into milk).
7. 20 piglets.
8. A long intestine will give a greater area for absorption than a short one.
9. Oxygen.
10. The products of digestion.
11. Carbon dioxide.
12. Vein.
13. Artery.
14. To ensure that any virus present on boots or clothes does not pass to the pig herd.
15. The second application of insecticide is to destroy lice that hatched after the first application.

6. Commercial Rabbits

1. A food conversion rate is the weight of food eaten by an animal to produce unit increase in weight.
2. Doe's number, date of birth, date mated, date given birth, number of young, food allocation, etc., all appear on the record card in the cage.
3. The rabbits are Californian.
4. A disorder of the lungs, nose or adjoining tubes.
5. A rabbit has 28 teeth.
6. Canines are missing in the rabbit.

7. Power for Crop Production

1. Wind does not use a fossil fuel.
2. If the engine is not level, the dip stick will probably give an incorrect reading.
3. The end of a bicycle pump warms up in use.
4. 30 N.
5. 5 N.
6. Oil will not freeze, it protects metal parts from rust and it lubricates the moving parts.
7. The weights on the front of the tractor help to balance the weight of the disc harrow. If there is not enough weight on the front wheels, steering is impossible.
8. The plough has been rotated.
9. It is a two-wheel drive tractor.

8. Farm Crops

1. Barley is the most extensively grown cereal crop in the U.K.
2. Grass occupies the largest area in the U.K.
3. The first six crops on the list are cereals; they occupy 3 825 000 hectares.
4. Rough grazing and 'other' (roads, buildings, etc.) are never ploughed.
5. The grass under the cages will not have lost any of its leaves to the grazing animal and will have grown more quickly than the grazed grass.
6. The electricity in the wire is running into the ground and is therefore not available to give the animal a shock.
7. If two, or more plants are growing in the same plot, none will produce a satisfactory root.
8. The average weight of sugar from one hectare is 16% of 35 tonnes is 5.6 tonnes.
9. Sugar beet sown on 5 May yields 2 tonne/ha more than sugar beet sown on the 19 May.
10. Sugar beet eelworm is controlled by the law.
11. The Brassica seed crop is being protected. The cross-pollination of the rape flowers would make no difference to the yield of oil seed. The cross-pollination of Brassica seeds with oilseed rape would make the crop useless.
12. Many of the nutrients in the roots would be returned to the soil in the animal's dung.

Glossary

Ad lib Always on offer (food).
Altitude The height above sea level.
Amphibian A cold-blooded vertebrate that developes from a water-dwelling creature, breathing with gills, to a land dweller breathing air.
Anaemic A blood condition where the ability of the blood to carry oxygen is reduced.
Anemometer Instrument that measures wind speed.
Annual A plant that completes one life cycle in one growing season.
Anterior Head end of animal.
Anther The part of a stamen that produces pollen.
Aorta Main artery.
Aphid A species of insect that lives by sucking plant juice.
Arable Cultivated land.
Arboreal Tree living.
Artery Blood vessel taking blood from the heart.
Ascaris Internal parasite of pig.
Atrium Chamber in heart that receives blood from the veins.
Auricle Small extension of grass leaf blade.
Auxin Growth-regulating chemical produced in plants.
Awn Spike on the seeds of some grasses, e.g., barley.

Bacteria Extremely small life form.
Bastard trenching A method of cultivating the soil to a depth of two spits.
Beaumont period A period of weather that favours potato blight.
Biennial A plant that requires two growing seasons to complete its life cycle.
Bile Secretions of the liver.
Bird A warm-blooded vertebrate covered with feathers.
Blanch Kept white by excluding light (vegetable).
Boar An entire male pig.
Brashing-up The removal of the lower branches of conifers.
Brassica A plant family – containing cabbage, turnip, etc.
British saddleback A breed of pig.
Broadcasting Sowing seeds by scattering them upon the surface.
Broilers Table chickens reared for the killing at an early age (10–14 weeks).
Brood chamber A box of frames in a beehive in which the queen lays eggs and young are reared.
Brooder Equipment for keeping baby chickens warm.
Broody hen Hen in condition to incubate eggs and rear chicks.
Browsing The eating of leaves, shoots, etc., from the tops and side branches of trees and other large vegetation.
Buck Male rabbit or deer.
Bud A compact cluster of tiny leaves (or flowers) on a very small stem.
Bulb Roughly spherical plant structure having a reproductive and overwintering function, consists of layers of swollen leaves on a very short stem – e.g., onion.

Caecum Part of the gut of birds and some other animals.
Caesarean section Birth by cutting baby from mother's uterus with scalpel or similar instrument.

Calcium carbonate Chemical substance from which egg shells are formed.
Calcicole Plant that requires alkaline soil.
Calcifuge Plant that grows well in acid soil.
Calomel A fungicide.
Calyx A ring of sepals on a flower or fruit.
Candling Looking into eggs by means of a bright light.
Canine A tooth for flesh tearing – large in carnivores – often absent in herbivores.
Canopy The area covered by the spread of a tree's branches.
Capillary Very fine tube.
Carbohydrate Organic compound containing only carbon, hydrogen and oxygen (sugars and starch).
Cardinal points The points of a compass N. S. E. and W.
Carnivore An animal that lives by eating other animals.
Castrate Removal of testicles.
Caudal disc Area around base of tail.
Cellulose Substance that gives strength to plant tissues.
Cervix Passage between vagina and uterus.
Chalaza Twisted, thickened area in egg white which holds the yolk in position.
Clamp An outside store of vegetables.
Clutch One sitting of eggs.
Coccidiosis A disease of rabbits and birds.
Colon Part of the large intestine.
Colostrum The first fluid produced by mammary glands of mammal after giving birth.
Compost 1. Decaying organic matter. 2. Material for filling seed boxes and plant pots.
Conifer Trees that bear cones (yew and juniper have berries, and are also conifers).
Contractile roots Strong roots on some corms and tap roots that contract and pull the plant deeper into the soil.
Coprophagous pellets Special droppings produced by rabbits at night which are immediately ingested
Corm Underground swollen base of stem, stores food and produces new shoots from its buds.
Corolla The complete whorl of petals on a flower.
Cotyledon (a) The part of a seed in which food is stored; (b) The first leaf(s) produced by a seed.
Crankshaft A rod with right angle bends for converting up and down motion to revolving motion.
Creep Area available to young but not parents.
Crop Storage organ in bird for undigested food.
Cross-pollination Pollination of a flower with pollen from another flower.
Crown The uppermost parts of a tree.
Crown board Cover on top of a beehive to prevent bees entering the roof space.
Culm Flower stalk of grass.
Cutting Part of a plant which has been cut off to grow a new plant.

Deciduous Tree or shrub that bears no leaves in winter.
Derris dust An insecticide manufactured from the root of the Derris plant.
Dewlap Fold of loose skin hanging from the neck of cattle.
Diameter The distance across a circle, measured through centre.
Diaphragm Sheet of muscle dividing lung cavity from abdominal cavity.
Dicotyledon A class of plants.
Doe Female rabbit.
Dormant Alive but not growing or changing in any way.
Dorsal Back part of an animal.
Double digging A method of digging the soil to a depth of two spits.
Down Small fluffy feathers growing underneath the main feathers on ducks and geese.
Drake A male duck.
Drey The nest of a squirrel.
Drill A shallow trench drawn in the soil tilth in which seeds are sown.
Duodenum The part of the intestines nearest to an animal's stomach.

Edible Fit to be eaten.
Egg tooth Hard tip on bird's beak used to break out from the shell.
Embryo Baby plant or animal inside seed, egg or parent.
Entire Not castrated.

Enzootic pneumonia Disease of pig.
Enzyme A substance in animals which cause chemical changes to take place.
Ephemeral Short lived.
Epididymis Coiled duct attached to testis.
Erode Removal of top soil by natural forces.
Etiolated Plant growth with long internodes due to insufficient light.

Faeces Undigested material passed from an animal's gut.
Fallopian Tube Duct from ovary to horn of uterus.
Farrow Pig gives birth.
Fawn Young deer.
Ferret Half-tame variety of pole-cat, kept for driving rabbits from burrows.
Fertilisation The fusing of pollen and ovule, or sperm and ova.
Fertiliser Chemical material, rich in one or more plant nutrient.
Fibrous (a) Consisting of many fibres (e.g., peat); (b) Fibrous root – slender root, often with slender branches.
Field capacity The maximum amount of water that a fully drained soil can retain.
Filament The part of a stamen that holds the anther.
Fish A cold-blooded vertebrate, covered in scales, confined to an aquatic environment.
Flocculation Numbers of clay particles sticking together to form crumbs.
Flower The sexually reproductive part of a plant.
Fruit The fertilised ovary of a flower containing seeds.
Function Purpose.
Fungicide Chemical substance that kills fungi.

Gall bladder A sac, situated on the liver, in which bile collects.
Gamma BHC An insecticide.
Gammexane An insecticide.
Gander Male goose.
Geotropism The response to gravity by part of a plant.
Germination The breaking of dormancy by the embryo in a seed.
Gestation period The length of pregnancy.
Gilt Young female pig.
Gizzard The part of a bird's stomach that crushes the food.
Glume Protective layer around the flowers in a spikelet of grass.
Gosling Baby goose.
Graminae Grass family.
Grazing The eating of grass, or other vegetation, from the ground.

Haulm The leaves and stem of potatoes.
Hay Sun-dried grass.
Hectare Area equal to 10 000 m^2.
Herbaceous plant Soft-stemmed plant – as distinct from trees and shrubs.
Herbicide Chemical substance that kills plants.
Herbivore An animal that lives by eating plants.
Hermaphrodyte Individual plant or animal that has both male and female organs.
Hexagon Six-sided figure.
Hibernation An extended period of sleep during the winter months when food is not available.
Humidity The amount of water vapour in the air.
Humus Organic material in the final stages of decay.
Hybrid Animal or plant produced by crossing two separate pure breeds.
Hydraulic Movement of liquids through pipes to give motive power.
Hypocotyl The length of 'stem' between the root and seed leaves of a seedling.

Incisor A tooth at the front of the jaw for biting.
Incubator Apparatus designed to keep eggs at constant temperature and humidity until the young hatch from them.
Inflorescence Flowering shoot containing many individual flowers or groups of flowers.
Ingest Eat.
Inorganic Substance that has never lived.
Insect An invertebrate with three body parts and six jointed legs attached to the middle part.

Insecticide Chemical substance that kills.
Insectivore An animal that lives by eating insects and other invertebrates.
Insulator Material that will not conduct electricity.
Internode The part of the stem between one node and the next.
Intestine The part of an animal's digestive system where food passes into the blood stream.
Invertebrate An animal without a backbone.

John Innes compost Mixture of loam, coarse sand, peat and fertiliser, for growing plants in pots and boxes.

Kidney Animal organ that filters waste products from the blood.
Kilowatt A unit of power.

Landrace A breed of pig.
Larva (plural larvae) The feeding stage between egg and pupa in the life cycle of invertebrates. A larva usually looks very different to the adult form.
Leach The removal of soil salts in the drainage water.
Leatherjacket Larva of crane fly (daddy long legs).
Leguminosae A plant family – peas, beans, clover, etc.
Lemma Part of the case that protects the sexual organs in a grass flower.
Ley A crop of grass or grass and clover mixture sown to last a limited number of years (1, 2, 3 or 4).
Ligament Band of strong tissue attached to bone.
Ligule Small transparent vertical projection on a grass sheath where leaf blade commences.
Litter The young produced by a single birth.
Liver Animal organ that stores food and produces bile.
Loam A soil formed from a mixture of sand, silt and clay particles.
Lodicule Very small part of a grass flower.

Macro-organisms Living things large enough to be seen with the naked eye.
Malathion An insecticide.
Mammal A hairy vertebrate that suckles its young.
Medullary rays Food storage cells in wood.
Membrane A single layer of skin.
Micro-organisms Living things too small to be seen with the naked eye.
Micrometer screw gauge An instrument for accurately measuring the thickness of materials that are too thin to be measured with a ruler.
Micropyle Tiny hole in the testa of a seed.
Mineral salts Inorganic chemical substances.
Molar A grinding tooth, situated at the back of the jaw.
Mole plough Plough that makes drainage tunnels in soil below the depth of normal cultivation.
Monocotyledon A class of plants.

Nectar Sweet watery substance produced by flowers to attract insects.
Nematode Unsegmented worm.
Newton Unit of force.
Node The place on a stem where the leaf stalk is attached.
Nursery Area where young plants or trees are raised.
Nymph A young insect that, except for size, resembles its parent.

Oesophagus Tube connecting mouth to stomach.
Oestrous The period during which a female will allow the male to mate.
Omnivore An animal that has a mixed diet (part plant and part animal), e.g., man
Organ Part of an animal or plant that performs a special function, e.g., leaf or lungs.
Organic Substance that is living or has lived.
Ovary (Animal) The organ in the female that produces ova (eggs).
Ovary (Plant) The part of a flower that develops into a fruit.
Ovule The part of a flower that develops into a seed.

Palae Part of the case that protects the sexual organs in the grass flower.
Pallets Squares of wood upon which loads are stacked for transport.
Palpation Pregnancy test of rabbit by handling.
Pancreas Animal organ that produces enzymes.
Parasite Organism that obtains its food by living on or in another organism (its host).
Penis Male reproductive and urinary organ.
Perennation The survival of a plant from year to year.
Perennial A plant that flowers each year.
Pesticide Chemical poisonous to pests.
Petal One of the parts of a flower – often brightly coloured.
Petiole The leaf stalk.
Phototropism The response to light by part of a plant.
pH The scale by which the degree of acidity is measured.
Ploche Circular cloche.
Plumule Small shoot inside, or just emerging from, a seed.
Poach The destruction of soil structure by treading.
Pollen The male sex cells produced by a flower.
Pollination The transfer of pollen to the stigma of a flower.
Porter bee escape Metal appliance which allows bees to pass from one section of the hive to another, but not to return.
Posterior Tail end of animal.
Preen gland Oil-producing gland on a bird's back, just forward from the tail.
Pregnant Refers to female that has young developing inside her uterus.
Prevailing wind The most frequent wind direction.
Propagation Increasing the numbers of plants from seeds or parent stock.
Propolis Sticky yellow substance collected by bees.
Prostate Male gland of mammals producing substances to add to sperms.
Protein An organic compound that contains the element nitrogen.
Proventriculus The enzyme-producing part of bird's stomach.
Pullet Female hen under 18 months old.
Pupa The non-feeding developmental stage between larva and adult of many invertebrates.

Queen excluder Sheet of metal punched with holes, large enough for worker bees to pass through but too small to allow queens or drones to pass through.

Rabies Fatal disease of mammals.
Radicle Small root inside, or just emerging from a seed.
Rectum Last part of large intestine.
Reptile A cold-blooded air breathing vertebrate, covered in scales, which reproduces by laying eggs on land.
Respiration Breathing (animal) obtaining energy from sugar and oxygen (plant).
Rhizome Horizontal underground stem.
Rodent Gnawing mammal with continually growing incisors.

Salmonella Micro-organism that causes food poisoning.
Sapling A young tree.
Scrotum Sac that contains the testicles.
Seed A tiny dormant plant with a store of food surrounded by a protective coat.
Self-pollination Pollination of a flower with its own pollen.
Seminal vesicle Male organ which stores sperm.
Sepal The outermost, leaf-like structure of a flower.
Shrub A moderate size woody perennial with many branches at the base.
Sigmoid 'S'-shaped.
Silage Partially decayed, stored grass.
Silt Mineral particles, larger than clay and smaller than fine sand.
Sink Wedge-shaped cut in a tree made as first part of the felling operation.
Slurry Very wet dung and mud.
Smoker Beekeepers' appliance for puffing smoke.
Sow Mother pig.
Spikelet A cluster of individual flowers in a grass plant.

Spit The length of the blade of a spade.
Spline Rectangular key fitting into grooves in a shaft.
Stamen The male part of a flower.
Sterile Unable to breed.
Stigma The female part of a flower that receives pollen.
Stimulus A change in the external environment of plant or animal which produces a response in that plant or animal.
Stolon Horizontal stem that grows above the ground along the soil surface.
Stool The roots and lower stem of a perennial.
Straw Dead leaves and stems of cereal crops left after the grain has been removed.
Stubble Stems of plants remaining above the soil after the top parts have been harvested.
Style The part of a flower between the stigma and the ovary.
Subsoil The layer of lighter coloured material directly underneath the topsoil.
Super Box of shallow frames in which bees store honey.
Syrup A strong solution of sugar in water for feeding to bees.
Systemic Moves through the systems and tissues of a plant or animal.

Tap-root A single main root that grows vertically downwards.
Tendril A slender outgrowth from a plant that curls around objects to give the plant support.
Terminal bud The bud on the tip of a branch or shoot.
Testa Seed coat.
Testis Organ in male which produces sperm.
Thigmotropism The response to touch by part of a plant.
Thinning The removal of some plants or trees to allow more space for the ones remaining to grow.
Thorax 1. Insects – the body part, behind the head to which the legs are attached.
2. Vertebrates – region of body that contains heart and lungs.
Tiller Bud of a grass plant.
Tilth The fineness of the structure of the surface soil.
Tonne 1000 kilograms.
Trachea Wind pipe.
Transformer A device that changes the voltage of an electric current.
Trichlorphon An insecticide.
Tropism A plant's response to a stimulus.
Tuber Part of a root or stem swollen with food stores.
Tuberculosis (T.B.) An animal disease, usually infecting the lungs.

Ureter Duct from kidney to bladder.
Uterus Female organ in which young develop.

Vagina Duct of female that receives penis during mating.
Variety A strain of plants within a species that have similar special charactistics.
Vein Blood vessel taking blood towards the heart.
Vena cava Main vein.
Vent The outlet in the back of a bird through which faeces and eggs pass.
Ventral Underneath part of animal.
Ventrical Chamber of heart that forces blood into arteries by contraction.
Vermin Animals which damage crops or food store.
Vernalisation A change in plant behaviour induced by abnormal temperature.
Vertebrate An animal with a backbone.
Viable Having the ability to germinate (seeds).
Villus Finger-like projection on inside wall of intestine.
Virus Extremely small form of life, that can live only in other living things.
Vitamins Chemical substances essential to animal health.
Vixen Female fox.
Vulva Exterior part of the female organ.

Warfarin Poison used against rodents.
Wean The removal of the baby animals from their mother as they are old enough to take adult food.
Weed A plant growing where it is not wanted.

Index